A Primer for Counseling the College Male

●

Walter S. Nosal, Ed.D.

Professor of Education
Director of Counseling Center

John Carroll University

WM. C. BROWN BOOK COMPANY
An Affiliate of
WM. C. BROWN COMPANY PUBLISHERS ◆ Dubuque, Iowa 52001

JAN 6   1969

Printed in the United States of America

To

Ruth, Pat, Jean, Sally, Connie, Bobby, Kathy, David, and Jay, (my immediate family,) and those thousands of counseled young people who are my adopted family.

PREFACE

Typically, one finds a book dealing with college youth presented in a highly logical manner. There is the usual definition of terms, an examination of premises and assumptions, followed by a presentation of findings, and concluding with guarded or cautious conclusions. Such efforts are directed at the scholar or researcher and are a necessary addition to the growing body of information for many future uses.

The present work will depart from that format, and instead, present the major recommendations at the beginning of the book in language that is addressed to the college student and his parents. This departure from traditional practice is deemed appropriate because many youth, perhaps too many, do not have access to competent counseling and information in a manner that can be easily understood and then put into practice without great delays.

In translating the technical information to a meaningful message to young people, I have developed a conversational and "sketching" approach in sharing important ideas about themselves to them and their parents. As a working motto for the past twenty years, I have adopted the idea that it is important to "see through people in order to see people through."

ACKNOWLEDGMENTS

The help of a number of individuals is hereby acknowledged. The completion of a project such as undertaken in this instance is rarely the solo performance of the chief investigator.

Gratitude is expressed to the Committee on Research of John Carroll University for making available the "seed money" to defray some major expenses in the initial study on Leaders and to the Cleveland Foundation for support in carrying out the study on Beginners.

Then in the order in which they appeared and helped in substantial ways, I want to thank publicly: Dr. Jack M. Lorenzo, Electroencephalographer; Miss Gladys Hill and Mrs. Jean O'Toole, E.E.G. Technicians; Dr. Francis T. Huck, Statistician; Miss Dolores Klavon and Mrs. Alice Mittinger, members of Counseling Center Staff; Mr. Joseph Gulvas, Miss Marian Kilbane, Mr. John Keshock, and Mr. Bernard Duber, graduate students; Dr. John M. Wittenbrook, medical consultant; Dr. Charles E. Henry, Electroencephalographer, Cleveland Clinic; Mrs. Margaret Henry of Medical Writing Associates; Mr. Manuel Salabounis, Director of Computer Center, Kathie Keane Skully and Mrs. Mary Ann Reed, typists.

In addition I would like to thank all the authors and publishers who have allowed me to use quotations from their works. A listing of these works will be found in the Reference. Each reference is identified either by its date of publication or Reference listing.

Walter S. Nosal

LIST OF TABLES

LIST OF FIGURES

TABLE OF CONTENTS

CHAPTER 1

Introduction

Considerable information has been accumulated from many fields of investigation about how human beings grow, develop, and shape their lives. Much of this information is written in such a manner that the valuable help that should come from such knowledge is not readily understood by college men, nor their parents who often feel "left out" when trying to advise the son in starting well and continuing through his studies to the point of graduation.

After a period of more than twenty years of counseling with young college men and conducting many studies on the major characteristics of student leaders, failures, and beginners, I will present a "blueprint" or guide that has been gradually developed to counsel such students.

A very important aspect of this effort will be to outline the major concepts that will continue to give order and sense to the specific recommendations that will follow in the next chapter.

It is impossible to present every fact of human development to a student in order that he might make the right decisions and move under his own power. What is possible and, I think, necessary is that the student have some meaningful picture of what has happened to him in the past, what is happening to him at the present, and some preview of what will likely occur in his future.

It is a very elementary observation that individuals change from birth to adulthood in physical proportions, in the amount of "self-care" they exercise, and in their activities. What is not so visible is the realization that they "have gone through and are going through stages" which are fairly predictable and are the basis of their present and future adjustments.

It is helpful to devote some time to the major developments between birth and high school graduation in order to "see" the picture of yourself for purposes of making decisions about next moves to make. Figure 1 is the model that includes the major developmental "hurdles" and the concept of individual differences.

Any discussion of each stage must of necessity be sketchy. But the important message to the reader is that you understand how it influences what goes on

1

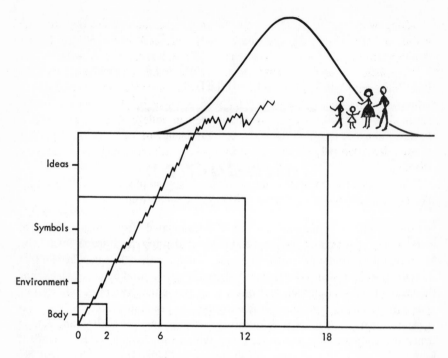

Figure 1. Developmental Tasks.

within yourself. No serious counselor would argue that the picture is complete. There is always the influence of the world and the people around us that produce many changes. In brief, no man grows up in a vacuum, but in a setting that has many subtle effects on him. Chapter 4 will present a long treatment of the conditions within the individual that are influencing his behavior; chapter 3 will provide a discussion of the influences of society and the college that must be recognized in any full discussion of the adjustments that must be made by young people in higher education.

GAINING CONTROL OF ONE'S BODY

The first stage is essentially covered in the first two years of life. It is a spectacular change from a helpless infant at birth to a fairly well-moving youngster at age two. The importance of developing large muscle coordination in walking, running, climbing, reaching and handling is the basis on which more specific and small muscle coordination will occur in the next stage.

Along with the great importance of moving around, inspecting the small world of the child, and "keeping one's balance," there is the internal development of gaining control over one's bladder, bowels, and stomach.

Very little attention is devoted to such early childhood developments unless there has been some interruption or delay in having them come to pass. On the other hand, the importance of keeping these systems in good shape seems to be lessened in the thinking of many young men in college. Because so much of these actions become automatic, there is a tendency to "take them for granted" or even deny that they are important for dealing with more important matters of the mind.

The factor of good health and maintaining a good physical condition cannot be denied in carrying out the many challenges that confront a young man.

GAINING CONTROL OF ONE'S ENVIRONMENT

The second stage that emerges concerns itself with learning to travel over many kinds of physical obstacles, such as stairs, distances, and heights. Early in this two to six year period, there is the challenge of learning how to handle toys, tricycles, balls, blocks, and objects that are found in the home and neighborhood. Toward the end of this period, the boy will have developed to the point where he can ride a bicycle, tie his shoe strings, button and unbutton his clothing, dress and bathe himself, learn to swim, and in general have a reasonable mastery over the concrete objects in his world.

This stage has great significance for the reason that a "sense of self confidence" is one of the major outcomes of a successful or reasonable achievement in this period.

If a child has not achieved a reasonable control over the practical affairs of his life, such as eating, playing, entertaining himself, and engaging in activities with other children of his own age, he is likely to approach the next stage with uncertainties about his own abilities and thereby be handicapped in terms of being able to pay attention and concentrate on what is the main activity of school programs.

GAINING CONTROL OVER SYMBOLS

Up until this stage, age 6 to 12, the boy has been exercising and operating in a practical world where his experiences are very real and comprehensible.

With the advent of formal schooling, there is a shift to another type of learning activity that is removed from the concrete experience, but still refers to the world that the child knows from experience. We now find the emphasis on symbols that are primarily of three types: words, numbers, and spatial figures.

With the emphasis on developing tools for reading, counting, and drawing, the child is forced to shift from being a mover to becoming a sitter who works with smaller muscles and is forced to learn, what to him, is a foreign language.

The acquisition of good learning tools and gaining control over the use of symbols permit the boy to expand his rate of learning far beyond anything possible by direct experience. It is now possible to learn about people and events far removed from the boy's setting in terms of time and distance. The importance of such tools cannot be overstressed, and the importance of keeping such tools in good condition must be emphasized.

Much self learning can be achieved and a tremendous fund of information secured for immediate usage, and particularly, for the building materials or knowledge out of which the next stage will be achieved.

GAINING CONTROL OVER IDEAS

The fourth stage that has great significance for the college male is roughly the period that is described as puberty and adolescence. It is during this period that the meaning of many experiences and facts becomes clearer to the young man. Whereas he was a great collector of information in the previous period of development, he is now able to read "between the lines," to read "beyond the lines," and to understand ideas that are conveyed by the words that he was busily learning in the earlier stage.

Although it is fairly easy to state that this period is important for gaining control over ideas, the case does not rest there. It is not only important to understand the concept; but it is increasingly important to make comparisons or form judgments of competing ideas, to be able to reason from one position to another, and to be able to postpone judgments until sufficient evidence is presented to form a conclusion.

With the emergence of these mental processes, the young man has arrived at near adulthood. No other major types of thinking abilities will be forthcoming. What is now important to realize is that the processes of forming ideas, making judgments, and reasoning to new conclusions will be foremost in the male's life for the college years and beyond.

Unfortunately, for many young men the conviction is held that college and the professions are exclusively devoted to thinking and communication of ideas. It is true that ideas may be intoxicating and interesting, but they are not the whole of development in college. The three earlier stages are never outgrown or become obsolete. In fact, they are the foundations on which the last stage is erected and by which it can be maintained.

INDIVIDUAL DIFFERENCES

The second major idea that should be understood by the collegian deals with the matter of individual differences. It is true that the Constitution states that we are all free and equal in a political sense, but the obvious evidence is that we are very different in many traits, abilities, motivation, adjustment, and values.

Elementary psychology has presented us with the following design to show us how people are distributed on a scale from very low to very high on many of the important characteristics that our society values.

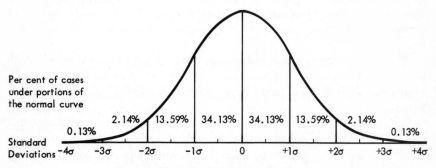

Figure 2. Methods of Expressing Test Scores.

Two important observations can be made at the very beginning of this discussion. First, at any and every age, people are found to range in ability from very low to very high. This is what is described as being "put on a curve to see how you compare with others of your own age." The second observation that is quickly made is that college students are, for all practical purposes, drawn from the upper half of the curve. This means that the typical college student is above average when compared to all of the people of his age across the country.

Turning to more specific examples that have been found to be related to progress in college studies, we find the attention of many investigators focused on the following types of individual differences:

1. *General Intelligence.* This is one of the major factors that has been identified as being very important in being able to compete in studies against others who are of the same age.
2. *Differential Aptitudes.* Many aptitudes have been identified and tests have been constructed to measure such abilities as Scholastic Aptitude, Mechanical Aptitude, Numerical Ability, Clerical Abilities, Artistic and Musical Aptitudes, to name some of the more recognized ones.
   On the other hand, there has been an increasing awareness that people have aptitudes that schools do not put a special premium on. Included here, would

be such aptitudes as social relations, athletic talents (other than the major competitive sports), and what might be called practical judgment.

3. *Motivational Differences.* It can be shown that college people differ in their interests, values and beliefs, aspirations, and adjustment to the challenges that everyone must deal with in his development.

4. *Hereditary or Genetic Differences.* By this stage of your life, one of the "facts of life" that you don't argue about is that "people are born different" in such obvious characteristics as color, sex, height, body-build and eye color. Scientists have been able to identify many other traits or characteristics that are related to genetics, but these are not as visible as the first group.

Many studies have been conducted for the past fifty years attempting to show the relationships of the above types of factors to academic progress. At this time, and for the foreseeable future, it is likely that no single factor nor combination of several factors will fully explain why some succeed and some fail.

What you can do is to learn what your chief abilities are, combine these with your major interests and values, secure the necessary training to convert such talents into skills that will help you in "learning how to live" and "learning how to make a living."

Whatever else can be said about point 4 above, it must be emphasized that you are a unique individual who is different from every other person in the world in some way. Somebody once put it very aptly by saying that every human being is an unrepeatable event.

If you can understand that every human being undergoes constant changes from conception to death, that he is never static, and if you realize that people of the same age have great varieties of abilities, aptitudes, interests, beliefs, and adjustments, you should be better able to begin the struggles of the college years.

The next chapter presents twelve suggestions that I have found through the years to help young men "keep on the track" or to "get back on the track" when they have slipped or fallen out of the race.

CHAPTER 2

How to Succeed in College

Success is not solely equated with academic achievement, although a minimal level of academic proficiency is required in order to continue to reap the many benefits that can be derived from the college experience. The chief focus will be on the development of the individual as the major goal of this stage of life. Although there is no dispute with the specific objectives that are the proper concern of the many academic disciplines, the larger goals are not completely the business of any one subject area.

In view of the diversity of forces that have contributed to an individual's development to the point of his college enrollment, many of which cannot be changed, the chief reliance for dealing with the present and the foreseeable future must be in the basis of learning. In the previous chapter, attention was called to the major developmental tasks that confront all normal persons. These were designated as gaining control over one's body, gaining control over one's physical world, gaining control over symbols, and gaining control over ideas.

By the time a young man arrives at college, he will have gained reasonable control over the systems that characterize the first three stages of life. However, the mistake is frequently made that having gained a degree of mastery that one can ignore or postpone further attention to those first three stages and devote oneself primarily or exclusively to the intellectual pursuits during the college period. This shortsightedness often continues into the professional careers of college men who ignore the tasks that were associated with their childhood and adolescence, on the one hand, and show a disinterest to look too far into the future on the other hand.

If the goal of "individual development" is a worthy one, then such development requires the individual to be active in his own behalf. We smile when someone speaks of "putting old heads on young shoulders" because the operation cannot be performed literally nor figuratively. We nod in agreement when the expression is "great oaks from little acorns grow" because experience has taught many adults and some youth that the course of development is not rapid nor spectacular. Since we cannot prepare a person to perform his career roles upon completion of studies, we prepare him primarily to enter upon the

7

first stages of a career or profession. So too, we do not achieve the fullness of maturity at the completion of a college experience.

Moving away from the easy generalizations and sermonizing, one counseling strategy will be detailed in a series of distillates that some refer to as the "wisdom of the ages." No claim to originality is made. I have documented throughout the text the many sources of my data, and now I prepare some prescriptions whose ingredients are widely available in various forms.

1. *"See your doctor for a checkup or appraisal of your abilities, aptitudes, interests and adjustment."* In this case, the doctor may be a psychiatrist, psychologist, or counselor. Although the findings in the last section of this report do not make results as complete or sufficient predictors, the proper use of such results can reduce the gamble or strangeness of the venture. This may be viewed as a psychological X-ray that provides clues to the next steps.

Minimally the counselor should be able to inform you of the class profiles in terms of ability, student origins, previous class failures and successes. In other words, you should have some knowledge about the type of student with whom you will be living, studying, and competing. Such information should be reduced to odds that permit the student to be able to make intelligent decisions about his specific fields of study and even the college in which they may be taken. Risks are involved, no matter what one's decision. But defined risks, consciously chosen, can often encourage an individual to his utmost. The process of choosing among colleges needs to be informed and deliberate, so the student can muster and strengthen his resources for a great effort of self-development for self-fulfillment. (Gibson, 115)

It is difficult to see what can be gained by denying any facts about yourself. You do exhibit machine-like and animal-like characteristics; rather than refuse to acknowledge these aspects of his nature, a man might base his claim to be something more than an animal or robot on his ability and indeed his yearning to recognize and overcome such tendencies. The systematic study of such tendencies is helpful in that endeavor. The critics sometimes write as if they believe we could not possibly like man once we really got to know him, or as if, once his illusions about himself were shattered, he would go to pieces. (Freedman, 103)

In the face of mounting pressures and the need for some guides for the individuals who must ultimately make decisions, the timely observation by Astin (8) director of the American Council on Education office of research is presented:

> Since our knowledge about the comparative impact of different higher educational institutions is still in a relatively primitive state, any attempts to rank or otherwise rate colleges in terms of "effectiveness" or "quality" are premature. There is, of course, considerable folklore about colleges, particularly about the more prestigious and visible institutions. At best, any system of rating institutions based on available

data would simply reinforce this folklore. At worse, the ratings would introduce additional unconfirmed evidence concerning quality to compete with the existing folklore.

Perhaps the greatest danger in using existing rating systems is that they imply that certain kinds of students should be "matched" with certain kinds of institutions. Normally, this involves simply a matching of students in terms of academic ability with institutions in terms of their selectivity. There are several problems with this approach to college counseling. First, it greatly oversimplifies the characteristics both of institutions and of students by implying that there is only one dimension (selectivity or ability) which is of any import in the college choice process. Our research evidence and that of many other investigators has shown that there are many other, perhaps more important, ways in which colleges and students differ. Secondly, the concept of "matching" students and colleges implies that each college would ideally enroll only one type of student. There is no evidence that I know of to indicate that homogeneous institutions are necessarily desirable for all students. It is important to make a clear distinction between "ratings" of colleges and objective descriptive information about the institution, its environment, or its student body. Obviously, more good information about institutions is needed in order to enhance institutional self-understanding and also to provide college-bound students with more meaningful information on which to base their decisions. The difficulty arises when such descriptive information is equated with institutional "effectiveness." Hopefully, systematic research in higher education will soon provide us with better information about how certain institutional characteristics affect the development of the student. But until such information is available, it is premature to assume that *any* known institutional characteristic is synonymous with institutional "quality." In short, institutions and prospective college students should take the available college rating systems that purport to give information concerning institutional effectiveness with a grain of salt.

Any attempt at getting the "proper fit" for a student in terms of college or even a study program within a college is likely to produce disappointment. There are no institutions where the molding can produce a standard product for the obvious reason that the inputs (students) are quite different at the outset. Freedman (103) humorously commented on the search for the "right institution" by stating that "while we may get fresh milk from contented cows, we get pearls from irritated oysters."

2. *"Sharpen your tools."* "A poor workman argues with his tools" has long been recognized as a rationalization for one's failure to do his best. The availability of many programmed materials to increase one's academic tools such as reading and math skills through "operation bootstraps" does not doom one to be burdened with poorly developed skills and study habits even though poor foundations were laid in an earlier period. The consistently high correlations of measures of ability in this connection with academic achievement warrants putting such skills in better working condition.

Interestingly, one of the unusual developments in the present study of beginners was the high relationship found between the writing of stories on the pictures and the subsequent achievement in formal studies. The practice of composing answers on the spot seems to be a very important aspect of the learning that is expected in studies. Practice in this regard can be carried out independently by rewriting one's notes before they "grow cold" and remain frozen in skeletal form; by beginning the practice of writing one's impressions of professors, current events, or incidents in a spontaneous fashion. This is likely to be the typical manner in which one responds to most of life's challenges rather than preparing outlines that are scrutinized before they are transposed into copy.

3. *"Never study after the sun sets,"* except in emergencies. It is quite obvious that the bulk of the world's professional work is done during the daylight hours, and this system is likely to continue. Moreover what limited research has been carried on in terms of when a group is most efficient (Wada) supports the view that daylight hours are most productive. This means that with an early start each day and by carrying a typical course load of 16-17 hours of class work, most students can complete the assignments and have evenings for other important learning experiences. Not only is there sufficient time to do the job during the daylight hours, but the sense of having completed the work permits one to engage in other activities without having assignments hanging over his head.

The "stress" during an examination is a condition that is inescapable. Everyone who is called upon to perform for others is subject to this "stress" in one way or another. The "anxiety" which precedes examinations for days can best be reduced by applying oneself to the preparation rather than "wringing one's hands."

4. *"Expand your consciousness by expanding your lungs."* An interesting departure in EEG examinations is the hyperventilation phase of the procedure. In that three or four minute interlude of heavy breathing many interesting sensory experiences are had. In a comparable fashion, the practice of vigorous exercise produces both temporary and long range experiences and benefits. Expressions such as "gaining your second wind," "clearing out the cobwebs," "turning off one engine and putting another one into use," "keeping all systems on the go," are all reflections about the value of systematic exercise and play. What is strongly recommended is that in addition to games that people engage in for both exercise and the competitive aspect, there is a personal value to be derived from engaging in activities that have physical activity but not a competitive aspect built into them. Such activities as hiking, swimming, handball, and weight lifting can be undertaken with a minimum of preparation and equipment.

The position is taken that every aspect of the individual's functioning is contributory to full development, irrespective of age. The Greeks were hailed for having advanced the thesis that a sound mind requires a sound body.

A commentary about the role of exercise in the life of business and professional men may point up the value of such pursuits. Not infrequently, many men plunge into their professions and careers with such complete force that they ignore the imperatives of keeping themselves in shape until some physical condition commands their attention. Then, a preoccupation with getting in shape appears for the person over forty.

The collegian appears to have some of the traits of the young professional worker. He is so caught up in matters of the mind, social issues, his "identity," and "making the grade" that he permits the physical to be tabled.

Greenwald (132) in an article on "Play Therapy for Children over Twenty-one" noted that executives who managed to maintain their humor and treated work like play were more productive, more energetic, more creative, more efficient than grim, hard-driving, hard-driven executives.

Sullivan frequently spoke of the basic tendency towards health, both mental and physical; man has somewhere in himself a will to recuperate; the organism is not indifferent to the alternatives of illness and health. Educators need a similar assumption. There is embedded in every man and woman a will to grow, mentally and physically. The personality is not indifferent to the alternatives of unfolding or stymieing the rational faculties. The normal person deals with problem situations in one of three ways: he gets on with it, he gets out of it, or he gets help with it.

Ciardi in an address to a group of business leaders stated "An ulcer, gentleman, is an unwritten poem." This could easily be expanded to include the postponed exercise, the tabled recreational plans, and the unopened painting kit.

Despite very little scientific knowledge of LSD and the other hallucinogenic drugs, nearly a million Americans have taken the psychedelic trip in the past five years. The spread of the usage of such drugs cannot be called an epidemic according to Dr. Albert Sattin, but physicians are worried about it. Sattin denied that the drugs were "mind expanding." He argued instead that they allowed the user to rid himself of his feelings. The main function of a drug like LSD is to remove restraints in the mind. It is dangerous, because no one can predict the consequences in the individual. In no case has LSD gone beyond the strictly experimental stage and there are no common medically accepted uses for it. According to McCaughy, the college generation is "methaphysically starved: and most of the college drug takers use them on an experimental basis." (Sattin, C.P.D., 318)

Recent research in neurochemistry (Ordy, 1967) points up that manipulation of the environment which leads to personal motivation is the chief basis of producing changes in behavior. The recourse to drugs, surgical procedures, and the like is primarily in terms of pathological conditions. These intrusions in the lives of individuals do not produce the salutary changes that come from learning models and programs. More people rust out than wear out. (Personal Communication, 1967)

5. *"Learn the game."* To be a student today is almost by definition to be one who has learned how to stay ahead of the game. Students didn't invent the

college game, which now ranks with Big Business, Big Labor and Big Government as Big Education. You have to play it long and hard for the simple reason that adults who run things haven't devised any socially acceptable options to college-going. Moreover, you will learn that there is less prejudice here than parallel entry into professional, business and social life. (Palmer 274)

Study the playing field. No college has a single student culture. All colleges have varying numbers of students who belong to the "collegiate subculture" for whom enjoying the experience before moving on to the adult world is emphasized; the "professional- vocational subculture" for whom preparation for adult life is the major task of college; an "intellectual-subculture" in which the search for answers to many of life's problems is eagerly sought; the "academic subculture" in which getting grades is viewed as the passport to the good life and secure future; and the "alienated or disenchanted" for whom the college provides a base from which to mount attack against the Establishment or to "find themselves." Whatever your personal inclination, you are able to align yourself with others having similar postures.

Find a professor or counselor who knows the atmosphere and will relate to you some of the roadblocks that loom up in whatever associations you make. Such a person might be likened to a coach who not only knows your special aptitudes but coincidentally knows something of the "opposition." Keep in touch with such a person.

Start modestly in terms of the amount of class work taken. Our findings on the seriousness of falling down in grade point average in the first semester of school (reported in Chapter VIII) suggests that a limited or reasonable load, maintained at least at the average level, can be a major factor in continuation until graduation. The pay-off in college studies, whatever else you hear, is still in academic grades.

Aside from the visible curriculum which is spelled out in the catalogues, "the invisible curriculum" has to also be taken. Here you are confronted by the styles of professors, the conflicting rules, the power plays between different segments of the university, the student organizations and at times unreasonable demands. This invisible curriculum is tougher to pass than the formal one. Several suggestions are in order which can help you weather these ambiguous challenges: an old Arabian observation that "all sunshine makes a desert" can help during periods of stress, and the "neglect of students is a|tradition," notwithstanding claims to the contrary.

6. *"Practice what you learn."* The value of laboratory experience in science courses is of unquestioned importance in tying together the theory and application. In a similar vein, every course should have its practicum. Learn parliamentary rules and stand up in a meeting; volunteer in a social agency for purposes of testing the theories about people you learn in psychology and sociology; a part time job in a business, industrial, or governmental establish-

ment will begin the serious task of seeing whether words and labels are representative of processes and realities.

Parents, teachers, and ministers often talk in such vague, abstract terms that the listener doesn't know what to do. We are asked to build for world peace, to become more humane, to invest our money wisely, to guard our health. But we are not presented with a tangible task, no simple steps to start out with. Those who make suggestions for action have a responsibility for defining the appropriate responses to be made. (Stevenson & Dale, 1967)

Woodrow Wilson gave the following advice in regard to the training of the political scientist: "He must frequent the street, the counting house, the clubhouse, the halls of legislatures. . . he must hear the din of conventions, and see their intrigues. . . he must keep his generalizations firmly bottomed on fact and experience."

The only way to develop dedication to the democratic process or to any ideal is to permit the learners to "take a hand" in it. They must respond to an experience in its concrete setting, not merely as a neat abstraction in a textbook.

Rokeach (303) observed that we are all motivated by the desire, which is sometimes strong and sometimes weak, to see reality as it actually is, even if it hurts.

Curiously enough, students accept drudgery when someone is bold enough to make them see that it is a pathway to excellence. Look at the football team. The coach doesn't entertain the members of the team. He demands strenuous efforts that resemble drudgery more than entertainment. Good performance is both their incentive and their reward. So it should be in everything else. The professional athlete, a linguist, mathematician, musician, and artist have a way of making their performances look easy. Think of what effort went into achieving the effortless appearance of an ice skater. If we are going to be diffident about the effort that must be invested and feel that we must entertain students, we err, but it does not mean that we must get tough. When discipline is imposed upon an individual without regard for his own purpose and without his acceptance, it may lead to anti-intellectualism. The football coach can "pour it on" because he knows that the students share his purpose. They want to be made to do well because of the common purpose of the team. But it is very difficult to use this model in the classroom, where students are encouraged to compete with each other. We cannot expect to create a group spirit in the classroom as we do on the athletic field. But students will go out into the community and work with an enthusiasm that approaches and at times exceeds that of an athlete.

7. *"Tailor your program to your needs and aspirations."* The large variety of studies, the wide open opportunities for working in your post college days, and the importance of finding a "labor of love" are all considerations that should enter into your stay in college. Nobody can lay claim to knowing what is best for you in studies, recreation, hobbies, diet, etc. Therefore, you have both the

opportunity to choose a variety of experiences and also the responsibility to carry out the imperatives of each choice.

The great emphasis on excellence is visible on all sides and on many lips. The difficulty with such preachment is that it leaves so much unsaid or unclear.

One consideration is to choose professors as you choose courses: ask successful upperclassmen who have weathered or traveled that way. Despite the resistance of many professors to be evaluated or sized up, the fact of college life is that they cannot escape such appraisal. It may be informal and inaccurate, in part, but some information is better than none when making decisions on what to do.

There is a fallacy that has widespread acceptance: namely, you failed out of such and such a college. The correction is that you may fail a program of studies within a college, but that there are numerous other choices to exercise before having the judgment made in a wholesale fashion. This means that you can shift programs, adjust size of loads or proceed along different lines before leaving an institution.

In a similar vein, it is important to recognize that pacing one's education as well as fitting one's education should be an individual process and not an event. You don't receive an education in the sense that a degree is conferred upon you at a particular time; you engage in a constant or intermittent manner to increase your knowledge, skills, insights, and competencies both in and out of the classroom. It is very likely that the bulk of information and facts that were memorized for purposes of passing tests will have been forgotten within a short time after their acquisition. The habits of application and the larger ideas and meanings will become increasingly clearer with the passage of time.

For the above reasons two generalizations should be kept in mind: those who go the furthest take the longest time to get there, and the longest journey begins with a single step.

8. *"Get smart."* You aren't as smart as you could be, because you don't know your strengths and weaknesses, and thereby stumble into the future. Adults are likely to underestimate the student's dormant powers and overestimate his ignorance. It would be helpful for teachers to diagnose or test the extent of a person's ignorance at the beginning of a course rather than at the close. The teaching or therapy should be based on what is revealed instead of merely noted at the close of the experience.

You aren't as smart as you could be because your life goals may be unrealistic. They may suffer from sentimentality or over-inflation. The college girl enrolled in commerce says she is going into "international trade" but she can't speak or write fluent English. *We all have a huge capacity for self-deception.* Realistic goal setting requires a long look ahead coupled with plans for daily steps in the planned direction. The person who is becoming smarter carries both a compass and a yard stick.

You are not smarter than you are because you don't associate with people who know more than you do. A good way to give your mind a sharp honing is to see, listen to or read a critical thinker whose point of view differs from your own. *We tend to avoid the kind of conflict that educates.* Controversy itself does not educate, but it is a necessary ingredient. While it has often been said that the key role of the teacher has been to trouble the comfortable, *the fact is that the student has the same opportunity to challenge the teacher by raising big questions.*

To learn how to use the two terms "implication" and "implementation" in every course would soon stamp you as being perceptive and inquiring.

You aren't smarter because you choose to be spectators in the stands rather than a responsible player in the field. The uncommitted, passive, disengaged, and excessively humble excuse themselves by protesting that they are not very good at such things, or it's not their field. If you can read, you can become knowledgeable and subsequently competent in most fields. While it is comfortable and easier to learn by being tutored, it is not the only or necessary way to develop.

The epitaph of a failing student or an imcompetent research worker is: He couldn't sit still.

We talk a great deal about underdeveloped countries, but the key problem is the underdevelopment of man. We emphasize material poverty but forget that spiritual poverty also prevents growth toward wisdom and maturity. (Dale, 64)

The counselor or teacher often hears the complaint that the student wasn't completely ready to take the test, or play the game, or make the decision. The fact of the matter is that rarely, if ever, is any person completely ready to carry out an assignment. The comforting aspect of this condition is that others are in the same circumstance. The most you can do is to prepare over a reasonable period of time the materials or gain the skills that will make you an adequate performer in comparison with your peers.

9. *"Get rid of your inferiority complex."* Frequently, this excuse for failing to achieve more in the world is nothing more than a summation of the facts. Since this condition is often associated with social skills which are the basis for easy communication and meetings, the need is to take stock of what is being done in your immediate subculture and likely to be carried on in your later adult life. Then cultivate or develop some of the social skills. These might include bowling, card playing, dancing, golf, chess, social conversation and dialogues, pool, etc. These may be likened to desserts that follow a hearty meal but are sufficient in small portions.

Interestingly, Menninger and many others have commented on the fact that most failures in business and the professions are not due to technical incompetence but due to social inadequacies or interpersonal awkwardness.

A future dilemma will not be on how to keep alive in terms of food, shelter, clothing and medical care, but how to spend the leisure time that increased industrial productivity is forcing upon large segments of our population.

While it is equally demonstrable that successful men in the professions spend more than the average amount of time in their careers, the best way to maintain *personal* productivity is to have a variety of outlets from the *main* commitment.

Every human life is sort of a handicap run toward the liberation of the full rational faculties. Few are able to come anywhere near the goal for a combination of reasons; first, unloving parents may divert the individual into a life long process of proving himself worthwhile; second, a precarious self-esteem may lead him to a constant quest for social approval and popularity, and the school and college become mainly an arena for developing social skills; third, the worries induced by a competitive society may make the individual acutely conscious of the hazards of an uncertain future, and the school and college experience is marked by a frantic striving for the improvement of his future prospects by hard work on assignments and striving for good grades; fourth, if his career ambitions become disappointed and the individual goes "down in the world," then his social anxieties and the need to rationalize or to hate may occupy the front of his consciousness for the rest of his life; or fifth, if his ambitions become gratified the chances that he will come to see his own identity in terms of his role, in the sense that his vision will be limited by his status. He reflects as a lawyer, doctor, man of wealth, executive, labor leader. (Rokeach, 303)

10. *"Be a Manry."* Travel the silent sea of books or as Pelican suggests take a break from the "grind" by a visit to the Hospital for the Soul, otherwise referred to as a library.

In the great struggle to assert your autonomy and independence, which is viewed as removing your dependence from the past, the easiest course of action is to know that past. Practically stated, the more you know about the past, the less likely you are to repeat the mistakes of the past (which included your parents and other adults).

It has been suggested that the most astute psychologist in modern times was Shakespeare, but that he used the language of the times rather than couching it in technical terms.

Two of the most exciting figures in the western world in the past thirty years were Winston Churchill and John F. Kennedy; both men devoted much time to reading history and literature for clues in dealing with their assignments.

11. *"Claim your inheritance."* Whatever else can be documented about you, the inescapable fact is that you are an individual that is an unrepeatable event. This makes you very special and unique, and that much is up to you to write the rest of the story. Opportunities are available to translate the potentiality into many types of noteworthy as well as notorious outcomes.

The individual liberty or freedom which is the birthright of Americans provides opportunities to undertake many types of training, travel, and commitment.

In this so-called "Era of the Student" in which uniqueness of the human "condition" is emphasized, the importance of maintaining an historical perspective is inescapable. One of the major functions of religion and ethical philosophy has been to help man meet his existential perplexities, but psychologists have tended to ignore the problem. (Mowrer, 255)

It is indeed true that when life is going well, death often seems remote, unreal; and that it looms largest in our thoughts when we are physically ill or emotionally troubled. But death is also a problem for the physically and emotionally healthy person. Thomas Aquinas begins his book, *My Way of Life,* with this statement of what is in many ways *the* human problem:

> The Road that stretches before the feet of a man is a challenge to his heart long before it tests the strength of his legs. Our destiny is to run to the edge of the world and beyond, off into the darkness; sure for all our blindness, secure for all our helplessness, strong for all our weakness, gaily in love for all the pressure on our hearts. (p.1.)

To what extent can "learning theory," as we now know it, contribute to a better understanding and more courageous confrontation of this enigma?

With other living organisms man shares many, many characteristics; truly he is a part of the Animal Kingdom. But only man is religious; and this characteristic reflects his efforts at "salvation" following Adam's "fall," or following man's rise to the point of being godlike in his intelligence and awareness, but still too human in his mortality. (Mowrer, 255)

Psychology doesn't have much to say on the fates of man in a religious sense, but it has much to say about the social aspects. How interesting it is that the story of Cain and Abel brings to our attention the observation that man can survive physically and psychologically, only if he becomes his "brother's keeper," concerned, compassionate, generous, helpful, related.

To Freud death was not the ultimate test of human character and courage; man was said to have an "instinct" for it. But to Fromm (1955) the mentally healthy person is the person who lives by love, reason and faith, who respects life, his own and that of his fellow man.

I share with Frank (99) the conviction that the view of the college world from one campus or region is likely to be not only quite distorted but also quite provincial. Rather than pretend to a knowledge of other schools, I would like to discuss what I see on my own campus, digress from there, and trust that at least some of what I say will generalize to other colleges. My contacts with students, and they are many and varied, lead me to the conclusion that the vast majority of them are deeply concerned with moral values and have high standards of personal conduct. Unfortunately, these concerns are not nearly as well publicized as are other occurrences which verge on the aberrational. Our communication media tend to deal more with the latter, and the public, consequently, becomes preoccupied with them.

12. *"Mortgage your own future."* In the final analysis only you can directly invest yourself and thereby create your own future.

Many spokesmen have recorded their views on what that future holds in store. Obviously, these range from a very pessimistic to a very optimistic one.

It is easier to attack and challenge than to erect or construct. Being for something, although it is imperfect, is better than withholding commitment until you are sure or possess a guarantee. No aspect of life has temporal assurances, whether it be a happy marriage, a good job, a happy life, etc. The most you can ask is for opportunities to struggle, to search for answers without demanding that somebody or some institution insure your success.

Rotter (310) reports on an unusually consistent set of findings about the influence of expectancies in human behavior. His investigation supported the view that the individual who has a strong belief that he can control his destiny is likely to: (a) be more alert to those aspects of the environment which provide useful information for his future behavior; (b) take steps to improve his environmental condition; (c) place a greater value on skill or achievement and be generally more concerned with his ability, particularly with his failures; and (d) be resistive to subtle attempts to influence him.

The attitude about whether you are truly a person, capable of carrying out your own plans, or a "thing" that is handled by parents, teachers, or friends is a major factor in your future development. The evidence is overwhelmingly in favor of your personhood.

If students sense that everything in the college can be understood only by the professionals, then the discussion stops and you will have problems because our problems will remain. Students develop a variety of strategies to deal with the almost inevitable dissonance between expected present, actual present, and hoped-for futures. Certain strategies have higher survival value in one academic setting than others. The institution, more than the student, sets the odds on the various strategies and coping patterns that will win. Students need to deal with the discrepancies and dissonance, not by innocence nor denial, but by honest attention to how they come to terms with these conditions. (Snyder, 336)

One reason why many persons do not feel a sense of power to control their own destiny is that they do indeed lack power. They do not think they can change themselves or society, and weak people do not make a strong society. Laswell noted that a mark of a democratic society is that we share power and respect. The disadvantaged have known neither power nor respect. Many of today's struggles are attempts to secure equality of power. (Dale, 65)

Not all of the above prescriptions are required in any case, nor is it likely that none of the prescriptions is called for in any case. Rather it can be shown that the college male has incompletely developed in some respect. The danger may lie in oversimplification of the problem which in no way is the path to the solution of the problem.

At this point I would like to introduce you to an important learning principle. Having read the previous pages which contain twelve suggestions for promoting your college development, take a sheet of paper and list those twelve or as many of them as you can. Having recorded the main idea of each suggestion, then write a few sentences on the specific items that are covered under each point.

It is very likely that you find yourself in an uncertain state and that less than half of the items were recorded. What you probably did was to read the information largely for making a superficial acquaintance with the subject matter and assumed that you would recognize the points if someone brought them up for discussion. Without the presentation by someone the likelihood of recalling them is considerably lessened; in fact, very improbable.

The major point that I make in this case is that most students do not distinguish between *reading* and *studying.* In the first case, you cover the material with the expectation that the material will be reproduced on a test and you will be expected to *recognize* it in the form of a multiple choice item, a true-false item, a matching item, or a short completion question. On the other hand, the professor may be evaluating your ability to *recall* the idea or the points of the discussion. There is a greater difficulty in recalling items than there is in recognizing them.

Studying some subject matter is closely related to recalling the pertinent items and concepts without having many props or cue cards to help you. When you make this clear distinction in your thinking, you will have added a very important foundation to your future learning. Now, go back over the twelve points and *study* them for future application.

In summation: young men you are forced to fend for yourselves, don't romanticize your college experiences, the adults in those setting are struggling with their own identities, and such identities do not generally have their focus in being helpers or counselors; they appear to be centered on being scholars, researchers, consultants, and administrators, who might, if honest, state, "This would be a nice place to work, if the students weren't around." This is especially true of large universities and small colleges in metropolitan areas.

The conflict that frequently rages between different segments of our society on the topic of whether *individuation* or *socialization* is to be the main objective of our educational programs is mirrored in the "heat" that is generated on the ranking of these two processes. Strong support is marshalled by Sanford and Freedman and others that the primary focus of college work should be on the process of individual development. This emphasis logically brings concurrence from young collegians because of their strong needs for emancipation, freedom, and exercise. On the other hand, the "needs" of society for the socialization of the new breed or crop of youth impose restraints that are viewed as authoritarian, dogmatic, and unwarranted. The conflict between generations which is highlighted in so many ways can be reduced to this impasse: How can society's institutions be sustained while at the same time permitting the maximum development of the individual in a pluralistic society? The struggle is not likely to be resolved by any negotiated peace for the future, but remains the perennial task of every individual in every generation to resolve with his older generation. The dynamic character of the principals precludes that one or the other will "lay down his arms" and submit to the other. The historical dominance of institutions over the lives of individuals is being challenged by philosophies that place the individual at the crucial-determining point.

The perennial task of providing opportunities and training for individual development while at the same time preserving institutional forms that require cooperative endeavors will provide future generations ample challenges to wrestle with as the physical survival issues become less urgent.

You may want to secure more information and ammunition for understanding and challenging the propositions outlined in this section. If so, proceed to the next section, where many ideas have been assembled for your examination and study.

Part II

In Part II, I will assume a different posture and perspective. The shift in this section will be to a counseling framework. Since no imperative strategy or practice emerges from studies, whatever their nature on humans, it follows that the counselor must fashion his own theory and consequent practices. The validity of his construction will be ascertained by critical examinations by his professional colleagues and by the efficacy of the program in assisting clients. The two types of validity are often referred to as construct and empirical validities, respectively. Systems do not force a single type of practice. Fielder's (1950) efforts in assessing the outcomes of therapy and counseling pointed out the great variance in theories held by counselors, but the similarity of outcomes resulted from personal competence, irrespective of the claimed theoretical position. Additionally, the work of Kelly and Fiske (186) sobers the enthusiastic acceptance of any diagnostic or evaluation procedure as a sufficient basis for predicting larger behavior outcomes or subsequent performance in a profession.

In the chapters that follow, the writer presents the major forces that are operating in individual behavior. In Chapter III the effort is directed to the presence and influence of external factors that intrude in the development of the individual. The influence of cultural or societal press is acknowledged as having very telling effects in the emerging or developing individual. The next section focuses on the differential effects of smaller segments of the milieu, which is the institutional setting wherein the impacts of student subcultures and faculty-administration activities are briefly outlined.

Chapter IV addresses itself to the longitudinal factors that help to shape the current functioning of the student. Considerable emphasis is placed on current personality integration and the learning resources that are available to the college male in coping with his challenges.

Then follows an attempt to formulate a strategy for dealing with the myriad of forces that impinge on the student.

CHAPTER 3

External Factors Influencing the College Male

THE LARGER SOCIETY OR CULTURE

Lerner (210) insists that we are in an age of revolution; foundations of our values are being shaken and world power structures and ideologies are changing. Moreover, our political thinking about the world of nation-states is being subjected to special scrutiny. Since we have the power of over-kill, it becomes necessary for education to develop two types of elites to handle such problems. These will become the commanding and creative elites, and it is imperative that they learn to work together. Tragedy is part of the very constitution of the universe ... no man, no nation is immune to it. But there is a difference between the tragic and the pathetic. The pathetic is man-made, and because it is, it can be resolved; poverty is not tragic, but it is pathetic and should be reduced or eliminated.

In developing the theme that behavior change can be induced by guidance, Weitz (381) reviewed the role of values in that context. He observed that to a large extent, the general view of man and his society held in the early part of the twentieth century involved a picture of man doing God's work. Man's purpose was seen in terms of performing good and moral acts, a reasonable inventory of which could be found in religious documents available to many, if not all, people. It was the stable, almost rigid majority that determined by their acts the texture of their society's values. Despite small but continuous and progressive revisions, there was little change in the Professed Values of the culture for almost thirty years after the first stirrings of organized, formal guidance. The standard virtues of honesty, charity, respect for authority, brotherly love, and the like continued to be honored in the texts of sermons, political speeches, and social studies syllabi. As time went on, however, the "Infinite" appeared less and less frequently in the official expressions of society's values. These virtues, over the years, came to seem good in themselves, without needing to be associated somehow with a Deity.

Weitz continued:

> The cataclysmic developments of the past forty years that made physical survival valuable, now shifted the importance from physical survival to psychological survival. Man's purpose since the war appears to have been to maintain his phenomenal self, to achieve physical and psychological survival through freedom and security. It is, as if each individual were saying, "Look at me! I'm somebody. I am: therefore, I am entitled to freedom and security." Van Kaam applies this system of values to guidance: Counseling is essentially a process of making free a humanizing of the person who has lost his freedom in sectors of his existence where he can no longer transcend his life situation by freely giving meaning to it.
>
> In America, at least, these changes may be summarized as a shift from a value system centered on moral responsibility to a higher law, to a system centered on individual freedom, security, and self-actualization.

We are in a period when images are viewed as important coin in human relations. Most of us are quite familiar with the efforts of Madison Avenue to increase the receptivity of products and individuals. One hears that the images of man guide an age. Parents raise their kids to conform to an image. Man is made in the image of God, but the Bible enjoins to make no images of God. Blocher (30) states that humans are in a bind. They are damned if they have no explicit images of human possibility and actuality, and they're damned if they take their images too literally. Frankl (101) notes that man is free and responsible to life. Each man's life is his answer to the questions that life puts to him. It is not a quest for pleasure, tension-reduction or power, but aims at the fulfillment of his creative values (work), experiential values (beauty and truth), and when life affords no alternatives to suffering and death, there are still attitudinal values. Man can choose to be an object or he can assume his freedom and responsibility and live his life rather than drift with its biological and sociological "determiners."

There is no dearth of commentators who have addressed themselves to the matter of values and the role of such values in current society. In order that the college, an institution developed by society for various purposes, be seen in its conflicting roles, a sampling of views will be included here.

From Rudolph (314) the assertion is recorded that the maturity of free man is anchored in his moral and intellectual capacity to cope with the insecurity that is unavoidably interwoven with the pursuit of values which are all in some measure and in some degree in conflict with one another. The ability to cope with tensions and with polar values has been recognized as the criterion of a free man by social philosophers as widely divergent as deTocqueville and Buber.

Sanford (318) writes that of all the effects of the cold war, the most serious has been moral deterioration in our national life. As Thomas Mann observed, the worst thing about totalitarianism is that its opponents are led to imitate its methods. We must seek to develop in the student the capacity to look upon other people, all kinds of people, and feel that we share with them a common humanity. The individual who cannot do this is, fundamentally, one who cannot admit into his consciousness some of his own dispositions. Whatever he cannot recognize in himself is likely to be attributed to some "outsiders," who are then regarded with suspicion and hostility.

The most significant thing about a society is its ruling beliefs and values. Adults make the world in which youth grows up, and therefore strong support can be marshalled for the notion that every generation of adults gets the type of youth it deserves. Moreover, no society will tolerate any institution that effectively undermines its values, but history is strewn with the wrecks of civilizations whose young people, following the lead of their elders, suffered a failure of nerve and a failure of will. (Lerner, 209)

In this pluralistic period many philosophies and many psychologies are available to provide a rationale for many diverse programs and activities. What is more, these are found to be operating side by side in various institutions, even visible as contradictory facets of the same person. Some examples:

We are living in an age when our educational institutions are valued to an unprecedented extent. The pendulum has swung from expecting too little to expecting too much. (Wilson, 395) The depersonalization of the student can lead to a grave threat to the purposes of higher education.

Historically and currently, the role of government in the lives of individuals is polarized along the positions outlined by Hamilton and Jefferson. According to Hamilton, government was for the purpose of providing stability and preserving order. Jefferson maintained that the main function of government was to provide for the freedom and happiness of its citizens, to use the resources of understanding that masses offered, and to respect the rights of the individual states. (Stewart, 348) Jefferson, moreover, maintained that America would not survive unless it could develop an aristocracy of virtue and talent which we could call today a set of elites of character and ability.

The country is populated by a large number of people who believe that it is every man's natural right to have children who are smarter and more successful than he. This expectation is treated in Dewey's "What the best and wisest parent wants for his own child, that must the community want for all its children. Any other ideal for our schools is narrow and unlovely; acted upon, it destroys democracy." It is not surprising that children, reacting to this expectation, are less than wholly deferential to their elders. (Frankel, 100) Coupled to this conviction has been the growth of a new attitude of child rearing in which the parents have made a genuine effort to understand their children and not impose parental authority in ways which might inhibit the young child. As a result, it is extremely difficult for the child to rebel, since he is understood rather than repressed. This has complications in developing an attitude of self-understanding before there is a great deal of self to understand. Most sixteen-year-olds are sufficiently sophisticated not only to know the limits of power possessed by their parents if it were to be put to a test, but are also prepared to live an independent emotional life by depriving the parents of a return of affection. Having staked everything on a warm and affectionate relationship with the child, the parent cannot then resort to older methods of authority with the expectation of respect and obedience. The tension of opposites, so often a part in the healthy emotional situation of the adolescent, disappears in a warm bath of parental affection. The parent, therefore, in fact, has not control over the child; the child often has not yet a sufficient experience to exert control over himself. (Sanford, 315)

It is possible to challenge the older progressive theory that absence of institutional authority and the award of freedom to the young in a radically democratic system will develop an understanding of democracy. The fallacy lies in assuming that because students have student rights and equality of status with other members of the campus community, including faculty and administration, therefore, the role of the student is of the same character (and equal in sense) to the status and role of the others. Laying claims to and possession of competencies or qualifications are not equitable. The dialogue that is so much heralded in our contemporary society as the means to solving many issues is misunderstood. Dialogue obtains when the principals are in comparable circumstances or of comparable resourcefulness. Otherwise, what is likely to be the nature of an exchange is one in which those in authority are listening with an open ear but not compelled to act on the petitions of the other group.

Most college generations in American higher education have, in varying degrees of intensity, questioned or rejected the moral codes of their day. Gallagher (107) noted:

> They are self-righteous in social matters and determinedly deliberate in experimentation in personal matters. They are caught between the compulsions of a new social morality and the license of the new personal immorality. One of their spokesman, Paul Krassner, opined "I believe that existence has no meaning, and I love every minute of it." Up until this time, most college presidents and faculties and students accepted the words of G.K. Chesterton: "Art, like morality, consists of drawing the line somewhere." The current dysphoric generation claims the acceptance of the aphorism is precisely what is wrong with the whole world.

The interdependence of the college and the larger social system is both close and complex. If most of the college graduates who are now influential in government and business are disposed to tolerate or even support a considerable amount of anti-intellectualism, it is evident that they did not become intellectuals; social and academic anxieties and incentives dominated their college years, and they never developed their full powers of rationality.

Anti-intellectualism exists in all countries, and it has existed in all countries at all times. Most of mankind's progress has been made over the violent objections of the majority of mankind and by men and women who were despised and feared by the majority. The world has never been safe for the intellectual. The intellectual has always been an outcast, a freak, an object of fear and derision. We are dealing with one of the eternal millstones that mankind wears around its neck. (Havemann, 146) It is because the intellectual life is essentially the discovery, contemplation, and evaluation of alternatives that conformity to any given pattern is its death warrant. It is for the widely shared concern about intellectuality that social scientists concentrate so heavily on the restraints upon freedom: both those within the individual and those in the social situation.

There appears to be some sense of uselessness in the world. ... the unacknowledged god of the modern world is productivity, higher standards of material living, and as much respite from work as possible. Huxley, a keen student of the human drama, stated that "the sense of uselessness is the severest shock the human system can endure," and this is reflected in Baldwin's "the most dangerous creation of any society is that man who has nothing to lose." This was the social dynamite that Conant spoke of when he surveyed the American Secondary school.

Sanford (315) further noted that every failure of rationality in a social system, as in personality, surely is a symptom of insecurity. It is most important to restore the responsible individual who is being lost in a tangle of organized social roles and group memberships. Images, roles, and committees act in such a way that it is hard to find who is responsible for what. Instead of good and bad decisions by responsible officials, we now have mediocre decisions by anonymous committees. Education should give the student a sense of himself instead of a feeling of impotence because of the vast and complex social processes and organizations that impinge on his life.

The American college is embedded in our culture and in our society. The colleges are expressive of persistent trends and persistent conflicts in the American value system, and they have a diversity of important functions to society. This means that fundamental changes in the colleges can come about only when there is a shift of emphasis in our general social processes. At the present time, the majority of our articulate citizens value the non-academic benefits their children derive from college and do not really want to see things change. (Reisman & Jencks, 293)

Our lack of confidence in the fundamental rightness of our comfortable or even privileged ways causes us to be suspicious of any knowledge that could expose and challenge our position. The Copernican heliocentric system was rejected because it upset the topographical notions which at the time required that heaven should be "above" and hell "below." If there was no particular place in the world for heaven and hell, religion itself was thought to be in danger. To be sure, religious doctrines have changed. But few would argue that we are worse off for having lost the belief in ancient cosmologies. (Stewart, 348)

The shift from reliance on external institutions, including formal religion, to a greater dependence on self or at least thinking about oneself is readily documented. The history of the past sixty years records many failures of powerful institutions to intervene in the direct assistance of many individuals. The stress on individuality is matched by the increase in the size and power of corporate groups. The movement toward impersonality in carrying through the task of making a living for the larger majority of Americans forces the "expression of individuality" on other aspects of living. Adults caught up in such arrangements bind themselves to unions, syndicates, associations, and combines for the purpose of holding their own in the larger struggle. As the preoccupations of adults become fixated on affiliations within their adult alignments, the younger generation perceives this as a struggle in which individuality is sacrificed for group survival. The urgency of finding one's "identity" in the peer group, rather than in a disinterested adult generation, gives expressions to many forms of dissociation. With the decline in the emphasis on God as the lawgiver and the lessened influence of strong adults in the lives of the young, the efficacy of the notion "the sanction for a law depends on the nature of the lawgiver" is met with doubts, and rebellion by many who question the adequacy and integrity of their visible authority figures.

The great appeal and popularity of the Existential movement derives much of its force from the disillusionment with the existing institutional arrangements under adult direction. Instead of heavy emphasis on invisible powers being responsible for one's fate, the individual is deemed sufficient to devise his own tactics for personal fulfillment and salvation. The baptism is shifted from an emphasis on "water" to one of "desire" and "fire." Contemplation through expanded consciousness and activism are derivatives of these new commitments. The "tuning in" and "turning off" phenomenon is a manifestation of the former conviction, while Peace Corps volunteers, civil rights marches, sit-ins, voter registrations, black power, and burnings are practical demonstrations of the latter motivation. Some support is given Freud's observation that young children are given to "an omnipotence of thought" in which their views are deemed sufficient to produce changes in their world. The disengaged group noted above is well characterized by such a childish level of rationality.

The preoccupations and activities of large segments of the American adult population are sufficiently adolescent in character that it is small wonder that intellectuality is not deemed an important commodity or goal. The strangeness of the view that "virtue is its own reward" or "playing the game well is more important than winning" or "learning has its own demands and prerogatives" brings puzzlement and surprise to many who are accustomed to rewards and prizes for merely surviving or attending.

Cogley (54) editorialized in the following vein:

> The generational gap is becoming so wide that some of us oldsters are beginning to believe that no one under 30 can be trusted. We do not trust their moral judgment, their political wisdom, or their fidelity to the traditions of civility. We are afraid to pass on the world to them, even though we can't do anything about it because their time has already come, or soon will.
>
> They in turn don't trust us. They don't trust our moral judgment, our political wisdom, or our fidelity to their future. They tell us we are great at making war, and point to Vietnam, but not very good at making love, and point to our racial record, our manifold other prejudices, and our indifference to another. We seem to be more concerned about keeping their hair short than about lengthening mankind's stay on earth, they tell us.
>
> They (the young) lived in a world that was so obviously different from the ideal one projected by parents, teachers, politicians and pastors that at least some have decided to do something about it. They have decided to stop obeying the disobedient; to stop paying attention to self-proclaimed peacelovers who spend a great part of their income on deadly weapons; to turn off when a sleek prelate denounces materialism; to close their ears when an embittered, loveless spokesman for old style morals denounces sexual laxity. "The simple fact is, we don't believe you. You have never given us any reason to. That's the real hangup."

The lack of awareness on the part of many members of each generation is that what it is "clamoring for" is the freedom to follow its own goals and insisting that the other side stand still. Anyone who has designed "perfect plays" in athletics or "prepared a stirring speech" knows that the outcome is far from perfection because the "other side" didn't stand still or the "audience" wouldn't listen. The consequences of many such disappointments is to belabor the other group rather than acknowledge personal lack of competence. This is witnessed in labor-management sessions, faculty-administration meetings, professor-student ties, government-industry expectations, in international relations, and in parent-child relationships. Redl's work (1951) led him to state, "In America, we have a love of kids, the neglect of children, and a hatred of youth." The distrust and hatred may be related to a familiar mechanism in which we tend to "hate in others our own worst faults!"

An elementary observation that is lost sight of quite frequently is that individuation is natural. We arrive in this world as unique individuals. We become socialized over a long period of time, but never lose the individuality we received at conception. It is easier to subscribe to and practice the credos of "enlightened self-interest," or "rugged individualism." It is more difficult and demanding to subscribe to and practice the "golden rule" or the Samaritan position: "Hands that serve are holier than lips that pray," and Keller's "It is better to light one candle than to curse the darkness."

The "cult of the individual," while having strong historical impress and plausibility in a setting with unexplored frontiers rests shakily when the economy of nations and the welfare of individuals are tied to cooperative efforts.

The struggles that beset the contemporary society derive from inconsistencies in the private and public attitudes that are derived from conceptions about the nature of man. The perennial task that confronts every man is vocalized in two historical eras:

> Men are qualified for civil liberty in exact proportion to their disposition to put chains upon their own appetites; in proportion as their love of justice is above their capacity; in proportion as their soundness and sobriety of understanding is above their vanity and presumption; in proportion as they are more disposed to listen to the counsels of the wise and good, in preference to the flattery of knaves.—(Edmund Burke)

Each Man's Right to Grow

> America's commitment is to give every person every chance to grow and develop to his best, his utmost self.
>
> Anyone can contribute. . . . A teacher strives to give honest individual attention to a child. An employer seeks to create the working environment in which employees can flourish and grow. A mother provides love and instruction that makes for early intellectual growth. A labor leader strikes a blow for equal employment opportunity.
>
> The government too is only a means to make the world manageable so that the individual human being may have the maximum amount of freedom. . . . to choose and to be what he has in him to be. . . . That's what our nation is about.
>
> I want to know what you have done lately about the basic American commitment?
>
> (Editorial, CPD, April 17, 1967)
> (re: John Gardner) (110)

> The riots were like a grotesque mirror, elongating and dramatizing the subtler thievery, disdain for human rights, and indifference to others that the rest of us have been getting away with for years.
>
> Cogley, (UB, 8/18/67) (54)

Most of us have lived within the fairly closed societies, and the behavior demands are fairly predictable. The moral revolution is calling the codes into question. Only if man can frame his own questions can he be really responsible for his own answers. Only persons who are responsible skeptics and responsible decision makers can make the breakthrough. Faculty and students and all thinking men are co-searchers. (Grennan, 133)

Taylor (356), in an address on "Higher Education and the National Purpose," observed that is is difficult to say how a country gets its purposes. Our national purpose is publicly stated in its greatest form in the Constitution of the United States. When one analyzes the Constitution, it can be seen as our own kind of blueprint for the society which we are in the process of building from day to day. But it leaves all the basic questions unanswered. As contrasted with the Soviet system it leaves open the means through which we achieve the purposes. When one looks at the meaning of the Constitution, it really comes down to the release of the individual into his society so that he may develop within himself those talents which are most appropriate to his particular character and to the needs of his society. Specific goals subsumed under the larger purpose are military, material, and political security for the United States.

THE COLLEGE ENVIRONMENT

In addition to the larger press that derives from the values and expectations of the culture and society, the institution designated as a college or university presents additional challenges and opportunities for the students as well as the adults. It is of recent date that serious and systematic studies of the institutional press or zeitgeist have been undertaken. The work of Pace (273), Stern (345), McConnell (240), Holland, (157), Wise (398), Brown (36), are available for more exhaustive coverage. Heavy reliance herein is placed on two excellent and recent treatises on the American College by Sanford, (315), and Dennis and Kaufman, (184).

The explosion of knowledge that is radically reshaping our intellectual, political, industrial, cultural, and military environments has been stimulated largely by research initiated in the colleges and universities. Paradoxically, the colleges have been relatively laggard in applying scientific methods to the understanding and evaluation of their own functioning. Practice in higher education, as in politics, remains largely untouched by the facts and principles of science. What our colleges do, tends to be either governed by tradition or to be improvised in the face of diverse—usually unanticipated-pressures. In the literature of the field there is much partisan argument and little evidence on the basis of which conflicting claims might be evaluated. (Sanford, 315).

The American college is a social institution, in which the complexities within our culture and society are mirrored in part. The inner workings of institutions, like those of individual personalities, are best revealed when the whole institution is under strain.

Recent research, both on student characteristics and on college environments, has exposed the limited usefulness of our conventional typologies of higher educational institutions. Even large universities may not be as distinct from small liberal arts colleges as one would suppose. The two groups of institutions obviously are different in complexity and size, but in the attitudes of faculty and students toward the basic purpose and values of higher education they may be quite similar. Both liberal arts colleges and large, complex institutions may be oriented more toward vocational training and vocational careers than toward commerce in ideas. (McConnell, 242)

The vast majority of institutions are characterized by environments that emphasize some degrees of conformity and constraint. The major source of diversity among institutions lies in the level of their intellectual press: modesty in human relations appears to be more uniformly emphasized than modesty in intellectual aspirations. (Stern, 345)

From a study of curricular changes since 1870 in fifty small or medium sized independent liberal arts colleges, McGrath and Russell (1964), concluded that "vocational or professional programs which differ in the degree of specialization in no substantial respect from comparable programs offered in undergraduate professional schools are now almost invariably a part of the offerings of the liberal arts colleges that were studied."

The really serious question is: what are our best colleges doing for the great mass of the uncommitted, the vocationally oriented, the anti-intellectuals? It is a remarkable fact that a culture that places relatively little value upon learning or the intellectual life, and has little understanding of it, or sympathy for what professors are trying to do, nevertheless regards college . . . the experience of college for young people as one of the greatest goods, virtually as one of the necessities of life. (Webster, Freedman, Heist, 378)

Our high regard for a culture of efficiency has led to an uncomfortably close analogy between educational processes and industrial processes. In a culture that is "thing oriented," it may lead to seeking standardized products. Increasing numbers of students seem to view college as some kind of maturational ritual, or initiation rite leading automatically to a good job and the Good Life. (Frankel, 100)

A college is people, ideas, and plant—in that order. On the other hand, it is necessary to understand the attitudes of colleges which are, in an important sense, corporate enterprises. Much of their activity has to be devoted to surviving, expanding, maintaining a strong position relative to other institutions.

The field of higher education is so controversial since it is confronted by questions of how to promote maximum freedom of the individual in a planned society. (Sanford, 315)

The college should not be locked in with government and business establishments. The college is a meeting ground where four major influences converge (family, economy, polity, and the community of scholarship). It is more than an institution for the student's self-discovery, or an instrument for society, and the imperatives of learning. (Frankel, 100) It is a hierarchical affair; some people know more than others and these exercise varying roles in the complex activity.

In the pluralistic pattern of our society, many educational philosophies are operating through our college programs. Very briefly, one is able to detect programs that have their chief foundations as rational, neohumanist, and instrumental. These are rarely found in pure states, but are likely found in varying amounts within any institutional setting.

Our professors and intellectuals are not without support, and not without sanction, in their efforts to supply the necessary criticism of our society and to raise the level of our culture. Society expects the colleges to look after the ideals, whatever else it may demand and however many obstacles it may put into their way. Our society suffers from addiction to practicality, power, success, social adjustment, excitement, and the gratifications of popular culture, but in a sense society has asked our colleges to "get us out of this, no matter how much we protest from time to time." The mandates of these schools are from the people, but they come from the peoples' better selves; they were given when people were thinking well or had found spokesmen who could express their higher aspirations. (Stewart, 345)

The colleges find themselves in the awkward positions of having promised more than they can sometimes deliver. Note how the public is told that the college experience will "liberate the mind," "build the capacity to make value judgments," and "inculcate the attitudes and values of democracy." These easy claims that are hard to substantiate because such outcomes are not fixed or static enough for easy measurement.

Even enlightened citizens have often been victims of considerable bamboozlement. They do not know what goes on in the colleges and have no ready means for finding out. Nor are there means of evaluating the effects of college programs. If the general public has little interest in improving the colleges, it must be said that many of the colleges seem to have but little more. (Sanford, 315)

Several explanations can be advanced for this state of affairs. First, many professors are primarily aligned with their disciplines rather than devoted to the institutions in which they work. There seems to be little payoff for working with undergraduates; the rewards in the coin of the college faculty—rank, prestige, respect and recognition from colleagues—emerge repeatedly as the compelling incentives. Many faculty groups do not see themselves as agents for social change; students on the other hand do conceive of themselves as agents of social changes. (Goldsen, 123) Second, during recent years faculties almost everywhere have gained immensely in their rights and privileges, and justly so, but perhaps the time is overdue for some of our institutional faculties to codify the responsibilities they should assume to go along with their freedom and influence. The house of intellect is visibly a house divided by internal dissensions as well as subject to increasing doubt by the larger society. If the student is an apprentice in the academic community and the colleges cannot abdicate to the students the primary responsibility for policy, it remains the residual right of students to be taught by people who are paying attention to their tasks as teachers, and who might regard this task as a central responsibility. Regrettably, it must be admitted that large numbers of students are being shortchanged. Professors who accept the protections and privileges of tenure or who want those protections surely have a personal moral responsibility to measure and balance their commitments to research and to teaching. (Eddy, 80)

In 1965, the Year of the Student brought some college administrators and faculties to the awareness of them in a manner, perhaps, that the civil rights disobedience has brought attention to problems in that area. The absence of any clear philosophy of higher education in America has permitted the development of many varieties of institutions with varying goals and consequent tensions. *What is a college?*

Some refer to it as an academic pressure cooker; some describe it as a retreat from the real game of life; some view it as a playground or custodial institution for the young; others find it a place to develop the talents to play in the adult world where the rules and motivations are not genteel; some want it to be the watch-dog of the middle class; others insist that it be the laboratory for finding better solutions to man's problems; some see it as a factory where one's hands are not soiled; some want to liberate the mind while others wish to liberate the libido.

No ready solutions can be located for the dilemma outlined above. But several bases are available to undertake the seeking for answers. If we view college as a culture which is more than books and lectures and grades, on the one hand, and focus on the individual development as the primary purpose of higher education, then some determinations are available.   We can expand on the quotation attributed to Schweitzer: "Example is not the main thing, it is everything." Sanford (315) continues in this view:

> We can best guide the student's development by exhibiting that which we wish him to achieve. Let the college show its students something of its own efforts to find the truth, especially the hard truth about itself, and we may be sure that many students will find in this a model and an inspiration to use their intelligence in trying to solve their own problems. By the same token a college that does not strive for rationality, fails its students. Let a college blindly defend its institutional features, adhere strictly to an "educational policy" whose theoretical features remain unexamined, make and enforce demands in the interests of purposes whose meaning cannot be made explicit to students or that cannot be justified as conducive to ultimate democratic goals, permit its officials to do things or say things, in the interest of public relations, that are not consistent with what has been said to students, or betray the essential idea of a college by accepting some kind of external restraint upon its freedom of inquiry, and the effects upon students are apparent and serious; they become passive or cynical and alienated from the major society and from themselves.

Studies by Jacobs, Eddy, Stern, and Newcomb have identified influential institutions sharing one thing in common: a consistent and pervasive educational philosophy. The existence of considerable personal freedom for the students, a sense of community, emphasis and respect accorded to the performing arts, a fusion of academic and off-campus experiences, a preoccupation with individual and small group problem solving, and a concern with the personality or character outcomes of education all appear to be manifestations of a definite educational philosophy. (Mayhew, 234)

In other investigations, Hassenger and Wise (144) used three measures of the college environment: the College and University Environment Scales, the Environmental Assessment Technique, and the College Characteristics Index, on a cross section of American Catholic colleges that indicated variation in academic and social atmospheres so great as to discourage generalization, especially in the matter of school encouragement of student freedom and responsibility. With wider variation, the pattern indicated average ratings below the norm in both encouragement of academic excellence and scholarship and cultivation of personal, political, and psychological "soul-searching." The Catholic colleges were generally above the norm in the encouragement of group and community loyalty, social consideration, conformity, and caution. No scales have been developed for general use that specifically recognize moral and spiritual differences.

Students for many years surrendered to the "in loco parentis" concept because it implied discipline but generous, personal help. As colleges have grown and "raised their standards," the nurturing functions have lessened. In a family, the child who is ignored except when it is necessary to punish him may soon be on the road to becoming a rebel or a delinquent. Now the students demand their "rights" as citizens rather than expect the care that formerly obtained.

If we adopt the view that the college is people, ideas, and plant—in that order, the roles of the adults in such settings must loom large. The brief overview of societal values operating in our culture was intended to show that the adults in higher education institutions are functioning with similar motivations. One of the most pervasive influences in the American picture is the importance that is attached to freedom or liberty. For many, it has become a matter of delayed preoccupation since the reports have begun to emerge from Vatican II. In the more than 250 Catholic institutions, it has become a matter of lively discussion, as well as heated words. The usual recourse to lines of authority for ready answers on how to conduct oneself as a member of the academic community is met with considerable ambivalence, hesitation, and uncertainty on how to proceed.

Two major considerations are noteworthy in any discussion of academic freedom. The first of these relates to the German origin of the concept that certain members of society were promised immunity from interference or coercion in the pursuit of scholarly inquiries and in the discharge of teaching roles. Civil liberties, a more comprehensive concept as outlined in the United States Constitution, provide all citizens with intellectual liberties in which one may inquire into any subject and announce the results of one's inquiries without asking anyone's permission. But no citizen in his status as a citizen is guaranteed access to the materials necessary to conduct inquiries or to audiences through whom he can make his conclusions public. (Frankel, 100)

The second element in the idea of academic freedom is the principle of academic self-government. Professors determine who shall be a member of the club. They lay down rules for degrees, licenses, what shall be taught. Academic freedom, in short, entails the recognition that scholarship is not simply an individual practice, but a social enterprise. The enterprise shall be controlled by an autonomous community which lays down its own laws for the conduct of its business. It doesn't have the obligation to present all points of view or all ideas. The right of any opinion to be heard, which is a right outside the campus, does not apply to the classroom. And this is not because the college does not practice free inquiry. It is because free scholarly inquiry is controlled and governed by scholars in accordance with their own standards. (Frankel, 100)

If we make the mistake of assuming that freedom is an end in itself, something good in itself, to be achieved at almost any cost, we will probably make the further mistake or assuming that such freedom must be without any limitation or restriction whatsoever. If, however, we accept it as a means to an end, we will more easily understand that, in practice, this freedom may in fact be restricted and that it should be used only to the extent that it is actually helpful in striving for the end desired. It will be more readily understood that, good though they be, freedom and individual rights do not exist in abstracto, but are enjoyed by and exercised by individual human beings who, in turn, exist not in abstracto, but in a real world in which they are but individual members of various societies which happen to have other members with similar rights and privileges. (Britt, 34)

Our universities do not govern themselves. Nor are they governed by any visible agency on the outside. Rather they live by rules which have been devised by a variety of authorities and whose origins are often lost to memory. It is not likely that an academic community will come to exist so long as students, faculty and administration feel that they are ruled by regulations not of their own making. It is a paradox that we have been rather lax in directing the cultural life on campus, while consenting to the continuance of rather strict controls over the student's personal conduct. It is our responsibility as teachers to guide our students towards the knowledge of genuine thought and beauty. I cannot agree that we should, in the name of democracy and freedom, maintain an attitude of benign tolerance toward any and all forms of thought and style that students may wish to express or espouse, often because they are uneducated; censorship and suppression is one thing; the absence of authoritative sanctions, quite another. For the business of the university is the furtherance of truth in its two forms: verifiability and genuineness. And truth is not a matter to be subjected to a democratic vote; rather, it is determined by standards whose validity we accept and which, as intellectuals, we are determined to maintain. (Wilson, 395)

The faculty must be given responsibility for all educational matters; for if our responsibility is restricted to giving of lectures and of grades, we will be dispensers of information instead of teachers. Let us close our gates. For the academic community needs to be protected from the dictation of the multitude. Let us first of all be masters within our walls. (Wilson, 395)

In addition to needing freedom, so as to nourish criticism of society, the university also must have discipline and order, so as to foster respect for law. For the students, it is intended to be neither a country club nor a perpetual debating society, but a place where they can learn to be happier and more useful members of the larger society. (Wilson, 395)

The crisis in higher education is chronic. The great problem today is not essentially different from what it has been for a long time. It is the college faculties who will have to take the major responsibility for the needed reforms. The burden of carrying out educational policies rests mainly on them, and, as professionals, they have the right to a major voice in the determination of these policies. There is no denying, however, that when there is a movement toward reform in colleges, it is the collective faculty who usually seem to be dragging their feet. There have been few fundamental innovations in higher education in the past 30 years. The reasons are found first in the fact that the typical faculty member is a specialist in an academic subject who has organized himself in such a way as to make deliberate and concerted change of any kind difficult, to protect his freedoms, securities, traditions, prerogatives, and secondly, because there is a lack of scientific basis for educational practice. In many respects, most education is experimental. It is designed by trial and error, and the practices are frequently related to unexamined or implicit philosophies of education.

Despite many differences in views on the subject of what is a college and how it is to be managed, some convergences are evident. Note the positions taken by the different pronouncements in the next paragraphs.

The real genius of the liberal arts program, the most essential distinctions between liberal and servile education, has been described by William Cory (1860), one of the great Eton masters, in the following terms:

> You go to school at the age of twelve or thirteen; and for the next four or five years you are not engaged so much in acquiring the knowledge as in making mental efforts under criticism. A certain amount of knowledge you can indeed with average faculties acquire so as to retain; nor need you regret the hours that you have spent on much that is forgotten, for the shadow of lost knowledge at least protects you from many illusions. But you go to a great school not for knowledge so much as for the arts and habits: for the habit of attention, for the art of expression, for the art of assuming at a moment's notice a new intellectual posture, for the art of entering quickly into another person's thoughts, for the habit of submitting to censure and refutation, for the art of indicating assent or dissent in graduated terms, for the habit of regarding minute points of accuracy, for the habit of working out what is possible in a given time, for taste, for discrimination, for mental courage and mental soberness. Above all, you go to a great school for self-knowledge. (ETS. 1964)

Then there is the position outlined by Sanford (315):

A college is not a therapeutic community, but its educational procedures must be guided in part by knowledge of how unconscious influences and developmental tasks are related to education. Educators must assist students to find "self-knowledge in depth." There are many procedures which can be used, such as giving support, offering advice and direction, letting the student talk about himself, adopting new social roles. By making available to the individual the symbols of our culture, it may vastly expand his capacity to find gratification in imagination rather than compulsive action or in mere sensation. Reading is essential, and once the necessary symbols have been acquired, books can help to gratify as well as to refine some of our most primitive emotional needs. It is sad that many children read without enjoyment, perhaps because they have been introduced to reading, not as a means of satisfying their impulses, but as a duty.

At the present time the hard sciences are not on the defensive. It is the social sciences and humanities that are on the defensive. Students look to these disciplines to help them approach answers to the explosive questions that trouble us. Teachers in the physical and biological sciences have known for a long time how to use the laboratory as a means of keeping concepts tied to observable phenomena but the neglect of this principle in the social sciences is distressing. (Goldsen, 123)

Protestations, claims, "exercise of prerogatives," and the like, are loose in our language. What a sobering and salutary influence would obtain if we could invoke the suggestion made by Adlai Stevenson. In one of his last appearances before an academic community he stated that no proposal for reform was socially responsible if it did not include consideration of how that reform was to be accomplished. (Dixon, 70)

For the professor the academic world is psychologically dangerous, competitive, uncharitable, full of disappointments and other threats to the spirit. The shortcomings of professors are better known than the shortcomings of their environment. Professors are not worse than other people; they simply live in a less tolerable situation. In many, perhaps most, of our institutions of higher education there is much confusion of the policy making and the administrative functions. There is such an erosion of the former function, with policy being made under the guise of administration, that the professor who would look after his interests is virtually forced to become a politician and take his place in the exhausting game of institutional intrigue. (Ostroff, 271)

The college professor in America has been asked to perform three quite disparate functions: first, the reconnaissance of the frontiers of knowledge; second, the imparting of "information," and third, the inculcation of values and the development of character. The difficulty in most colleges derives from not knowing how to mix these roles. The obvious one in the evolutionary development of the profession has seen the progressive decline of the character-development function, with a strong tendency of the research and informational functions to part company and to form two separate callings.

In terms of the three basic functions of the professorial calling, it would seem fair to conclude from the data surveyed that professors tend to esteem and respect themselves primarily on the basis of their research function. Students and administration, however, especially in smaller institutions, tend to value most of the informational and character-developing functions. On the other hand, the public at large is probably inclined to attach great significance to what is called the character-building function (probably because the job was not done well enough at home, although perceived dimly). Thus the different segments of the population that the professor must in some degree answer apparently expect different kinds of performances. If the lack of adequate studies of the college professor is apparent, the need for them is equally evident.

What we must do is to recognize the pluralism in teaching and the many styles of influence. Teaching styles are so diverse that they can be categorized in a great many different ways. Sanford (315) summarized the work of Jackson in grouping the five distinct modes of healing: shamanism, magic, religion, mysticism, and naturalism. The shaman heals through the use of personal power, using craft, charm, and cunning. The magician heals through his knowledge of arcane and complex rules and his ability to follow the ritual precisely; the priest claims no personal power, but achieves his healing capacity as an agent or vessel or an omnipotent authority; the mystic healer relies on insight, vision, and wisdom, through which he cures the sick soul; the naturalist is impersonal, empirical, task-oriented. This typology may be a useful one for treating other forms of interaction, such as that which obtains between teacher and student.

The teacher may also serve as a negative or anti-model. Here the student sees the teacher as a lodestar, from which he sails away as rapidly as he can. He may breed disciples, but also enemies. In witnessing the internal struggles that go on in every teacher or at least recognizing them, one can learn that moral courage is possible, but that it is uncommon.

Few of us are content and willing to be who we are: part of the human multitude, and yet ennobled as bearers of the world's intellectual heritage. Thus, we are, both similar to our students and different from them. The main difference is this: we have experienced change within ourselves, and they have not. We are not too sure of our position in the world; they are too sure of theirs. Their status-striving has the determined push of careerism; our status anxiety is a gnawing worry lest we fail to live up to the expectations which we ourselves and others attach to our position.

This is our condition. . . . this is the condition of our universities. We cannot make ourselves over, nor our students, nor the institution, simply by hopeful wishing or grim determination. But, understanding our condition, we can deliberately try to create circumstances more conducive to new learning. And in each university we can set ourselves the long-range task of building a community devoted to the pursuit of excellence according to our standards of truth and beauty.

For the teacher, education is forever an act of self-revelation. In the dissensual sciences, self-revelation is even more important; almost, invariably questions of value are mingled with questions of theory and fact, and if the student does not learn to be articulate about his values, if he takes them for granted, he has not begun to penetrate into his field of study. Self-revelation is the surest path to self-awareness. Education is a public process, therapy is a private one. Science and the arts are public, personality is private. (Sanford, 315)

Truth is forever the product of search. It is forever acquired and never possessed. The student who leaves the college without having understood the tentative, developmental nature of truth should never have come to the campus. But nothing about the nature of truth will ever be communicated by a cold intellectualism which divorces knowledge from human experience. If he is to learn about truth, the student must be present as his teacher struggles to obtain it, and as his own powers grow, he must begin to join the battle. Teaching and research are not alternatives. Both are part of the same process of education, complementary activities in the academic community. SEARCH as well as RESEARCH are modes of exercise.

Recently the United States Commissioner of Education stated that "despite our national pride in diversity, a surprising 'sameness' permeates most of American Higher Education. At a time when public schools are realizing the importance of individual differences and are adopting individualized instruction, independent study, flexible scheduling, team teaching, nongraded classes, and similar practices, most colleges and universities still subscribe to a uniform four-year, 125 unit system."

In another criticism, Howe observed that an area "noticeable by its absence" is "a rational, informed concern for student growth in that somewhat frightening and highly personal matter of feelings and emotions." He said he did not know whether this calls for new educational programs, or whether the problem can be handled by "a more sophisticated attitude" on the part of college and university administrations. "I do believe," he said, "that faculty and administrations must recognize the profound influence their attitudes toward students have on emotional and personal development. It makes a great difference, for example, whether a college president regards a sharp manifestation of student dissent as a revolt of the palace serfs, to be put down as rapidly and quietly as possible, or as a legitimate protest from full citizens of the academic community who are entitled to be heard and negotiated with—not just dealt with." (Howe, 164)

Howe found some student causes and activities disturbing and is deeply concerned about the increasing use of drugs on major campuses. "It is clearly time we mounted a major program of drug education—not propaganda—for your generation and mine," he said. "My generation needs to understand that a combination of preaching and rigid discipline won't solve the drug problem; both our generations need a new willingness to engage in an exchange of ideas about that problem."

CHAPTER 4

Internal Influences on the College Student

Having focused attention on the external forces that influence the development of the college student in the previous chapter, attention will now be drawn to a large variety of *intraindividual* factors that are operating in the development of the student. Each category will present a very limited, in fact too abbreviated, treatment of the influence of the particular aspect under discussion. The justification for this departure derives from the realization that it is necessary to call attention to many areas of investigation without compelling scholarly competence in each one for the counselor, the teacher, and *possibly* the parents and the student. The behavior that is relatively easy to describe is more difficult to explain, and even more elusive to predict and control.

Many approaches are open to the investigator for purposes of organizing his information. In this instance, a developmental framework will be used. Beginning with genetic foundations, then moving on to a brief commentary on neuro-chemical foundations, pausing longer at the important phenomenon of learning, and concluding with the personality-adjustment-values state hopefully will provide both a longitudinal and cross-sectional description of the college male as seen through the efforts of many investigators and writers.

GENETICS

In a fine tribute **Heritage from Mendel**, Brink (33) and many colleagues point out the brilliance of Mendel's conclusions on the role of genetic factors in producing individual differences. Many conclusions about the processes, variations and principles of genetics are recorded. For counseling, the importance of "uniqueness or individuality" cannot be minimized. Statistics based on groups, notwithstanding, do not provide answers and solutions to individual human problems. They are bases or predictions on which decisions for the individual within the group must be made.

Baldwin (1964) extending the point made about individuality mentioned that all traits have environmental and genetic components. Thus it is appropriate only to inquire as to the relative proportions of the population variable which is due to differences in genetic and environmental factors. The hoary "nature-nurture" controversy must be replaced by a concept of "nature-nurture" collaboration. Each individual is a unique and unrepeatable event, but considerable similarity can be noted in the manner in which he proceeds through the various stages of life and the communality of many of the behavior forms he demonstrates.

NEUROCHEMISTRY

Pribram (288) in a provocative article, **The New Neurology: Memory, Novelty, Thought, and Choice,** supports the work of Rosenzweig (306) and Ordy, et al. (1965) in pointing out the dynamic, growing, versatile role of the central nervous system, particularly the brain, in behavior. The concept of a fixed instrumentation that severely limits the behaviors possible or equates structure to function is rejected. The sophisticated and expanding use of modern techniques of investigation have opened vistas for studying glial materials and chemical agents in developmental and learning stages. Fiber growth, directed by its own excitation, is supported by investigations on histological and histochemical analyses of neural tissue obtained from animals raised under conditions of sensory deprivation. Chemical analyses pointed out the roles of RNA and DNA as correlates of behavior alterations.

The processes that govern development of language in the infant are roughly the same as those involved in the development of thinking, according to Pribram.

The significance of this area for counseling is that "exercise and activity do not produce deterioration or transitory changes, but that structural and histochemical changes occur that are cumulative, permitting subsequently, a higher level of activity to be engaged in."

"The brain," as more and more experimenters find, "is truly made to accomplish what it must, behavior being what it is." This should hearten all those who in any way are associated with the development of competence.

LEARNING

The topic of learning is a central problem for psychologists. The major learning approaches have been treatments with a psychological framework as represented by Thorndike, Hull, Guthrie, Skinner, the Gestaltists, Tolman, Mowrer, and others. In recent years, a number of other models have appeared on the scene, viz., mathematical, analogical, neurological, and neurochemical.

Both the mathematical or symbolic models (Bush & Mosteller, Estes, and Overall) and the analogical (Miller, Weiner, Rosenblatt) are of extra-organic nature, i.e., they utilize external models to apply to the organism. On the other hand, the neurological and neurochemical are intraorganismic in that they deal with the internal aspects of the organism. Lashley, Hebb, and Pribram are associated with the former approach; Krech, Rosenzweig, and Ordy are representative of the neurochemical orientation.

The counselor's chief reliance will be models that have a psychological basis for their derivation. His setting is very unlikely to permit and provide him with the techniques and materials for adopting neurological approaches.

Consistent with the rationale that has been professed, viz., a developmental model, the brief selection of pertinent literature will reflect that position.

Piaget (282) and Bruner (38) postulate that learning follows a developmental sequence in which acquisition of motoric skills, imagery, and symbols are the bases for learning to cope with one's world.

Mowrer (255) in a revised two-factor theory of learning encompasses dynamic forces and cognitive conditions in describing the learning process. His theory maintains that all learning is sign learning and that solution learning is a derivative thereof. In short, as far as "types of learning" are concerned, the current version is "one factored," but it remains two factored as regards reinforcement.

Cattell (48) makes a distinction in two types of conditioning that assists in viewing the panorama of learning. The early development of the field focused on states (conditions) which are inherent and that demand attention, e.g., food, sleep, etc. The role of the adult was to provide consistent relief and support for these conditions. Much of the emphasis was placed on associative learning in explaining the manner in which the connections were made. Later investigations focused on instrumental learning, in which speech, cries, gestures, movements, etc., brought relief and opportunity or pain and restriction to the learner. Much of the current work in learning is centered on instrumental learning and serves as a backdrop for one of the currently featured theories of counseling that will be mentioned in the next paragraph.

The relatively recent emergence of behavior therapies and behavior counseling has roots in theories of learning that are associated with Thorndike, Guthrie, Pavlov, and Watson, which incidentally, form the major base of educational practice in the United States. The systematic preoccupation with only observable phenomena or the tangibility of behavior is central to this position. In counseling, the specificity of tasks and their completion offers concrete evidence to the learner-client that his efforts are rewarded. The relationship of self-confidence (which is a goal or concomitant, rather than a given state) is directly tied to competence in handling defined tasks.

The roles of intangibles, concepts, and ideals, are variously treated in the literature. Kemp (186) and Shoben (328), to mention just two, place such forces at the stimulus end of the learning relationship. Krumboltz (203) and Bijou (27) place such conditions at the derivative end of the learning sequence. This writer reconciles the two positions as outcomes that can also become stimuli in subsequent situations for further learning. For example, the lack of confidence or doubt that occurs when an individual is ignorant of a process or information can be improved by training or supplying information so that the subject will undertake to gain skill or information without intervention by others.

Glasser (118) in **Reality Therapy** uses a learning model in developing responsible behavior in clients. To him, responsibility and respect (which are values and processes) are gained by learned responses to concrete challenges. The focus on goals may interfere with activities that would eventually lead to that outcome. He affirms "people don't act irresponsibly because they are ill; they are ill because they act irresponsibly." He states that needs are given, but that individual capacities vary and change to satisfy them. The satisfaction of these needs cannot be done in vivo, in vitro, but in situ. The dissection of the need in a laboratory or counseling office is of little value. The individual resolve and vicarious rehearsal of achieving the needs satisfaction requires a social setting and can only be fulfilled in that context. The counselor or therapist must show the client the unrealistic or unsatisfactory modes of his functioning and then teach him better ways to fulfill his needs within the confines of reality. *What* are you doing, not *why* are you doing it? What are your plans for going on? .. . .are questions that set the stage for concrete behaviors. Waiting for attitude change stalls therapy, whereas changing behavior leads to change in attitude.

In a philosophical vein, Glasser (118) states that reality may be painful, harsh, and dangerous; and it changes slowly. All any man can hope to do is to struggle with it in a responsible way by doing right and enjoying the pleasure or suffering the pain that must follow. This is strikingly similar to Frankl's view about every man's freedom to be creative in a productive, experiential or attitudinal manner.

The emphasis in **Reality Therapy** is on strengthening mental weaknesses rather than curing mental illness. The medical model is inappropriate. Illness is cured by removing the causative agent; weakness is cured by strengthening the existing body to cope with the stress of the world. Responsibility in overcoming illness rests heavily on the doctor; responsibility in overcoming weakness rests heavily on the patient, client, or student for self-improvement.

If tools fashion the thinking of an age, and the zeitgeist or times influence the values of that period, then attention must be directed to providing individuals with competence in the use of such tools or devising new tools and providing opportunities for practical demonstration of skills.

Gilson (in Bruner, 38) observed that it is as impossible to paint by means of words as it is to speak by means of pictures, and Freud (1926) adverted to the "omnipotence of thought" in children. There is considerable preachment on the need for serious thinking, critical reasoning, and the like. What is frequently overlooked by sloganeers is that it is easier to translate from one language to another than from one psychology to another. The priority of experience before logic is aptly summarized in the concept that "whatever is in the intellect is first in the senses."

Learning is a complicated process; there are many gaps in our knowledge about it. However, we do know that, in part, it is modified by various emotional interactions occurring between the students and his total human environment. The college teacher with whom the student is in almost daily contact plays an important role in his emotional as well as his intellectual growth. Good teachers have always used their subject matter, their knowledge and trained judgment to help students develop.

The basic enthusiasm for a subject which makes a first-rate scholar effective in research and publication also tends to make him a first rate teacher. For the most part, such a teacher is not apt to be intimidated by prevailing political taboos which often carry with them a loss of freedom of expression in the classroom. Unfortunately, the ease of evaluating documented professional contributions and therefore of rewarding it tends strongly to create the illusion that "good teaching" is not rewarded and thus to inhibit its development in a staff member's formative years. The difficulty for the administration is that this illusion is often fostered by the incompetent who considers himself a good teacher in order to justify his failure to himself. Every effort should be made to discover means of encouraging distinguished teaching, especially where it is not coupled with research and writing (Group for Advancement of Psychiatry, 1955).

The times demand that we learn more, learn it faster, remember it better, and apply it more skillfully. Teacher and learner productivity must rise sharply. How much change can we get if we apply known principles of teaching and learning? Tyler, director of the Center for Advanced Study in the Behavioral Science at Stanford, recently stated that "we now know enough about the conditions which contribute to learning to double the productivity of the college years."

Modern learning theory can help secure this increased productivity. Some psychologists do not believe that the state of their science permits such optimism; but we need not depend only on principles of learning nailed down by psychologists. Technology both precedes and follows science. As Hilgard puts it, "Pure science does not lead automatically to its own application. A state of invention lies between."

Dale (63) outlines some generalizations about learning that have been winnowed from the laboratory and classroom experience:

1. The clearer, the nearer, the more realistic and relevant the statement of desired outcomes, the more effective the learning. If you can't see the target clearly, the chances of hitting it are reduced. Many teachers do not work from a carefully planned course and unit outline in which the desired goals are carefully differentiated into information, intellectual processes, skills, and values.
2. We learn what we practice. The most commonly practiced skill in school and college is memorizing for temporary learning and many students are highly proficient at it. Effective practice requires a model to be imitated. Does the classroom instruction provide models of persons skillfully thinking, painting, writing, composing, or solving problems?
3. You must teach for transfer. Old learning doesn't automatically transfer to new learning. All of us have a large reservoir of inert knowledge which does not help us solve new problems because we haven't practiced ways of transferring it to new situations. Perhaps this was what Whitehead had in mind when he stated: "The most useless bore is the individual who is filled with information but doesn't see the relationships within it."
   Transfer may be thwarted by premature verbalization. We may talk too much before we do. Some intuitive doing is probably a necessary condition for fruitful verbalization of principles. Dewey stated, "An ounce of experience is better than a ton of theory, simply because it is only as an experience that any theory has vital and verifiable significance." A theory apart from an experience cannot be definitely grasped even as a theory.
4. There is a motivation factor in all learning. Immediate rewards usually produce more learning than extrinsic ones. We can learn to be motivated by both present and remote awards. Immature persons must have all their rewards right now rather than deferring them.
5. Learning is increased by knowledge of results. If correct responses are to be rewarded, the learner must know how well he has done, get "prompt reinforcing feedback."
6. We learn best what is meaningful. No one would speak up for meaninglessness in education, but everyday teachers and texts present unclear materials to students. Rote methods of teaching and learning are common. A typical remedy when students do not understand is "more of the same" . . . work harder, read the material over and over again.
7. Most people never reach their potential. The data from measurement of mental ability and achievement are sometimes accepted as defining the upper limits of student potential. But such data are not adequate predictors of college success. Further, low correlation between mental ability tests and creativity is well-known.
8. Learning must be organized for sequence and cumulative effects. A person's knowledge can accumulate without being cumulative. Logical subject matter is easier to learn, and use, but this logic must become a part of the individual's organized repertoire of experience.
   We must teach, in depth, a more limited number of systematized generalizations, organize learning around a few key, persistent issues. But basic, as always, is the intent of the individual. The will and dynamics of the individual remain central in all principles of effective learning.

Repeatedly, one is struck by the efforts of teachers and parents to "put old heads on young shoulders" with the subsequent anguish on the part of the principals because the assignment was not successfully handled. Elsewhere, it was stated that an emphasis on verbal conceptualization may interfere with understanding in other dimensions. The necessity of experience in the rediscovery of the "wisdom of the ages" by every generation cannot be stated too strongly.

PERSONALITY

The emancipation of psychology from philosophy did not terminate its preoccupation with the problems on the nature or essence of man (metaphysics), nor with the role of methodology (epistemology) in securing answers to this question. The physical sciences, working with less complex phenomena, were able to effect a more decisive separation in their investigations of the world, man excepted.

Several plausible and tenable theories of personality are available that are based on developmental needs to help provide some rationale to the functioning of the college male. A distinction is here proposed that when thinking of the individual, this investigator claims that the person is unchanging, but the personality is changing. From the moment of conception, the individual remains the same person throughout his existence. Hopefully, he will undergo great alterations in the direction of becoming increasingly mature, independent, and contributing to society.

The dynamic conception of needs is essential in understanding the behavior of individuals. Two formulations that are rarely juxtaposed are those of Maslow and the other one that is accorded an Aristotelian origin. The hierarchies of needs are strikingly similar. See Figure 3.

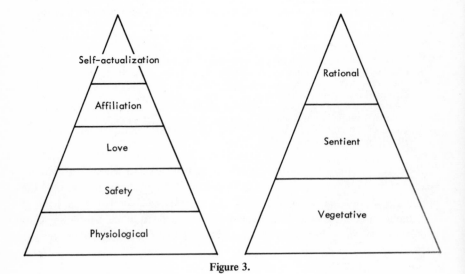

Figure 3.

In a developmental sense, "lower" needs take precedence over "higher" needs until maturity, self-actualization, or rationality are achieved. However, the constancy of and the simultaneous interaction of the various levels is readily demonstrable. Man is characterized as having properties that are found in nature, e.g., inanimate objects subject to gravity, plant life responding to chemical forces, animal life with sensory capabilities, and rationally being able to transform or alter his circumstances instead of being forced to adapt to them, as well as inquiring into his origins and destiny.

Other theoreticians have expanded on segments of the various levels. Erickson's (84) excellent treatment on personality development, Frankl's views on the role of rational and intellectual forces in man, Murphy's insistence that lower needs can be subject to but not supplanted by higher needs, Shoben's and Maslow's formulations emphasizing creative forces are all challenges to the thesis that a "Galilean" notion of equi-importance to all activities is necessary. Instead, the thesis is presented that while man is capable of many types of behaviors that can be judged to be equally important, still that physical and safety needs must be satisfied in order to free man for pursuit of the remaining higher needs.

Freud's contributions are heavily documented in demonstrating that biological needs, unconscious or non-conscious influences, early childhood emotional experiences, all produce an influence on adolescent and adult behavior. Unfortunately, the strongly deterministic influences of childhood were held to be so influential in the socialization of the adult ego that counseling procedures derived from this position would necessarily emphasize release of emotional forces rather than increasing controls of them. Freedman (102 and 103) challenges the view that childhood experiences are so forceful that adolescent and adult behaviors are essentially reactions to the earlier developmental states.

> One can discern some regularities in the behavior and experiences of students. But personality changes then include changes in intellectual abilities and in thinking; changes in opinions, beliefs, and values; changes in what is often called character; and changes in internal psychological processes—for example, emotional stability versus instability, mechanisms of defense, and attitudes towards oneself and other people.
>
> The possibility of effecting significant changes in personality is, of course, the faith upon which liberal education is based.
>
> By contrast, until very recently, psychiatrists, psychologists, and psychoanalysts have tended to emphasize the fixity of the personality of the college years. The traditional view of personality development in the college years originates in the ascription of overweening importance to the events of infancy and early childhood. According to this view, the really important things occur in the first five or six years of life. At puberty, there is a resurgence of some of the conflicts of childhood. By age 16 or thereabouts, the personality is fairly well shaped. Short of psychoanalysis or deep-going psychotherapy, nothing is likely to change things appreciably.
>
> Very important changes in personality can and often do take place during the college years. They very much hope that certain things will happen, but they lack the confidence to try to bring them about on their own. As a result, they adopt a passive attitude and look hopefully to something outside of themselves, to the vague entity called "the college" which will bring by some magic the great things they would like

to see. It is this lack of confidence in their own ability or potentiality for development that makes for the essential tragedy to occur . . . the tragedy of turning them into seniors who have lost the spirit, the idealism, and freshness of the entering student. The students have been socialized by the college.

Farnsworth (90) has devoted much time and thought to the college male and outlines the college student's developmental tasks in the following terms:

1. Changing for relations of dependence upon one's parents and other older people to those of independence. Constructive rebellion may signify success; apathy and resignation reveal failure. Rebellion which is uncritical, unfocused, and indefinitely continued usually suggests the tragedy of long-continued psychological deficiencies in earlier stages of development.

2. Dealing with authority poses a special problem for many college students. Displacement of negative feelings from their parents to the college or to some of its officials is quite common. Their attitude toward the college's use of authority remains ambivalent; although they expect limits to be set on their behavior, they resent their enforcement. Many of them want all the advantages of independence without giving up any of the advantages of dependence on their parents.

3. Learning to deal with uncertainty and ambiguity, particularly in matters involving the balance between love and hatred. The art of disagreeing vigorously with others without hating them is an important aspect of maturity. In a democracy, this is an essential ingredient. One form that uncertainty may take that is painful to some students may be called the dilemma of choice. "He who has a choice has a problem."

4. Developing a mature sexuality. No more complex problem now confronts educational administrators in this country than that of fostering conditions in our colleges that permit the development of wholesome attitudes about sex, marriage, and the family. Such attitudes are necessary to the development of people of character and integrity.

5. Finding security, developing feelings of adequacy or competence, and attaining prestige or esteem. Recent research confirms a principle that has been accepted intuitively or as a result of experience; namely, that academic progress is more rapid when a student is stimulated to work to capacity and when there are frequent changes of conditions under which he works to permit and encourage the development of versatility. Because of the enormous influence on contemporary thought of the work of Erik Erickson, the concept of identity and its corresponding negative and role-diffusing phases are so well known that nearly every college student with personal conflict assumes that he is suffering from an "identity crisis" whether in fact he is or not.

6. Development of standards and value systems. If the original admirable desires of the students, the goals of the curriculum planners, and the highest ideals of education as expressed in philosophical terms could somehow be coordinated and implemented, the college experience might be far more influential than it now is. Unfortunately, many peer-group pressures, influences of mass media of communication, and attitudes displayed by persons outside the colleges show the balance of values, tastes and standards to be toward mediocrity or worse. Individual students should be aided in developing high ideals in the face of overwhelming pressures toward low ones.
    As Sanford (1964) aptly stated, "Intellect without humane feeling can be monstrous, whereas feeling without intelligence is childish." It is very clear that knowledge without virtue is dangerous. But we have not yet learned how best to develop character, nor are our institutions of higher learning sufficiently concerned about their responsibility or aware that the task in large part belongs to them.

7. Obtaining essential knowledge of delicate and complex matters. Students and many faculty members keep private many of their disappointments regarding the college experience. Exposure of such feelings may be painful or even dangerous. It is in the acquisition of knowledge-in-depth of a college that all types of counselors can be helpful, but in so doing, problems of confidentiality must be thoroughly understood.

In the next few years, we will probably see more and more friction between students and administration in American colleges. Relations between teachers and students are the heart of the educational process. Teachers should be as much concerned about the people they teach as the subjects they teach. Concern with the emotional development of college students should no longer be considered out of bounds by those who plan the programs of institutions of higher learning.

In considering the college freshman as a human being, it is well to remember that underneath the rather smooth exterior he is probably just as confused and complicated as the rest of us. Just as there are profound human resemblances, there are also marked individual differences. Individual differences have been vividly described by McConnell and his associates at the Center for the Study of Higher Education at Berkeley (1965). We know from their work that there is an enormous diversity among entering freshmen, diversity among colleges, and diversity among students entering any particular college. The range of scores is very wide with respect to any characteristic that might possibly interest us. If the intellectual abilities of all the students entering one institution are below the average of students entering another institution, then the program of introducing these two groups to the intellectual life is bound to be different. So it is with respect to values. If at one institution the students hold very high theoretical and esthetic values and are relatively unconventional, the task of introducing them to the intellectual life of the college is very different from what it is at a college where the students yearn primarily for social status and glamour or entry into a career that will provide them with many material benefits. (Sanford, 315).

The freshman is pretty strict in his moral requirements upon himself and others. This idealism of the freshman is partly caused by the necessity for being very, very different from what he was just a little while ago, when he felt more or less overwhelmed by his impulses. One of the good sides of this is the freshman's intolerance of anything hypocritical or phony. He wants a clear-cut and unambiguous picture of his hero, and he is not prepared for the discovery that his heroes have feet of clay. Another aspect of the authoritarian stage is the need for external support for the moral positions that have been taken. He is still under the sway of the family and community standards, but he can remain so only if he has external support for his system of values. It is this state of affairs that is responsible for the freshman's susceptibility to influence either by adult authorities of the college or by the student peer group. Since the freshman does not get much attention from the adults, he typically seeks support for his conventional moral position from the college peer culture.

In his uncertainty about himself, the freshman shows a tendency to over estimate what he is and what he can do, together with a tendency to fall into every serious underestimation of himself. One way out of this uncertainty is an early declaration of what his professional role is going to be. The trouble with this mode of adaptation is not only that the student often makes false or inappropriate choices but also that it often causes a premature closure of the personality.

The main purpose of the freshman year in any college should be to win the freshmen to the intellectual life. In most cases, this cannot possibly be done except by the faculty. Also, it is important to tell the freshman the truth about the college. Students generally hold three views on the purposes of college: (1) an academic philosophy (that a basic education and the appreciation of ideas are important in and of themselves); (2) a vocational philosophy (that vocational training and skills are necessary for effectiveness in one's career); and (3) an interpersonal philosophy (that the ability to get along with different people contributes to a satisfying life). Freshmen stress: "What work can do for me"; seniors: "What I can do with my work." (Sanford, 316)

Research on the growth and development of students as they pass through college is scanty and inconclusive. In a study by Medsker and Trent (247) the conclusion was reported that whereas tests of ability showed that numbers of college persisters, dropouts, and nonattenders had the academic ability to do college work, both the questionnaire responses and the measured student characteristics pointed to the appreciation of career values as likely to be focally related to the pursuit of higher education.

It is widely known that different higher educational institutions enroll different types of students. Several recent studies of higher educational institutions have drawn attention to the importance of differences between institutions in their student "inputs." For example, the characteristics of the entering student body have been found to be closely related both to the later educational achievement of the college graduates (Astin, 8) and to the characteristics of the college environment (Astin and Holland, 8).

The freshman classes enrolling at 248 colleges and universities were surveyed in the fall of 1961 to determine some of the major distinguishing characteristics of entering student bodies. Each of 127,212 students provided information regarding academic and extracurricular achievements in high school, educational and vocational aspirations, and socioeconomic status. A factor analysis of 52 student "input" variables revealed six distinguishing characteristics of entering classes: Intellectualism, Estheticism, Status, Leadership, Masculinity, and Pragmatism. (Astin, 1964).

Table 1 shows the intercorrelations among the six factor scores.

TABLE 1
Intercorrelations Among the Six Characteristics Factor Scores

Factor	2	3	4	5	6
1. Intellectualism	.29	.39	.04	.24	.25
2. Estheticism		.27	-.07	-.16	-.24
3. Status			.05	-.22	.31
4. Leadership				-.09	-.19
5. Pragmatism					.22
6. Masculinity					

Note—N = 246 institutions

There is no single student culture in the U.S. The new college generation has energy to burn, years of time, a grim determination born of surmounting the precollege roadblocks, a penchant for activism, organization skills perfected by summers in Civil Rights Movements, a deep sense of social justice, a healthy antipathy toward any Establishment, and perhaps most importantly, an ability to adjust to change, whether it be technological, economic, political, or social. (Dennis and Kaufman, 1966).

A strikingly familiar refrain was noted by another observer of youth more than 2,000 years ago. Aristotle spoke of youth being restless in the following manner:

> Youth are restless: youth have exalted notions because they have not yet been humbled by life or learnt its necessary limitations; moreover their hopeful disposition makes them think themselves equal to great things—and that means having exalted notions. They would always rather do noble deeds than useful ones; their lives are regulated more by moral feeling than by reasoning—all their mistakes are in the direction of doing things excessively and vehemently. They overdo everything— they love too much, hate too much, and the same with everything else. (Cited by Wilson, 391).

Somewhat dissimilar views are presented by other commentators. Greeley (130a) stated that in our approach to the present student generation we must avoid being taken in by the journalists who report on the attention-getting minority. Both the silent majority and the creative minority, however, share in the same spirit of alienation. The privatism, resistance, and sullenness of the current generation reflect the failure of the western intellectual tradition to provide youth with a vision of meaning and purpose.

Stern (344), who must rank with one of the most astute observers of the college scene, writes:

Social scientists have described three paths followed by today's youth in response to society's demands. The uncommitted ignore the absurdities of their situation and try to slide by with as little difficulty as possible, outwardly conforming while inwardly reserving for themselves a private sector of life. The alienated withdraw from the struggle and immerse themselves in pleasures of the moment. The rebels seek a casue with which they may flog the establishment and in which they may find identity. Yet, 1,540 incoming freshmen in 14 widely diverse colleges and universities, in stating their expectations for college by completing the College Characteristics Index, gave little evidence of any of the three orientations described above. They had extraordinarily high expectations for both the academic and non-academic activities they anticipated.

Upperclass students have lost the idealistic images of the entering freshman, and where the disillusionment is greatest, usually at large universities, student rebellion has been more acute.

Research has produced a great amount of information about the students who are entering college. Diversity is the striking fact. Diversity among institutions and diversity among students entering the same institutions. (Traxler, 1940, Fricke, 104, McConnell and Heist, 242). This holds not only for abilities but for a great variety of personality and social characteristics as well. In a significant contribution to research on students, Stern, Stein, and Bloom (346) and Stern and Cope (1956) categorized students into one of four major groups: stereopaths (authoritarians), nonstereopaths (non-authoritarians), rationals, and irrationals.

On the other hand, all too little is known statistically or experimentally about the relationship between personality characteristics students bring to college and their academic achievement, either in the conventional sense of grades and persistence, or in the more subtle sense of independent, critical, and creative intellectual competencies (which are seldom reflected in academic marks). Even less is known about the relationship between personality structure and the attainment of personal maturity and effectiveness. But the first step in making these studies is to know the entering student. (Douvan and Kaye, 75).

If we know little about the decision to go to college, we know even less about how adolescents choose the particular schools they enter. Who influences the choice, where potential students get their information about and knowledge of schools, how unconscious motives may enter the choice—these remain virtually untouched. The choice of school is not a uniform process that parents, counselors, and students engage in. (Douvan and Kaye, 75).

Recently, Chickering (49) found a high degree of congruence between institutional characteristics and student personality, with students of conservative religious beliefs attending colleges with similar emphasis and with altruistic students attending church related colleges where service is emphasized. This was obtained in a study of relationships between student personality traits and institutional characteristics based on 13 colleges.

In the face of mounting difficulties to be admitted to colleges and graduate schools of their choice, many students are subjected to pressures and uncertainties that produce anxieties that were not a major phenomenon in pre-World War II days. This anxiety forces students into conforming roles at the point of high school graduation. To be oneself requires the courage that not infrequently finds the student described as an "oddball." May (231) commented on the role of the university in an age of anxiety and concluded that anxiety is a normal corollary of freedom and can be handled by a person who has a strong sense of personal freedom and a firm set of values. Meyerson (252), in commenting on the change in the status of the college student, noted that today's student, though no longer the elect, is not allowed privileges of the electorate. "In loco parentis," standardized facets of housing and other facilities, and ineffective student governments leave no decisions for the students. These frustrations of mass consideration are responsible for anti-administration slogans, extreme proposals for self-government, suggestions for grading the faculty, and complaints against student grades and faculty neglect.

Rudolph (313), in an excellent review of the historical status of students, makes some incisive observations in the following manner:

> The neglect of students is a historical tradition. An examination of the record points out that if the administration and faculty could not bring the colleges to life, the students were prepared to prove that they could bring life to the colleges. Intercollegiate athletics, extracurricular activities, fraternities, student government, and similar extra-classroom activities were initiated by students. The agents of change were students. If a college cannot keep ahead of its students, students will surely get ahead of the college. Neglect demands response; the young do not refuse to act merely because they are not understood.
>
> The most sensitive barometer of what is going on at a college is the extracurriculum. It is the instrument of change, the instrument with which generations of students, who possess the college for but a few years, register their values. Interestingly, the literary societies of the 19th century college were organized by students who insisted on exchanging views without direct faculty interference. These groups found it necessary to secure written materials for their information, and in a large measure were the bases on which college libraries were founded.
>
> The neglect of students as alive human beings is a venerable academic tradition, a tradition that deserves inspection and repudiation.

The focus in this presentation is to bring attention to the prevalence of conditions that interfere with adequate discharge of the responsibilities that devolve on society and particularly the college to the students. Repeatedly, the charge is made that students are different than their predecessors, that they are spoiled, unappreciative, passive, Bohemian, etc. These need to be examined beyond the descriptive labels that provide some sense of justification to the adults, but rarely provide any relief to the situations that demand some constructive efforts. The wholesale indictment of college youth without specification of particulars, and more importantly, of devising practical measures, increases rather than decreases the tensions between the generations. In the previous chapter, the observation was made that every adult generation deserves the younger generation that it inherits or produced.

Frank (99) claims there are a number of ways in which the patterns of higher education could be reviewed and revised with an eye to reducing the number of factory seconds—human wreckage. It is dangerous to be a whole person because it means being vulnerable, and in the students' eyes not many adults are good models to imitate. He observed that students often find themselves in double-binds as follows:

> Too often a student entering college is encouraged to begin thinking for himself and then given poor or failing grades when his thinking does not match the teacher's. The student is told he must assume responsibility for his own behavior, but then he is faced with a set of parietal rules and required attendance at classes. He is expected and subtly told to revolt against control as part of the process of assuming what has been described as the "burden of liberty" but he may be suspended or expelled if he does. One of the more enduring double binds for students is found in sex. Our culture states unequivocally that sexual intercourse before or outside of marriage is forbidden. Equally unequivocally, it states that sex is an instinct that cannot be controlled, especially among the young and paraded in so many popular media.
>
> He is instructed by the teachers who are hired to teach, but who are promoted for their publications.

Berdie (21), after a long professional career in the student personnel field, sees the issue in the emergence of ambivalences leading to stress. Some ambivalences result in learning, creation, and invention. Other ambivalences result in indecision, discomfort, unhappiness, faulty logic, and riotous behavior. Everything the college student does and believes in is a potential source of stress.

Blaine (29), from a position in a highly visible university, commented on two of the most controversial topics in the college picture. In the area of sex, as well as in the area of drugs, there are not consistent statistics which determine whether or not there has been a significant behavioral change in recent years. Knowing what leads to the development of a morality which encourages students to take drugs, to be promiscuous, and to involve themselves in riotous behavior means knowing the psychological configurations of the late adolescent.

> Psychologically, the late adolescent is not prepared for adult sexuality. The average college undergraduate by his nature prefers an emotional and a physical relationship with the opposite sex which is intimate and private but not one that includes intercourse. Dr. Paul Walters (1965) puts it this way . . . "The sexual impulse of the adolescent seems to be diffuse and unfocused and consisting of vague longings for fusion with the loved object." By this he means an emotional fusion or indentification rather than a physical one. Premature sexual intercourse represents a serious failure in the development of the adolescent ego."
>
> Moreover, there is the fact that delaying sexual gratification until marriage does not cause a degree of frustration liable to lead to psychological damage, nor can sexual experiences before marriage be correlated with the greater compatibility after marriage. Much information of this sort can be transmitted by means of group discussions which include psychological as well as physiological and moral subject matter.

On drugs, those who routinely ingest such substances usually fall into a category best described as the inadequate personality. They feel less than whole, as though something had been left out of them when they were first born. Drugs provide a temporary respite from this feeling of relative ineffectiveness. Most of them do not prove themselves adequate by doing anything remarkable when under the influence of a drug, but they feel as if they could. (This is comparable to the psychology of the alcoholic.)

Counseling is far more effective than drugs in helping people who unrealistically fear they are inadequate to cope with the social and academic aspects of college.

Students expect authority to react to their rebellion but to react in a strong and unflustered manner and not to cave in no matter how strong the revocation. Binger tells a story which epitomizes neatly this ambivalent student attitude: "We are rioting, Sir."

A willingness to discuss matters of policy with students, combined with the reservation of the right to make, hold to, and enforce the ultimate decision regardless of student agreement with it, is usually the wisest administrative policy.

Student mores may have changed a little over recent years. Existentialism and the emphasis on science and technology have brought self-centeredness and cold logic into the ethical thinking of today's youth and young adults in place of the more emotional and spiritual absolute values of the Victorian era. But for all their arrogance and defiance, these are the most intelligent and the healthiest group of college students there has ever been. Each new generation seems to need to feel they are different.

Two recent studies call attention to characteristics of students as well as institutions in the United States. Stern (344) surveyed 3,300 freshmen entering four dissimilar colleges. Using the College Characteristics Index, the freshmen indicated what they expected college to be like. They were realistic in their appraisal of the degree of freedom to be expected in college, but highly idealistic with respect to the areas of intellectual and social activities and self-expression. These expectations were evidently shared by significant persons in the student's earlier environment— parents, teachers, and counselors, but contrasted sharply with the more realistic views of upperclassmen and faculty members.

The freshmen expectations of a consumer-oriented college that fulfills needs and allows full social and political participation contrasts with the actual functioning of the producer-oriented college. Student demonstrations are sparked by this failure of naive idealism, with disillusion especially evident at large universities. Some colleges are now beginning to conform to expectations of consumers by attempting to combine the goals of scholarship and individual fulfillment.

A description of the American college freshman was attempted by Abe, Lutz, Holland, and Richards (1). Over 12,000 freshmen in 31 institutions, selected to be reasonably representative of the diverse types in the United States in terms of location, size, and program, produced a comprehensive view. A college for every level of intellectual capacity and for many different assortments of attitudes, outlooks, and personality types is available. Almost any student can find congenial people at every college because each institution contains a wide cross-section of individuals.

Wise (398) characterizes many of today's college students as rather cautious seekers after inner security in an outwardly insecure world. They are aware that this search may be fruitless, but they engage in it with courage nonetheless, concerning themselves more with day-to-day living, self-knowledge, and personal life plans than with problems of the larger world. They have, in other words, adopted an approach to mankind's eternal search for security whereby they seek to reduce the problem to a series of steps that may be taken in progression, rather than head straight for the goal and ignore intervening obstacles until they are brought up short.

Interest in student groups, clubs, even fraternities has steadily dwindled, except for the freshman who is trying to find his footing in this new world of college life. Interest in the world outside the college has also shown a marked decrease at least as gauged by an interest in youth groups, political and economic discussion groups, and the like. There is a widely shared impression (not yet supported by available research) among people who work with college students that these students are, however, showing a greatly increased interest in exploring religious ideas and participating in religious activities. Students are growing more and more resistant to organization, whether for student government or for fun. Even participation in sports is becoming more individualistic.

Dating, while still a major concern, has adopted new patterns. The status badge of having "several on the string" has somehow become worthless, and "going steady" has become the accepted procedure. The oddest thing about the revolution of the social life of youth in the last 20 years is that it constitutes the triumph of rural 19th century American mores in the urban and suburban society of the mid-20th century.

More than half of the incoming freshmen at the nation's colleges and universities in the fall of 1967 said they think faculty members are more competent than students to specify the curriculum, but that faculty promotions should be based in part on student evaluations. The estimated 1.3 million freshmen appeared about evenly divided on whether college officials are too lax in dealing with student protests on campus. These opinions emerged from second large scale survey of the nation's entering freshmen, conducted by the American Council on Education's Office of Research (4).

In the same study, when asked to rate objectives considered to be essential or very important to them, the highest percentage of students (82.9) chose "Developing a meaningful philosophy of life." Others ranking high with students were "Becoming an authority on a special subject in my subject field" (67.8 percent), "Helping others who are in difficulty" (61.8 percent), and "Keeping up to date with political affairs" (50.6 percent). A total of 46.4 percent listed "Being successful in a business of my own" as essential or very important.

Business was indicated as the probable major field of study by 16.2 percent. Other popular fields in the top five: education, 10.5 percent; engineering, 9.5 percent; fine arts, 8.6 percent; and psychology, sociology, or anthropology, 7.8 percent.

Students said the academic reputation of the college and advice of a parent or other relative were the major influences in determining where they would go to college.

CHAPTER 5

A Strategy for Counseling the College Male

Several courses or alternatives are open to the counselor in devising a philosophy and/or strategy for counseling. He may adopt a theoretical position that has been developed by others and then implement it as best he can with practices that derive from such a position. On the other hand, the practitioner may conclude that the variety of problems and tasks that confronts him requires a variety of insights and skills that extend from numerous theories. Ideally, the counselor will be conversant with the rationale of every practice that he adopts. In a realistic sense, the absence of a single theory, or even several comprehensive theories of human behavior, forces the counselor to construct or assemble one that is efficacious in dealing with the clients that he serves.

Oppenheimer (1954) concluded that professional workers and scientists are frequently forced to deal with phenomena by analogous reasoning because no direct route to, or observation of, certain principles are available. Moreover, scientists construct theories and models for the purpose of carrying out research and explaining events. Similarly, while no one equates a blueprint to the finished structure, the value of such a guide is obvious. Having an idea and establishing its validity is not so readily achieved.

The enunciation of a theory, just as the drawing of a blueprint, is relatively easy and quickly completed; the validation of the theory and the construction of the building are slow, oft-times tedious, and generally require adjustments while the activity is under way.

Continuing with the analogy, the construction of the building, based on the blueprint, forces attention to be centered on ingredients (building materials, future uses of the plant, geographic location, and sequence in construction activities). In typical home construction at least 22 sub trades must be coordinated for completion of the project. The contractor struggles with ordering the materials, assigning priorities to activities, and reckoning with unpredictables and unmanageable elements in the workers and the weather. The customer, on the other hand, is generally impatient with progress, doesn't always distinguish between his "needs" and his wants in housing and frequently expects that changes can be readily effected after a certain point in construction has passed.

Turning back to the counseling arena, several elementary considerations must be acknowledged. First, the counselor rarely has a finished blueprint or theory that suffices to guide his activities, and secondly, the client is not static but is, himself, proceeding along a course of development that is changing. In the face of these conditions, it behooves the counselor to avail himself of a large variety of insights, competencies, and skills to assist many individuals with different problems and at different stages of development.

Inasmuch as the counselor arrives at his position from a distinctly different genetic and historical past than any other counselor, it follows that personal styles in counseling are likely to vary. It is hoped, however, that principles and practices will derive from more substantial reflection and research.

Throughout the months of formulating and writing, the teasing out the relationships from the published information and seeking prescriptions, the constant intrusion of "live" materials, i.e., the students and clients, sobered the inclination and enthusiasm to write in definitive and unequivocal terms. Whatever else this "interference" may have accomplished, it precluded the equating of humans to numbers or conceptualized models. The imperative is . . . our services are for people, and that we must find our partial answers in many sources rather than register disappointment that cases don't fit the generalizations, "laws," expectations and hunches, which might provide a straight line to the desired changes.

We may, as Thoreau noted, be able to examine the branches but not the roots that sustain them.

Counseling in this context is defined as the diagnosis and treatment of minor (non-imbedded, non-incapacitating), functional (non-organic) maladjustments, and as a relationship, primarily individual and face to face, between counselor and client. (Pepinsky, 1948)

In assembling the ingredients (ideas, assumptions, information, and convictions) for this investigator's strategy for counseling college males, credit and appreciation are accorded to the large number of scholars, both historical and contemporary, who have addressed themselves to probing the general phenomenon of behavior or the special area of the college period.

In Chapter 2 counseling prescriptions were presented that appear relevant in terms of limited research conducted on the college male and on the accumulation of shared experiences of many student personnel workers and counseling psychologists who have labored in the field. Considerable recourse is made to the writer's own experiences over the past twenty years. While his major efforts have been devoted to the counseling of thousands of college males in that period, additional thousands of other clients have been counseled.

Counselors rely on various "roadmaps" or guides by which to discharge their assignments. Reasons for referral by others or self-referrals are likely to be made in terms of labels. Popular reasons include poor concentration, low achievement, confusion as to what courses are to be taken, inability to sleep, the artificiality of school work, anger and/or disgust with roommate or others in the student's life, weariness, and numerous other explanations. Weider (1966) listed 48 reasons that have been advanced as frequent explanations for underachievement alone.

Whatever the reasons for the student's presence in the counselor's office, his presence there will likely force the generation of some "hypothesis" about the case in the mind of the counselor. Many reasons may be operating to produce a single complaint, just as many complaints or questions may derive from a single explanation or reason. Providing some manageable basis for dealing with such matters forces the development of a strategy that will order the activities of the counselor. Insufficient time generally precludes doing a comprehensive case study on every student who comes into the counseling center.

Two broad types of responsibilities can be delineated for the counselor. These are:

1. The educative role in which the counselor provides the major information seemingly being sought. This might be likened to a coaching function in which the player is instructed on specifics that are important to him.
2. The adjustive function can be viewed as one in which the counselor's activity is visibly reduced and the student assumes a larger role. This might be likened to the actual contest that is played by the student with the coach on the sidelines.

Generally the "visibility" of the counselor and client shifts, but both are in the picture. From mathematics one might hearken to the topological model in which the relative roles of each dimension or segment alter as the other ingredients or parts change.

Attention will be focused on the activities that appear to have the counselor visibly active in the counseling relationship, but under no circumstance can it be concluded that the overt inactivity of the student is directly reflective of his involvement in the process. The counselor, in the current model undertakes to learn as much as he can about the client from records that are available and from diagnostic settings. This data is organized into four major categories that have been found to correlate with academic progress and adjustment to school. It must be noted here that intercorrelations are typically found in varying degrees among the four categories, and this fact will preclude the use of any one category as a single or sufficient explanation for success or failure.

The four areas or categories that have served as a workable schema for both the educative and adjustive functions of the counselor are:

1. Level of intellectual functioning.
2. Aptitudes and learning tools.
3. Motivation and adjustment.
4. Maturation and health considerations.

LEVEL OF INTELLECTUAL FUNCTIONING

Considerable consensus can be shown that college students are drawn from the upper half of the population of their peers. The estimated IQ of the high school graduate is 108, and at the present time approximately one-half of high school graduates matriculate in college-level programs. It can be reasonably concluded that the average WAIS IQ of 110-112, with a S.D. of 10, will be characteristic of the college population in the United States. Just as intra-group differences will be found within an institution, it can be readily demonstrated that there will be differences between the mean scores of institutions. At the present time colleges are available that characteristically attract students from the high average range, to other schools that with few exceptions are attended by students from the above 120 IQ range.

The significant point in the previous paragraph is not that colleges vary in the intellectual caliber of their student, but that students find institutions where they will be competing with others who are not extremely higher or lower in this major cognitive dimension. The sometimes expressed alarm or fear that we shall get a homogenized product if we serve youngsters of comparable abilities fails to recognize that differences are present even when the total scores may be identical. How one arrives at a total score is based on a series of tasks in which differential weights or resources are readily determined.

One of the major considerations, therefore, of a counselor is to ascertain the level of a student's intellectual functioning by some adequate measure of intelligence. The task does not end here, but requires that the student be apprised of his relative position in the test norms and in the particular institution that he is attending or might attend. The sentimental argument that such information might injure the student's self-image if the results are not high, can be countered by the observation that students are more perceptive about their relative standings among peers and that a selective winnowing is occurring without design. Moreover, it is of greater harm for a student to be asked to compete in settings where he is clearly out of the running in terms of intellectual capacity. We don't enter four-cylinder vehicles in the Indianapolis 500!!!! But we do find many uses and joys in owning such a low-powered automobile. As a general rule the counselor can adopt the principle that the best diagnosis is the one made nearest the time of a major decision.

After arriving at a clear determination of a student's intellectual level and informing him of his position, along with the odds of his maintaining a successful pace in the institution, the counselor will have the further task of speaking in terms of what alternatives might be entered into if the present alignment is deemed risky. It must be emphasized that this factor alone does not insure nor negate one's continuation in studies. The relationships that have been repeatedly found between intelligence and achievement in college settings are such that approximately one-third of the variance can be attributed to this factor. The mistake is sometimes made that because coefficients of correlations may not exceed .4, that very little relationship exists between ability and achievement. What is lost sight of is that a great deal of prior selection has occurred and that students in an institution may be very much alike in terms of brightness, and this condition tends to blur the importance of ability or intelligence. No great benefit accrues to the student who fails in a contest or program where he had only a slight chance. The "psychic scars" may be too great a payment for the temporary placement in a program or school.

Lack of assurance about one's abilities or the reverse condition (overestimation) of one's abilities can be checked and clarified in this arena of assessment.

DIFFERENTIAL APTITUDES AND LEARNING TOOLS

Aside from differences in overall ability, a more compelling observation is that students have varying aptitudes or abilities to carry on many tasks. These can be measured and should be related to the student so that he be knowledgeable about himself in order to choose various courses of action with some awareness of the probability of success or failure in those endeavors. One of the major developments in education and guidance growing out of World War II was the development of tests for measuring many aptitudes and assigning individuals to roles in which they could achieve satisfactorily.

Closely aligned to the presence of varying aptitudes in everyone is the development of or acquisition of "learning tools" to undertake the training that is envisioned. Here again, tests have been developed to a high order for purposes of determining the degree to which the student is ready to undertake the actual studies or training. As in the previous section on intelligence, much research has been conducted which shows that statistical relationships are clearly present between the extent of one's aptitudes and learning tools and his achievement in related training or educational ventures. While it is possible for individuals with sufficient abilities and aptitudes to fall down or fail in studies, it is improbable to find people "falling up." That is to say, lacking ability and skills, one can, by sheer determination or motivation pull himself up to the level of others who have both the ability and determination. For too long we have had commencement speakers and well-intentioned individuals exhorting youth to "hitch your wagon to a star," or "you too, can be president," or "if at first you don't succeed, try, try again." The net effect many times of such advice is to produce frustrations that spread to many other facets of a youngster's life and worsen rather than improve his chances for finding satisfaction in discharging roles that are compatible with his talents.

For a long time we have had the philosophy of education and guidance rooted in some well-meaning conviction that "a person can do anything he puts his mind to," which is a layman's translation of the behavioristic theory that learning is the answer to all of one's aspirations. Genetically and through the intervention of other physical forces in a person's life, limits are set that are not drastically alterable. To achieve commensurately with one's aptitudes is a defensible and commendable educational and counseling goal, but to enjoin or encourage all individuals to "shoot for the stars" is not warranted. When you stop "shooting for the stars" you may find it necessary to "just start shooting."

At the present time very little support can be marshalled for the transformation of individuals in terms of their basic intelligence levels. Stated in a vernacular sense we cannot through any systematic means currently available to scientists eliminate stupidity, but we can do much to reduce ignorance and illiteracy by systematic educational practices. The "waste in education" is phenomenal when one measures the amount of knowledge that is retained shortly after the termination of a formal course. It may well be that the emphasis in many courses is grossly misplaced and that the purposes of the professor rather than the needs of the student are being served.

Lack of information and lack of skills are two of the major types of interference in the progress of students, even though adequate intelligence is present to participate.

MOTIVATION AND ADJUSTMENT

One of the greatest preoccupations of counselors and psychologists in the post World War II period has been on the concept of personality. Its development, measurement, and implications for future strivings in an individual have been lively topics for debate, research, and commentary. Like the weather, we probably talk more about personality than any other topic, but we are not agreed in any wholesale fashion on what to do about it.

No dispute is had with the several major approaches to assessing personality, which, in this context, is defined as the characteristic manner in which the person moves toward the goals that he has set for himself, or which, while he is highly dependent, others have set for him. It is manifestly clear that many assumptions, rationales, and therefore procedures for assessing or describing the condition can be adopted and assist the student to a better understanding of himself. What is patently clear is that no single school or theory has been advanced to explain the many actions that are subsumed under such a heading.

The historical failure of measures of intelligence and aptitudes to account sufficiently for success and failure in education prompted the search for personality and so-called non-intellective factors to explain in straightforward fashion the events that transpire when youth are confronted by learning tasks. Because the comprehension eludes our firm grasp does not warrant giving up the search. It is becoming increasingly clear that a multiplicity of factors operating simultaneously will be the verdict in any attempt to explain simple as well as complex behaviors.

Turning to concrete practices that can assist both the counselor and student in the student's development, one is confronted by a large variety of inventories, tests, questionnaires, and procedures for measuring interests, values, adjustment, attitudes, motivation, and in a global fashion, the personality of the student. As in any other diagnostic procedure, the variety of tests administered and filed away, is of less importance than the frequent use and substantial understanding of a few instruments in a particular setting. Time and cost factors will preclude the exhaustive analysis of an individual in a college counseling center. Such an undertaking may better be reserved for clinical psychologists and psychiatrists who may wish to undertake a "major transformation" of a poorly functioning individual. In college settings it is very likely that the extent of dysfunctioning will not require major alterations in the individual's personality.

In view of the so-called "identity crisis" that emerges in the early years of college, there is a readiness, even eagerness, on the part of many young males to see themselves portrayed in a series of profiles or capsule descriptions. Especially receptive are those who are emerging from a dependency role to a relatively autonomous one in the college years.

Important consideration should be devoted to pointing out to the student the meaning of the many labels that are used by test producers and translating these into language that is comprehensible to the student. Moreover, the fluidity of personality, including its alterability or changeability, must be emphasized. It is regrettable that we have spent so much time in education preoccupied with reducing the ignorance of man about his universe and have devoted virtually no time to instructing man about his personal universe.

We speak of increasing our knowledge of the world and thereby being better able to cope with it, but we desist from increasing our knowledge about ourselves and thereby improving our resourcefulness. Just as it is important for knowledge about abilities, aptitudes to be shared with the student, so likewise, it is important to apprise the student about his major personality and adjustment characteristics. The adoption of a "learning model" posits the view that students can change their personalities in directions that will make them more effective, and not necessarily reduce their individuality.

Again, as was pointed out in the previous section, considerable variation will occur between individuals in terms of the many characteristics under examination as well as many variations within the individual. It is a truism that we are sometimes interesting contradictions or "that we may be our own worst enemies."

Sufficient gain from the existing instruments can be secured to quicken the interest of students in their own development and to provide them with a profile or portrait that will be intelligible when comparing them with others in similar academic pursuits or career aspirations.

Specific conditions that interfere with progress toward one's goals that can be noted in this category include dependency, self-conflicts that derive from cultural gaps between parents and child, intra-personal conflicts where preoccupation with physical and mental traits is exaggerated, and from choice anxiety in which many needs are straining for expression immediately but the conditions are not propitious for expression.

MATURATION AND HEALTH CONSIDERATIONS

Historically, the psychologist and counselor have abstained from direct use of data from this direction. The assumption was often made that the student who was upright and mobile was in reasonably good health and should be able to embark on educational and vocational tasks without further examination. Or, the failure to find clear cut explanations for poor achievement and misbehavior might lead to the conclusion that "something physical" was wrong with the student.

Increasing awareness of the interplay of maturational processes, health status, and sensory processes in learning activities has sobered the use of unequivocal explanations for success or failure. Interestingly, the confluence of research activities on learning finds neurologists, pharmacologists, optometrists, psychologists, nutritionists, sociologists, educators, moralists, mercantilists, and political scientists, to name a few, focusing their sights on the phenomenon of learning. While some groups are more concerned with describing, analyzing, and predicting the manner in which it occurs, all of the major segments of our culture are straining to control or guide it to their particular goals.

Just as it was noted in previous sections, the distribution of conditions of maturation and health also falls along a continuum from being in marginal condition to being in excellent development. Moreover, there is a variation in the pace or timing which characterizes the development of any individual that can be distinguished from his peers. What can be concluded here is that there is a continuous upward development in varying speeds from person to person, but learning tasks will vary less in college youth due to this consideration than in younger children. This is not to state, however, that every college youth is equally ready and able to undertake any task.

The decline in the popularity of physical activities in the college years is regrettable. Just at the time when many physical resources and systems are reaching their maximum development, we find many youth "retiring" from such physical activities. The findings of more and more investigators that "it is easier to rust out than wear out" seems to be lost on many college males. In their zeal to become "scholars" or thinkers, they have the erroneous notion that you have to park the vehicle. The reverse finding that activity in the physical realm can increase and sustain the mental processes is not a recent discovery, but somehow it must be rediscovered by every individual in every generation. It might be well to cast the motto: "A boy becomes a man before he becomes a scholar."

Counselors should increase their collaboration with specialists in the health field and help student's program courses of action that recognize physical factors as compelling ones in many of the choices and routes that are open to students.

Diagnosis based upon knowledge and understanding of causes underlying a client's maladjustment probably leads to more effective therapy than diagnosis based solely upon knowledge of the external situation. The dictum that the "counselor should be able to see through people in order to see them through" is adopted as a rule of thumb. It provides for clarifications of the roles of both counselor and client, and additionally, permits the evaluation of the merits of the procedures adopted. Considerable anticipation of both Glasser's and Krumboltz's emphases are found in Pepinsky's formulations.

Part III

Reviewing definitive studies on college students reported in the literature and reporting on intensive studies conducted in one institution will be the main purpose of this section.

The generalized overview reported in Part II provided a backdrop for the comprehensive assessment of college males who are described as student leaders, student failures, and beginners in a single institution.

The use of the most widely used clinical and counseling instruments for evaluation was supplemented by the adoption of an electroencephalographic (EEG) examination that is rarely used as a diagnostic departure in college studies.

CHAPTER 6

Rationale for Studies

Historically, in the United States a handful of investigators has concerned themselves with characteristics of college students. In a rough chronological fashion these included Cattell & Farrand (47), Toops (1923), Remmers (1928), Crawford (60), Whitmer (1931), Eurich (85), Strang (1937), Learned & Wood (205), Harris (141), Dressel (1943), Burnham (43), Iffert (168 & 169), Sanford (316), to cite some of the major undertakings.

The post-sputnik developments in higher education with emphasis on intellectuality for national interest and the very recent emergence of student movements and student unrest have focused attention on the college student in an unprecedented fashion. Witness the flood of reports generated by McConnell (240), Goldsen (124), Sanford (315, 317), Eddy (81), Freedman (103), Lavin (204), Goslin (128), Super (354), Tiedeman (1963), Williamson (392), Astin (8), the Group for the Advancement of Psychiatry (1965), the College Student Personnel Institute (1965, 1966), The American Council on Education (1959) Bolton & Kammeyer (31).

Webster, Heist, and Friedman (378) commented that investigation of student characteristics in an intensive way has hardly begun. Educators and the general public must be kept informed about the value of mental testing in this kind of research. Typically, studies undertaken and reported on have been prepared for a professional audience. The present undertaking will attempt to adhere to the format of reporting the findings in a manner that is couched in the language of the professional worker dealing with college youth.

The present studies, undertaken at a single institution – John Carroll University, were conducted on three groups of students with varying statuses. The major purpose was to ferret out the intellectual, personality, adjustment, motivational and electrophysiological (EEG) characteristics operating in outstanding students underachieving or failing students and freshmen who had not embarked upon formal college studies. Three major influences guided the investigator's efforts to increase the information on college males.

The first influential concept was ably stated by Zubin (404) who addressed himself to the discussion that persists on actuarial versus clinical prediction. Meehl (248) and MacArthur (1955) serve as the chief spokesmen for the two positions that address themselves to the prediction of outcomes in counseling and psychotherapy. Zubin declared that the issue was a pseudoproblem because these approaches were both sides of the same coin. He went on to state that the distinction between the actuarial and the clinical was heuristic rather than basic. The process of prediction for a group is quite different from the prediction for an individual. A distinction needs to be made between a prediction and a decision based on that prediction. The importance of developing individual statistics is leading to the emergence of interest in pattern analysis or typological analysis and that by providing like-minded or like-structured subgroups, it becomes possible to apply present day statistics to homogeneous groups in our clinical population. He continued . . .

> This is the first step in the rediscovery of the individual. Our second most important problem today is to find the pertinent variables for classifying the groups into homogeneous subgroups. Here a reorientation in psychology is called for. But what are the pertinent variables for the description of man? Factor analytic methods have attempted to answer the question. Factor analysis, however, has been applied largely to the conceptual responses of man. The psychomotor, sensory, and physiological levels of response have hardly been tapped in factorial studies. But the perceptual and conceptual functions are largely dependent upon man's past experience and to a lesser extent on the immediate "here and now" effects of brain function.

While Zubin was speaking of the benefits to be reaped to clinical populations by enlarging the focus of studies, the pertinence of his observations to college males is acknowledged. Moreover, this view is shared by Lavin (204) that investigations using students equated for ability but differing in grades or performance will yield greater information. Murphy's (1967) presidential address on "Pythagorean Number Theory and Its Implications for Psychology" supports the view that pre-occupation with numbers should not blind the investigator to the primacy of the individual. The observation that "hunch space and hyperspace are in the mind of the psychologist, not the client's" appears to be cogent in this context.

The second major influence on the design and conduct of the studies derived from the concept so well stated by Messick (251).

> Just as a test has as many empirical validities as there are criterion measures to which it has been related, so too may a test display different proportions of reliable variance or reflect different construct interpretations primarily because the motivations and defenses of the subjects are implicated in different ways under different testing conditions. Thus, the same test, for example, might measure one set of things if administered in the context of diagnostic guidance in a clinical setting, a radically different set of things if administered in the context of anonymous inquiry

in a research laboratory, and yet another set if administered as a personal evaluation for industrial or academic selection.

The awareness that student leaders and student failures were designations "after the fact" of college performance prompted the third phase of the study by selecting a sample of students for comparable analysis who had not begun college work. Yet, the disclaimer that they had not been exposed to the influence of the college climate, and therefore, unaffected, cannot be fully granted. The influence of previous elementary and secondary schooling had already developed self-conceptions as to roles in academic settings.

The third consideration that loomed large in the investigations derived from the Galton-Pearson tradition to the currently designated multivariate experimental emphasis. Cattell (48) reported that Galton's vision included in embryo the refined methods of analysis of behavior in situ and undisturbed. Recognition is accorded to the multiplicity of factors operating in any behavioral response. This same arena designates research, in part, to be exploration and hypothesis-generating. Cattell (48) observed that research need not begin with a hypothesis at all, and in its true life setting, a finished hypothesis is rarely the germinal point of research action. It can begin with noticing a curious and intriguing regularity. Theory serves to mirror the essence of nature, not to force nature into its specifications. Discussion often arises as to whether theory is a tool and stimulus for research, or whether it is the very goal and consummation of research. Although both of these organic purposes operate, the scientist at heart. . . .

will probably give priority to this second view, in which gaining a complete theoretical system is the meaning of science itself, for sheer curiosity would suffice to stimulate him to scientific experiment regardless of the existence of this and that competing theory; but theory is the sum total, at a given time, of our organized understanding and predictive power – our capacity to explain in a given area.

Any model, which is a theory reduced to some mathematical, physical, or symbolic essentials in which the relations of parts are determined by accepted rules, must be kept the servant, not the master of the data. Bereiter and Freedman (24) add their voices to this conviction in stating:

anyone interested in carrying on a comparative study of people in different fields of study will have no difficulty finding worthwhile psychological measures to apply. . . . future studies will do well not only to use a greater variety of measuring instruments but also to extract more information from the scores obtained. . . . . . . Multivariate techniques, which are ideally suited to studies in this area, are still used by only a few researchers.

Empirical research should produce information of considerable intrinsic interest, but it will become theoretically relevant only in the light of later developments.

Burnham (43), one of the pioneers in studies of dealing with college youth, pointed out the desirability of identifying two groups of students. One, the group demonstrating desirable forms of behavior and personal characteristics: the good citizens, the creative people, those who bring a variety of interests to the student body. The other group which we need to identify is the poorly motivated, the non-contributors to the student body in the broadest sense of the word. Once two contrasting groups have been identified we need to study their earlier histories and learn more about the developmental aspects of their personality characteristics. Burnham continued . . . .

> We need to know how these characteristics can be recognized, how they can be classified, and with what degree of reliability. Probably more important, we need to learn more about how students with such personality characteristics can be helped to make desirable adaptations and modifications. To introduce the academically qualified but personally submarginal applicant to a college environment in which he cannot adapt constructively on a personal basis is probably as cruel and indefensible as to introduce his opposite number with good personal characteristics but submarginal academic ability into a college environment where he is certain to meet frustration and failure through sheer lack of intellectual ability.

Tomkins (364) commenting on the ideology of research strategies in psychology made the cogent observation:

> Our field is admittedly a difficult one, and our progress to date is somewhat less than the heart desires. Despite the revolutionary insights of Freud and the promise of factor analytic methods, there is an enduring, gnawing discontent which generates the flamboyant, inflated self-assertion of the clinician and the factor analyst alike, and which also generates their mutually extrapunitive posture.
>
> In knowledge as in virtue, there is no royal road. Neither method appears to me to have opened the royal road though both have opened exciting vistas. I will defend the pre-Freudian, pre-Thurstonean dogma that science begins and ends in an active brain enclosed in a body comfortably supported in an arm chair. In between these reflective moments are interposed a variety of fact findings, hypothesis testings, and statistical analysis designed to illuminate the cognition before and after. Which method of fact finding, which methods of statistical analysis, appear to me of secondary importance so long as one has been bright enough, or persistent enough, or lucky enough, or all of these, to stumble onto something important. It seems highly improbable that any method will ever guarantee the discovery of truth.

In concluding this brief excursion into the literature, the relevance of an observation by Harris (142) is noted:

> Prehistoric men, like schizophrenic patients, undoubtedly have observed many new relationships in nature; but what usually distinguishes a scientific from a non-scientific endeavor is the fact that the investigator not only has a strong conviction about the conditions under which the relationship occurs and the conditions under which it does not occur, but that he also is willing to put his ideas to a test.

This may further serve as a challenge to the "mind expanding" sector of our intellectual leaders.

In carrying through on the above assumptions and convictions, the investigator undertook three separate studies of "homogeneous groups" in a single university setting for purposes of enlarging the awareness of factors contributing to success and failure in college.

Each study will be presented separately in succeeding chapters, and in each case the conditions under which the investigation was conducted will be delineated. It will suffice at this point to mention that the particular samples of students were Student Leaders, Underachievers or Failures, and the Beginners.

CHAPTER 7

Profiles of Student Leaders

The preoccupation of many investigators such as Stogdill (349), Shartle (325), McClelland (237), MacKinnon (219), Terman (359), Bass (11), Katz (182), Kelly (186), and Ginzberg (1964) attests to the importance that is attached to the phenomenon of leadership. Despite the widespread interest in leadership, many writers frequently present their findings in broad generalizations or recommendations that more attention be devoted to charting the characteristic. Moreover, one is struck by the failure to transpose findings from one discipline or procedure to another.

PROCEDURE

In this phase of the investigation it was proposed to assess student leaders in a college setting by a series of psychological tests and an electroencephalographic examination, commonly and hereafter referred to as an EEG. The leaders were all those who had been chosen for membership in "Who's Who in American Colleges" at John Carroll University in the academic year 1960-1961. This qualification produced a sample of twenty students. In order to increase the sample to a larger representation, sixteen student leaders were added to the study sample. This latter group was handled as a separate segment through the initial statistical work, but when no systematic or significant differences occurred, the two classifications (Who's Who and student leaders) were combined to provide the sample of thirty-six.

Every student who qualified was willing to undertake the extensive testing and further agreed to share information in the five-year follow-up that was planned and completed in 1966.

All of the original testing was completed within two months, in October and November 1960. In every instance, the assessment was carried on according to the strict procedures outlined for the technique by a trained worker. The students were briefed as to what general tests were to be used, how the results would be shared with each one, that "privileged communication" was the basis of the relationship between the investigator and the subjects, and that no communication nor sharing should occur within the study sample.

The study was intended to describe in a comprehensive fashion the traits and aptitudes of student leaders. Several hypotheses were entertained that might be supported by the findings. These included:

1. Leadership is correlated with fast waves (Beta waves—low amplitude, frequency between 13 and 18 per second).
2. Leadership is correlated with tension states and/or restlessness as evidenced by personality or neurological measures.
3. Personality and intellectual factors cluster in a fashion that claims "the laws of nature are correlative, not compensatory."
4. Leadership is correlated with superior standings on intelligence and personality tests.

In addition to the descriptive task, the rationale and some pertinent research carried on with each evaluative procedure were examined to provide some basis for comparative observations about the student leaders with other groups.

INSTRUMENTATION

Wechsler Adult Intelligence Scale, The Psychological Corporation, N.Y., 1955.

Concept Mastery Test, Form T, The Psychological Corporation, N.Y., 1950.

Rorschach Ink Blot Test, Grune and Stratton, N.Y.

Minnesota Multiphasic Personality Inventory, The Psychological Corporation, 1951.

Allport, Vernon, Lindzey, **Study of Values**, Houghton-Mifflin Company, N.Y., 1961.

Grass Eight Channel Electroencephalograph, Model IV, Grass Instrument Company, Quincy, Massachusetts.

LITERATURE

The review to follow in this section will concern itself with some of the general treatises on leadership. Further coverage will appear in subsequent sections dealing with specific techniques and behavioral correlates.

Wald (376) in preparation for his study on top level business and industrial executives reported that for more than thirty years studies have been conducted with the aim of gaining information about the phenomenon of leadership, and from these efforts two orientations have emerged. The first concerns itself with trait configurations and the second with situational contexts.

Research concerning leadership up to 1948 has been summarized by a number of reviews, including those of Smith and Krueger (333), Jenkins (175) and Stogdill (349). In 1960 Bass tried to gather together what was known about leadership contained in 1155 articles and treatises and attempted to organize this knowledge into a set of generalizations held together by reason as well as experiment.

Toynbee (365) traced the changes in abilities required of the leadership as a society proceeds through various stages of growth and decline. During its growth in response to physical or social challenge, strong, creative, heroic abilities predominate. During disintegration, the savior comes to the fore. Similar changes appear in the growth of business organization. The new, struggling business may require aggressive, "hard-headed," creative, high-pressure, non-conformists for adequate leadership; the old, well-established concern may require a conservative, relaxed, cautious, executive more sensitive to human and organizational relationships and demands.

On the jacket cover of **Talent and Society** (1958) is penned the crisp observation:

> This book tackles one of the most pressing questions facing our society today. How can we find our future leaders at an early age? Who are the best young scientists in our high schools, the boys and girls most suited to go to college, the most gifted in leadership or some special talent? Until now, in the recognition of talent, chief reliance has been placed on intelligence and aptitude tests, inadequate as they may be. Yet, personality and character traits, when combined with above average intelligence, have been known to produce significant achievement.

The Committee which produced the above named report adopted as its major field of study those aspects of talent which would not ordinarily be classified as "abilities." It concentrated on values and motives—non-academic determinants of achievement and on social skills. Concluding that comprehensive overview it stated:

> Research on basic theoretical problems in talent identification and development should receive additional strong support. . . . . in our rush to give every potentially talented child a break or to beat the Russians in the production of engineers, let us not forget that the quota of basic knowledge on how to solve such problems is not very great.

MacKinnon's (219) large research project at the Institute for Personality Assessment and Research at the University of California concerned itself with:

> The assessment method to survey the aptitudes and personality characteristics of a group of Air Force officers of the rank of Captain, with a view to establishing the patterns of ability, motivation, and personality which are associated with outstanding effectiveness in military and command functions. After three days of written tests were given to 343 Air Force Captains at their respective bases and three days of "living-in-assessments," 621 test scores, scale scores, staff judgments, and cluster and

factor scores were obtained. The collection of such an array of data permits a description of the average Air Force officer in this study. He is an above average, though not superior intelligence, rather well adjusted, more like a business man than a scholar, and with the interests of a military officer.

Clark (52) in reviewing the MacKinnon study concluded with "It is a pity that the promise of the report that functional relationships within the personality" be pictured is not fulfilled.

Stuit et al. (250) introduce **Predicting Success in Professional Schools** with the observation:

> Examination of the published research studies also reveals that investigators have been preoccupied with the study of factors which are largely intellectual. The personal qualifications of professional students, their adjustment and motivation to enter professional work have received far less careful study than they deserve. . . . . admittedly, research in the area of personality and interest factors is difficult and often disappointing, but if efficiency of prediction is to be improved, research work in this area must be undertaken.

Shartle's (324) **Executive Performance and Leadership** provided these views:

> A number of studies of the characteristics of executives can be found in the literature. Such studies are helpful in giving clues, but there is no assurance that the conclusions of one study can have practical value in any other situation.

Stodgill (319), who reviewed the literature extensively, concluded that:

> persons in leadership roles tend to exceed the members of their respective groups in intelligence, scholarship, dependability in exercising responsibilities, activity and social participation, and socio-economic status.

Terman and Oden (359), concluding the monumental work on the Gifted Group at Mid-Life, stated:

> Since the less successful subjects do not differ to any extent in intelligence as measured by tests, it is clear that notable achievement calls for more than high order of intelligence. After the 1940 follow-up a detailed analysis was made of the life histories of the 150 most successful and 150 least successful men among the gifted subjects in an attempt to identify some of the non-intellectual factors that affect life success. The results of this study indicated that personality factors are extremely important determiners of achievement. The correlation between success and such variables as mental health, emotional stability, and social adjustment is consistently positive rather than negative. In this respect the data ran directly counter to the conclusions reached by Lange-Eichbaum in his study of historical geniuses. A number of interesting differences between the two sub-groups were brought out, but the four traits on which they differed most widely were "persistence in the accomplishment of end," "integration toward goals," "self-confidence," and "freedom from inferiority feelings."

Gilmer (147), reviewing studies on executive behavior, noted:

> Progress in scientific prediction of executive success is severely handicapped by inability to solve the criterion problem. . . . . that there is a growing list of articles dealing with discussions of executive development, most of them at the nonresearch level.

Wald (376), summarizing his doctoral dissertation titled **A Psycho-Educational Study of Top Level Business and Industrial Executives**, reported that there is a definite pattern of background and personality making for executive competence. The executives were studied by three techniques:

1. A 140 item questionnaire covering home and background.
2. Three tests of intellectual ability, interests, and personality.
3. An interview of two to four hours.

Each of the men questioned was serving as an officer in an organization established for at least five years which had, during that time, maintained more than $5,000,000 of business each year. Each had served in such a position for at least three years, was in large measure responsible for planning and coordinating company policy, had received an annual salary of not less than $20,000 for the last three years and had been educated in American schools predominantly.

> 1. Thirty-three executives representing 29 different organizations were studied. With the exception of two who immigrated to this country as children, all of the group were born in the United States. Sixteen, or almost half of the participants, were reared in cities of 100,000 or more population.
> 2. With reference to home background, seventy-five percent of the group had two American born parents, 10% had one foreign born parent, and 15% had two foreign born parents. All but four came from families whose incomes were either average or above average in their communities. The parents' educational backgrounds were definitely above average. Somewhat more than half of the fathers were engaged in professional or managerial occupations. The great majority of the group of executives came from homes in which family relationships were harmonious. The parents of only one participant were divorced.
> 3. In terms of educational backgrounds, the executives themselves were well educated. The average level of formal education was slightly above third year college. Twenty-two of the participants, or 67%, were graduated from college, and of the 11 others all but two took higher level business and accounting courses. Of the 22 college graduates, four were graduated from schools of commerce, four pursued engineering degrees, and 14 received their degrees in liberal arts. The college subjects which were felt to have been most helpful in subsequent vocational pursuits were English, economics, accounting, and political science.
> 4. Of the collegians, seven were elected officers of their fraternities; six were elected to student government offices; two were editors of one of their college's major publications; and four were elected officers of various clubs.
> 5. Most of the 33 felt that their advancement was not entirely due to some superior's "discovering" their talents and pushing them ahead or to hard work, but a combination of both. All but one of the group felt keenly interested in their work. Rather than merely selling their services for a certain number of hours each week,

they received their greatest satisfactions from the increased importance of their organizations in the total economy.

6. A majority of the 33 stated that skill in human relations was most important in their own advancement. Important qualities were the ability to get along with people, social poise, consideration of others, and tact in personal dealings. Next in importance, mentioned by nine executives, was the capacity to analyze facts and to understand and correctly solve problems. Seven indicated that supervisory ability helped them greatly.

7. A high degree of personal ambition and desire to improve the overall value of their organization were believed by six of the group to be important in gaining business recognition.

8. The group members were found also to possess high moral and religious standards. Every one of them was brought up with church training; over two-thirds were continuing as active members of established churches. Less than 15% had ever been separated from their wives or had previously been divorced.

The functions of college and university education include not only the development of subject matter competence but also the stimulation and guidance of leadership potential. An indication of the increasing emphasis on this latter function is the effort with which colleges and universities seek to attract students who are potential leaders. Goldman (122) pointed out that such students are valued because of the contributions which they can make in such areas as student government, publications, and social activities as well as to future business and community affairs. Over a generation ago, Hunter and Jordan (167) reported "Only a meager beginning has been made in developing methods of discovering potential leadership ability and in giving specific training in order that the most able individuals will gravitate to positions of leadership." Mathewson (230) summarized the challenge to educators in the following words:

> Education of the future should be able to characterize and understand persons much more completely in terms of constitutional make-up, developmental potential, and temperamental idiosyncrasy, and thus be in a position to adapt educational experiences much more effectively to maximum individual development.

Several comprehensive and current bibliographies have been published on leadership research by the Continuing Education Service (1962) and Arlen (1957). Duber (1967) assembled eight different approaches on the identification of leaders in the literature. These approaches are shown graphically in Figure 4.

Ginzberg (1964), in the follow-up study that resulted in **Talent and Performance**, developed a fourfold system of classification that designated a *leadership* type. He spoke of this group as being strongly motivated to arrive at positions of dominance over others. They can be, and frequently are, just as deeply committed to their work as the individualistic type, but their efforts are directed towards securing, holding, and expanding their positions of influence or dominance over others. He found 18% of the total sample with this value orientation. In view of the outstanding ability of the respondents, the relatively

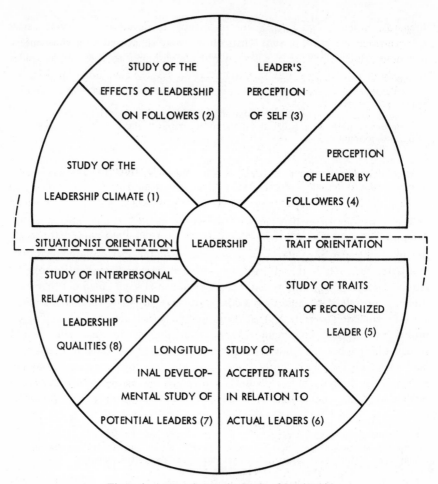

Figure 4. **Approaches to the Study of Leadership**

small number who were classified as the leadership type might at first appear surprising, since we could expect those with superior ability to seek and gain power. The small proportion who fall in this classification may reflect the fact that the key sector of contemporary life in which men can find an outlet for leadership proclivities is in corporate enterprise. But people heading for top positions in business do not have to pursue graduate or professional education; this was surely so in the early postwar years, and this fact may have introduced a bias into the smallness of the group with outstanding abilities having a leadership orientation.

Confronted by the widely recognized difficulty of distinguishing between academic achievement and student accomplishment outside of the classroom,

Richards, Holland, and Lutz (296) undertook to develop a device to assess non-academic accomplishments. Their efforts were supported by a wide variety of studies which suggested that academic accomplishment as measured by grades is largely independent of many achievements outside the classroom (MacKinnon, 219; Price, et al., 1964; Holland & Nichols, 1964; Holland & Richards, 158; Hoyt, 1965). The Richards' study was conducted on a freshman group of 1576 men and 1571 women enrolled in 6 colleges, a sophomore group of 2293 men and 2834 women enrolled in 31 colleges, and a senior group of 981 men and 585 women enrolled in 12 colleges.

Since the major focus of this chapter is on male student leaders, only that area of the Richards' investigation will be commented on. Correlations with college grades and thirteen college achievement scales produced only one significant relationship, and that was on Recognition for Academic Accomplishment. Intercorrelations of College Achievement Scales for College Seniors are presented in Table 2.

TABLE 2
Intercorrelations of College Achievement
Scales for College Seniors

Scale	1	2	3	4	5	6	7	8	9	10	11	12	13
1. Leadership Achievement	--	41	22	46	12	19	20	22	18	27	25	25	30
2. Social Participation	39	--	29	44	07	28	38	22	10	42	44	30	13
3. Artistic Achievement	16	25	--	31	22	27	35	17	17	37	23	26	02
4. Social Service Ach.	45	35	22	--	05	30	30	40	20	30	27	30	08
5. Scientific Achievement	05	07	05	05	--	10	09	02	12	14	06	05	31
6. Business Achievement	19	24	17	22	08	--	21	12	15	22	25	26	01
7. Humanistic-Cultural Ach.	22	31	23	21	15	15	--	17	19	41	40	35	09
8. Religious Service	23	19	12	47	01	08	20	--	23	18	17	27	04
9. Musical Achievement	10	03	09	09	02	10	11	20	--	23	14	27	10
10. Writing Achievement	22	34	23	15	03	19	38	16	09	--	32	39	10
11. Social Science Ach.	12	30	08	19	10	14	34	12	00	22	--	31	15
12. Speech & Dramatic Ach.	21	27	13	13	03	10	32	13	13	28	10	--	08
13. Recognition for Academic Accomplishment	35	11	02	20	20	17	26	12	04	13	09	09	--

Note—Correlations for males are shown above the diagonal and for females below the diagonal. Decimal points have been omitted.

Because the criteria of socially relevant accomplishment rested on the students' self-reports, the scales could possibly be "invalid" in the sense that some students may give distorted reports of their achievements. The evidence that students gave frank responses is so far indirect (Richards, et al., 292).

Much has been reported about leaders in non-academic settings. Relatively little substantive work has been carried on in which student leaders are distinguished from the student groups of which they are a part. Bay (13) observed that since most entering students are at a developmental stage where social acceptance is very important to them, they will tend to model themselves after the social leaders, not the studious types. Furthermore, those who become social leaders will tend to be recruited in part from those with a self-assurance and relative lack of concern for academic achievement associated with an upper-class of wealthy upper middle-class family background, and in part from star athletes.

STUDENT LEADERS AS FRESHMEN

The major objective of this section will be to describe the student leaders by a variety of measures and items that were available from records secured at the time of entrance to the University in 1957.

As part of the routine procedure for admission to the University and as a basis for placement in various class sections in English, mathematics, engineering studies, and reading improvement, a full day of testing had been required of all new students since 1949. The tests that were administered to the freshman class of 1957 were the School and College Ability Tests (SCAT), and the Cooperative Tests for English, Mechanics, Reading Comprehension, Mathematics, and the Pre-Engineering Test (ETS, 1951-1955).

TABLE 3

Percentile Means and SD's of Student Leaders
on Tests Taken as Entering Freshmen

SCAT			Coop. Reading		Coop. Math	
	M	SD	M	SD	M	SD
Verbal	75.0	18.3				
Quantitative	83.5	16.0				
Total	84.0	15.2	57.3	21.8	72.0	21.3

The SCAT is intended to measure four of the school-learned skills which research had shown to be closely related to academic success in school and college. Any score earned on this test was an estimate of the level of skill the student had attained in handling certain specific kinds of verbal or quantitative material. In developing the first norms for the SCAT, an attempt was made to represent as closely as possible the norm group for the 1954 edition of the ACE Psychological Examination for College Freshmen according to Melville (249).

In a John Carroll University study (1961) conducted with the entering freshman class of 1959, the SCAT mean percentile was found to be 70.0 with a SD of 21.0 for 609 students. The difference between the Student Leader SCAT mean of 84.0 secured at the freshman level and that of the 1959 freshman class was significant at the .01 level. When comparisons were made against published norms for students in liberal arts colleges, the SCAT and Cooperative Mathematics means for the Leaders exceeded the normative group by a magnitude to be significant at the .05 level.

In the correlation matrix presented on page 225, the freshman SCAT score correlated highest with the senior grade point average (GPA) $r = .465$ [in terms of intellective measures used at whatever stage of the investigation]. The r of .465 was significant at the .01 level. Further examination of the matrix shows high intercorrelations between the SCAT and the other measures of academic aptitude, viz., with Reading .654, with Math .601 at the freshman level. In comparing freshman level tests with senior level measures, the following significant relationships were noted: SCAT total scores showed an r of .53 with the Concept Mastery Test, an r of .42 with the Wechsler Adult Intelligence Scale, an r of .470 with the Religious Scale of the Allport-Vernon-Lindzey **Study of Values,** and a negative r of .566 with the Economic Scale on the Allport. The frequency of significant correlations exceeds that which would be expected by chance at the .05 level.

BIOGRAPHICAL DATA

Turning to biographical items as revealed by a Personal Data Form at the time of admission to the University, the following categories were extracted:

Family Relationships:

Number of Children	:	Mean 3.2, range 1-7
Position in family	:	Quite variable. No consistent rank in birth order noted.
Parental educational background	:	Elementary School - 10%
		High School - 47%
		Some College - 22%
		College Graduate - 21%

High School:

Origin	:	Private - 83%
		Public - 17%

High School: (Cont'd)

Activities	:	Mean number engaged in 2.75, tallied as	
		Athletics	- 67%
		Publications	- 47%
		Student Government	- 47%
		Music	- 36%
		Debate	- 28%
		Dramatics	- 28%
		Religious	- 25%
Hours studied	:	Averaged 12 per week, with a range of 5 to 20. No support can be secured for the view that leaders were "grinds" during high school.	
Career Plans	:	None	- 5%
		Law	- 14%
		Teaching	- 22%
		Science-Medicine	- 28%
		Business	- 33%
Future Plans	:	What do you plan to be doing 10-15 years hence?	
		Vague	- 14%
		Specific	- 86%
		Wishful	- 0%

Self-checked personality traits:

Friendly	- 95%
Reserved	- 20%
Stubborn	- 27%
Self-confident	- 33%
Irritable	- 1%
Cheerful	- 55%
Tactful	- 40%
Capable	- 50%
Anxious	- 14%
Nervous	- 14%
Quick-tempered	- 14%
Social	- 50%
Tolerant	- 50%
Pessimistic	- 11%
Cynical	- 8%
Self-conscious	- 27%
Average amount of poise	- 89%
Aggressive	- 21%
Conscientious	- 50%

Self-checked physical conditions-symptoms present in last six months:

Indigestion	- 8%
Sleeplessness	- 5%
Headaches	- 14%
Dizziness	- 0%
Easily exhausted	- 8%
Excessive sweating	- 0%
Eye strain	- 5%
Continuous tired feeling	- 8%
Muscle twitches	- 0%
Surgical Procedure	- 22%

Community origins of Leaders:

Commuters	- 25%
Residents	- 75%

A discussion of the significance of the above data will be reserved for the next chapter in which the leaders will be compared with Failures. One striking note can be made of the great variance that obtains between the community origins of student leaders. Historically and currently, the John Carroll University student population has been almost equally divided between commuters and residents. The proportion of student leaders drawn from out-of-town sources produced a chi-square value significant at the .01 level. Considerable credence is given to Sanford's (315) assertion that "leaving home to pursue studies has much value in the development of a college student." Moreover, Wald's (374) findings on business and executive leaders are mirrored in the student leader survey.

INTELLECTUALITY—AS SENIORS

This section will be devoted to the presentations of various measures of intellectual development and achievement. Specifically, the Wechsler Adult Intelligence Scale (WAIS), the Concept Mastery Test (CMT), and the Grade Point Average (GPA) were the bases for assessment. Academic achievement (GPA) was on a five-point system with an A equal to 4 and an F equated to zero.

Key to variables in correlation matrix:

1. GPA   - Grade Point Average
2. EEG-R   - Electroencephalogram Rating (see p. 141)
3. Alpha Index - EEG rating in terms of % of 8-13 frequency
4. CMT   - Concept Mastery Test
5. WAIS-V   - Verbal Scale IQ of the Wechsler Adult Intelligence Scale

Key to variables in correlation matrix: (Cont'd)

6.	WAIS-P	-	Performance Scale IQ of Wechsler Adult Intelligence Scale
7.	WAIS	-	Full Scale IQ of the Wechsler Adult Intelligence Scale
8.	SCAT-V	-	Verbal Scale of the School and College Ability Test, Form 1A
9.	SCAT-Q	-	Quantitative Scale of the SCAT, Form 1A
10.	SCAT-T	-	Full Scale of the SCAT, Form 1A
11.	Coop. Rdg.	-	Cooperative Reading Test, Form T, C2
12.	Coop. Math.	-	Cooperative Mathematics Test, Form XX
13.	MMPI-L	-	Minnesota Multiphasic Personality Inventory-Lie Score
14.	MMPI-F	-	MMPI Validity Score
15.	MMPI-K	-	MMPI Correction Score
16.	MMPI-Hs	-	MMPI Hypochondriasis Scale
17.	MMPI-D	-	MMPI Depression Scale
18.	MMPI-Hy	-	MMPI Hysteria Scale
19.	MMPI-Pd	-	MMPI Psychopathic Deviate Scale
20.	MMPI-Mf	-	MMPI Masculinity-Feminity Interest Scale
21.	MMPI-Pa	-	MMPI Paranoia Scale
22.	MMPI-Pt	-	MMPI Psychasthenia Scale
23.	MMPI-Sc	-	MMPI Schizophrenia Scale
24.	MMPI-Ma	-	MMPI Hypomania Scale
25.	MMPI-Si	-	MMPI Social Introversion Scale
26.	A-Th	-	Allport-Vernon-Lindzey **Study of Values**–Theoretical
27.	A-Ec	-	Allport-Vernon-Lindzey **Study of Values**–Economic
28.	A-Ae	-	Allport-Vernon-Lindzey **Study of Values**–Aesthetic
29.	A-Soc.	-	Allport-Vernon-Lindzey **Study of Values**–Social
30.	A-Pol.	-	Allport-Vernon-Lindzey **Study of Values**–Political
31.	A-Rel.	-	Allport-Vernon-Lindzey **Study of Values**–Religious
32.	R-W+	-	Rorschach Whole Response Total
33.	R-D	-	Rorschach Major Detail Responses
34.	R-M+	-	Rorschach Movement Responses
35.	R-FC+	-	Rorschach Form-Color Responses
36.	R-g	-	Rorschach Organization Score

(See Appendix 1.)

WECHSLER ADULT INTELLIGENCE SCALE

A great deal of information had been reported regarding the use of the Wechsler-Bellevue Intelligence Scale. Literature related to the use of the Wechsler Adult Intelligence Scale was available, but far less abundant. Research

Figure 5 shows the WAIS Record Profile of Student Leaders. Table 4 reports the mean scaled scores and the SD's for each subject.

WECHSLER ADULT INTELLIGENCE SCALE

TABLE OF SCALED SCORE EQUIVALENTS*

Scaled Score	Information	Comprehension	Arithmetic	Similarities	Digit Span	Vocabulary	Digit Symbol	Picture Completion	Block Design	Picture Arrangement	Object Assembly	Scaled Score
19	29	27-28		26	17	78-80	87-90					19
18	28	26		25		76-77	83-86					18
17	27	25	18	24	16	74-75	79-82	21		36	44	17
16	26	24	17	23	15	71-73	76-78	20	48	35	43	16
15	25	22	16	21	14	67-70	72-75	19	47	34	42	15
14	23-24	22	15	22		63-66	69-71	19	46	33	41	14
13	21-22	21	14	19-20	13	59-62	66-68	18	42-43	30-31	38-39	13
12	19-20	20	13	17-18	12	54-58	62-65	17	39-41	28-29	36-37	12
11	17-18	19	12	15-16		47-53	58-61	15-16	35-38	26-27	34-35	11
10	15-16	17-18		13-14		40-46	52-57	14	31-34	23-25	31-33	10
9	13-14	15-16	10	11-12	10	32-39	47-51	12-13	28-30	20-22	28-30	9
8	11-12	14	9	9-10	9	26-31	41-46	10-11	25-27	18-19	25-27	8
7	9-10	12-13	7-8	7-8	8	22-25	35-40	8-9	21-24	15-17	22-24	7
6	7-8	10-11	6	5-6		18-21	29-34	6-7	17-20	12-14	19-21	6
5	5-6	8-9	5	4	7	14-17	23-28	5	13-16	9-11	15-18	5
4	4	6-7	4	3		11-13	18-22	4	10-12	8	11-14	4
3	3	5	3	2	6	10	15-17	3	6-9	7	8-10	3
2	2	4	2	1	4-5	9	13-14	2	3-5	6	5-7	2
1	1	3	1			8	12	1	2	5	3-4	1
0	0	0-2	0	0	0-3	0-7	0-11	0	0-1	0-4	0-2	0

RAW SCORE

*Clinicians who wish to draw a "psychograph" on the above table may do so by connecting the subject's raw scores. The interpretation of any such profile, however, should take into account the reliabilities of the subtests and the lower reliabilities of differences between subtest scores.

Figure 5

SUMMARY

TEST	Raw Score	Scaled Score	S.D.
Information		14.5	1.85
Comprehension		15.4	2.39
Arithmetic		12.9	2.27
Similarities		15.0	1.93
Digit Span		12.9	3.22
Vocabulary		15.7	1.68
Verbal Score			
Digit Symbol		12.8	1.91
Picture Completion		13.1	2.41
Block Design		12.6	2.15
Picture Arrangement		10.7	2.39
Object Assembly		11.8	2.67
Performance Score			
Total Score			

VERBAL SCORE 86 IQ 127.4
PERFORMANCE SCORE 61 IQ 114
FULL SCALE SCORE 146 IQ 122.9

Table 4

findings that involved the variables of scholastic aptitude, academic achievement and general intelligence, as investigated and described in this study were limited.

Guertin (136) reported that the WAIS was clearly improved over the previously well received Wechsler-Bellevue scales, and that the WAIS, for the time being, stood alone as a measure of general intelligence with very little competition.

A factorial study on the WAIS by Cohen (55) resulted in a first and most important general eductive factor g. It accounted for about 50 percent of the total variance contributed by all the tests. The other factors extracted were verbal comprehension, performance or non-verbal organization, and memory. Lesser factors, accounting for less than 2% of the variance, were capacity to resist distraction and relevance of response.

A validity study involving 161 college freshmen correlating the WAIS with grade point average and the ACE Psychological Examination produced correlations worthy of comparison. The following r's were reported with freshman GPA:

	Test	r
WAIS	Verbal Scale weighted score	0.58
WAIS	Full Scale weighted score	0.53
ACE	Linguistic Score (raw score)	0.46
ACE	Total Score (raw score)	0.35
WAIS	Performance Scale weighted	0.31
ACE	Quantitative Score (raw score)	0.18

Intercorrelations of the four best predictors of freshman grade point averages were found between:

WAIS	Verbal Scale and ACE L	r = 0.53
WAIS	Verbal Scale and ACE Total	r = 0.58
WAIS	Full Scale and ACE L	r = 0.50
WAIS	Full Scale and ACE Total	r = 0.57

Additional data, by Plant and Lynd (285), using 361 college freshmen selected voluntarily from general psychology classes ranging in age from 17-22 who took all eleven subtests and completed their freshman year after WAIS testing, produced the following results:

	Verbal IQ	Performance IQ	Full Scale IQ
M	115.6	112.3	115.2
SD	8.2	9.8	8.8
Range	85-140	83-143	91-145

The authors concluded that collegiate educational predictions from WAIS scores were as good as or better than similar predictions from the ACE.

In an attempt to estimate the average IQ of college students Plant and Richardson (286) sampled 735 college freshman at San Jose State College and found the mean IQ to be 116.5, SD 9.6 on the Wechsler-Bellevue. Other studies which used the W-B produced mean IQ's from 117 to 127 for college and university students. In terms of the W-B, the IQ was most nearly correct when estimated to be 120.

The role of intelligence, as measured by the W-B in the appraisal of executive personnel was investigated by Balinsky and Shaw (9). The Richardson, Bellows, Henry & Company Incorporated, a middle-sized company, used the WAIS in appraising their personnel. Thirty-nine top management personnel, including the president, whose functions were either in accounting and finance or in some form of selling and commodity exchange operations, were given the WAIS.

The results were correlated with performance ratings that were based on a seven point scale going from one as "unsatisfactory" to seven as "outstanding." The mean age was 46.1 with a range of 32-63. The verbal IQ was the only scale in the WAIS that correlated significantly with performance ratings. An r of .32 was significant at the .05 level. The arithmetic reasoning subtest yielded an r of .42 that was significant at the .01 level. Although the vocabulary subtest was the highest scaled score for executives, arithmetic correlated highest of all the Wechsler subtests. The correlations of the three parts of the WAIS, plus the arithmetic subtest, with on the job performance ratings produced these results:

	Verbal IQ	Performance IQ	Full Scale IQ	Arithmetic
M	125.1	117.09	124.09	14.51
SD	8.09	9.81	7.90	22.21
r	.32	.08	.24	.42

Average performance rating ranged from 2.5 to 6.33, SD .54. The authors concluded that non-verbal subtests of the WAIS contributed to the lowering of the significance of the Full Scale IQ, showing a correlation which was only slightly better than chance. The vocabulary subtest was high but lacked correlation with performance on the job, while arithmetic, only moderately high in score, correlated highest with on-the-job performance of executives.

The WAIS and WB-I were claimed to be useful devices in counseling and guidance. Wechsler (380) cited a study by Simon and Levitt on the relationship between W-B IQ's and various occupational levels with norms for major descriptive categories. Most of the occupational groups studied showed a systematic 2 to 5 point higher verbal than performance IQ. Performance IQ was high for artists and skilled laborers. Engineers recorded the highest median, 133. Accountants were second with 128 and a range of 106 to 143. Teachers had a median of 126 with a range of 94 to 152. Business managers and executives were next with an IQ of 125 and a range of 92-146. Wechsler further speculated that so far as intelligence level and college success were concerned the WAIS and W-B seemed to indicate that individuals below 110 IQ had poor chances of completing the average course within the usual four-year period.

De Martino (Wechsler 379) who attempted to measure the relationship of intelligence to scholastic aptitude and achievement, using Verbal and Perform-ance IQ's obtained by 100 pre-engineering freshman students, correlated the WAIS with college grades and an aptitude inventory. The Verbal Scale, with a mean of 118.31 and a SD of 8.13, correlated much better with the criteria than Performance Scale (.516 against .097).

A validity study on a WAIS norm group, cited earlier in the (Plant & Lynd 285) study showed a Verbal mean IQ of 115.6, SD 8.20 (N = 361). To determine whether there was a statistical difference between this group and the sample study in Table 5, calculation produced a mean difference of 11.54 and a critical ratio of 8.48. A second similar study was cited by DeMartino on 100 Freshman pre-engineering students with a WAIS Verbal mean IQ of 118.31, SD 8.13. Comparison with the Student-Leader mean produced a C.R. of 6.05. A significant difference between the three sample means was clearly evident at the .01 level. The probability was low (one in 100) that the critical ratios of 8.48 and 6.05 happened by chance alone. The null hypothesis was rejected (that the three groups were equal in verbal intelligence). The Student-Leaders were superior to the pre-engineering students and those of the validity study.

An examination of the correlation matrix in which the WAIS is correlated with various types of measures reveals that its major relationships are with other types of intellectual achievement. Significant r's were found between the WAIS and GPA, CMT, SCAT-V, SCAT-T, Coop. Math, and these results mirror other findings.

The relationship of the WAIS to what are sometimes called non-intellective measures followed the expected outcomes. Two interesting developments did occur in the correlation of WAIS and Allport-Theoretical of .335, and in the WAIS vs. Allport-Economic with an r of -.398. No special significance can be attached to these findings because chance would account for almost two such relationships emerging in the array.

CONCEPT MASTERY TEST

The Concept Mastery Test, Form T, the Psychological Corporation (1950), was devised at Stanford University in 1939 for use in the follow-up program of the Stanford research with gifted subjects. This research, which was launched in 1921, was designed as a longitudinal study of intellectually gifted children. The subjects were selected from the school population in childhood or early youth on the basis of an intelligence test, the requirement being an IQ of 140 or higher on the Stanford-Binet or, for the older subjects, a group test score that placed them in the top one percent of the school population. This gifted group has been followed both by mail and by field studies for 45 years.

In 1939 the first field follow-up since the subjects had become adults was undertaken. A test was needed which could be administered to a group in a brief period, which would differentiate at a very high level of mental ability, and which would yield a statistically reliable measure of intellectual functions similar to those brought into play by the Stanford-Binet and other scales highly saturated with Spearman's "G."

Since no test was available that met the needs of the gifted study, it was necessary to construct one. After a survey of the results yielded by the leading types of intelligence tests... their reliabilities, their validities as measures of "intellect," and their relative efficiency per unit of time, two types of tests were chosen: the synonyms-antonyms and the analogies tests. The test was called the Concept Mastery Test because it deals chiefly with abstract ideas. Abstractions are the shorthand of the higher thought processes, and a subject's ability to function at the upper intellectual levels is determined largely by the number and variety of concepts at his command and by his ability to see relationships between them. Admittedly, the test does not tap all kinds of intellect one might like to measure.

Various types of groups (CMT Manual-1950) have been administered the CMT and these provide some tentative norms for comparative purposes. Some of these are presented here:

	N	Mean	SD
Stanford University Undergraduates	59	79.9	25.6
Electronic Engineers and Scientists	102	92.4	38.2
Undergraduate and Graduate Students and Teaching Assistants (Stanford and University of California)	148	95.6	39.4
Air Force Captains	341	60.2	31.3
Subjects of Stanford Gifted Group	768	136.7	28.5

The Student-Leader group achieved the following results in the standard administration (mean = 88.14, SD = 28.4).

In further analyses of differences, the student leader group was significantly higher than the Air Force Captains' sample, and significantly lower than the Subjects of the Stanford Gifted Group. It can be concluded that the John Carroll University student leaders are drawn from the same population as Stanford University undergraduates, Electronic Engineers and Scientists, and the undergraduate and graduate student and teaching assistants at Stanford and the University of California.

In addition to the correlations cited earlier in this chapter, several other relationships were studied. The major variables were:

Variable X_1	Grade Point Average (GPA)
Variable X_2	EEG-R
Variable X_3	Wechsler Adult Intelligence Scale-Full Scale IQ
Variable X_4	Concept Mastery Test Raw Score
Variable X_5	School and College Ability Test, Total Percentile
Variable X_6	Allport-Religion Scale

Table 5 provides a summary of the intercorrelations for the six variables mentioned in the preceding discussion.

TABLE 5

Intercorrelations for Five Independent Variables
and the Criterion Variable, Grade Point Achievement

	r_1	r_2	r_3	r_4	r_5	r_6 (Allport-Rel.)
X_1 GPA		.21	.38	.44	.47	.47
X_2 EEG			.18	.37	.27	.01
X_3 WAIS				.39	.42	.29
X_4 CMT					.53	.43
X_5 SCAT						.47

$$R_{1.23456} = .59$$

TABLE 6

Data for Regression Analysis

	Mean	SD	N
GPA	3.05	.52	36
WAIS	122.88	7.78	36
SCAT Percentile	84.00	15.16	36
Allport - R	45.14	7.78	36

The R = .59 cited above is significant at .01 level for 34 degrees of freedom. $R^2_{1.23456}$ indicates the proportion of variance of the dependent variables which is explained or accounted for by the independent variables. Hence, the total variance of GPA may be accounted for as follows:

.6 % by correlation with EEG-R
2.56% by correlation with WAIS
1.69% by correlation with CMT
3.24% by correlation with SCAT
7.84% by correlation with Allport - Religion
19.00% by indirect correlation between the variables
65.00% by correlation with variables other than above.

It is a widely accepted view that efforts to show relationships between measures of cognitive functioning and academic progress have reached a stage or plateau where typically the indices cluster between .5 and .6 on multiple correlations.

Departing from that format, two multiple correlations were performed with non-intellective variables selected from the correlation matrix against the predicted variable of academic achievement. In the first analysis the variables were:

Variable X_1	GPA
Variable X_2	EEG-R
Variable X_3	MMPI-Pd
Variable X_4	Allport-Religion
Variable X_5	MMPI-Mf
Variable X_6	Rorschach g

TABLE 7
Intercorrelations for Five Independent Variables
and the Criterion Variable, Grade Point Average

	r_1	r_2	r_3	r_4	r_5	r_6
X₁ GPA		.21	.01	.47	.01	.15
X₂ EEG-R			.23	.01	-.39	.17
X₃ MMPI-Pd				.13	.34	.08
X₄ ALLPORT-R					.22	.17
X₅ MMPI-MF						.08

$$R_{1.23456} = .5244$$

$R^2{}_{1.23456}$ indicates the proportion of variance of the dependent (predicted) variable which is explained or accounted for by the independent variables. Hence, the total variance of GPA may be analyzed or accounted for as follows:

5.76% by correlation with EEG

1.44% by correlation with MMPI-Pd

22.09% by correlation with Allport-Rel.

.16% by correlation with MMPI-Mf

.09% by correlation with Rorschach g

-2.04% by dampening effect or interference due to negative correlations.

72.5 % by variables other than those above.

In view of the three multiple correlation outcomes just presented, no definite combination of variables can be designated as showing a superior predictive value over the others. The fact should not be lost sight of that the sample of student leaders was a very homogeneous group and that reduced values of relationships would be expected.

The relationships between various types of intellectual or scholastic aptitude measures with academic achievement fall within the expected limits that have been found for the past thirty years. It must be emphasized that the magnitude of the r's or R's is constricted by virtue of the high degree of selectivity that is found in college samples. This was true of the Student Leaders used in this investigation. The tendency to minimize the role of intellectual abilities as a consequence of such statistical findings can be expected by readers not cognizant of the relationship between selection of individuals and scholastic achievement.

The pressure to accommodate more and more students, both percentage-wise and in absolute numbers, can only lead to an overall lessening of the quality of the college population in the United States. This fact has serious implications that will be discussed in a later section.

The conclusion is clear that the Student Leader group, without exception, was drawn from the top quarter of the peer group that it belonged to, and that mean IQ of 122 surpassed 92 percent of the adults in this country between the ages of 20 and 24.

The correlation matrix provides some interesting relationships beyond that generally found in the literature. Some commentaries on these conditions will be presented in subsequent section on personality and electroencephalography. However, a few must be pointed out here. The measure of intellectual functioning that correlated highest with the academic achievement of the Student Leaders was the SCAT, which was secured three years earlier. Moreover, the SCAT had high correlations with other variables deemed important for academic progress—such as Reading and Mathematics. Some support is provided for the view that whatever else may be operating in the progress of young men through college, nothing measurable to date surpasses the importance of well developed language and mathematical skills and comprehension.

Bay (13) stated that:

> Those who become social leaders will tend to be recruited in part from those with a self assurance and relative lack of concern for academic achievement associated with an upper class or wealthy upper middle class family background, and in part star athletes.

His conclusion cannot be supported by the findings secured on Student Leaders in this setting.

In concluding this section which has been concerned to point up levels of intellectual development as well as relationships among various measures of productivity, citations from a few more studies will be presented.

Hollingworth (159) reported that the leader cannot be too superior to those he leads. The leader must be more able to solve the problems of the group, but not much more able. She found that among children with a mean IQ of 100, the IQ of the leader was between 115 and 130. A child of 160 IQ had very little chance to emerge as leader of a group, although the same child might have been successful if the average IQ in the group had been 140 instead of 100. Hollingworth concluded . . . "the leader is likely to be more intelligent, but not much more intelligent, than the average of the group led."

McCuen (243) noted that leaders of college student organizations are selected who are only slightly above the average for their respective groups.

Bass (11), surveying the field of leadership, concluded that a large amount of experimental evidence supports the proposition that successful leaders are verbally high scorers. Green (151) found tested vocabulary correlated .30 with leadership in conferences. Thurstone (362) found that higher paid administrators surpassed lower paid ones in linguistic aptitude test scores but not in word fluency, per se. Positive relations between leadership and verbal aptitude were also reported by Terman (358), Burks (42), and Malloy (223).

In 1957, Mann, in Bass (11), reviewing 196 results from 28 studies, found that 88% of these correlations between intelligence and leadership were positive.

Spiller (337) commented that "one cannot be both truly great (an outstanding leader) and truly be a pioneer." From an analysis of the biographical data, he concluded that most outstanding leaders were not original thinkers, but popularizers profiting from the "innumerable" contributions previously made.

PERSONALITY—AS SENIORS

It is generally agreed that the present era of psychological assessment is concerned with the most elusive of concepts . . . *personality*. Consequently, the construction and use of personality inventories and tests are beset with special difficulties over and above the common problems encountered in all psychological testing.

The great variety of definitions and the numerous rationales that have been proposed for delineating the phenomenon have resulted in a production of personality tests that range from simple self-report inventories to highly esoteric projective devices. This development prompted White (389) to the observation that it is not unduly difficult to make up a personality test, but it is a gigantic undertaking to find out what it is worth.

Bereiter and Freedman (24), in reviewing fields of study and people in them, observed that personality measurement at the present time is at a stage of development where it is considerably easier to develop reliable measuring devices than it is to find out what they measure. As a result, it is possible to speak of personality differences between curricular groups but to remain vague about the nature of those differences.

In this investigation, three widely used scales were administered. Two of these, the **Minnesota Multiphasic Personality Inventory** and the Allport-Vernon-Lindzey **Study of Values**, represent the trait-oriented approach to assessment. The Rorschach Ink Blot Test is representative of the projective tests of personality.

Goldman (122) asserted that numerous well-constructed tests and a great deal of validity data exist to assist colleges in selecting students on the basis of scholastic aptitude, but that little material is available to define leadership behavior.

In a study of leaders and non-leaders on the Queens College campus, Beer (18) enumerated various attributes of leaders. These included: greater confidence and degree of realism, willingness to accept responsibility, greater feeling of personal worth, and more drive. Cobb (53), in a study of women leaders at the University of Nebraska, concluded that leaders are objective, emotionally controlled, broad in their views of the world, and have many interests beyond those immediately related to their personal lives.

Ludeman (217) conducted a study of the attitudes of five hundred college students towards the qualities of ideal and effective college students. The qualities most frequently designated were honesty, intelligence, ability to get along with others, participation in activities, cooperativeness, good scholarship, friendliness and setting of high goals.

Hunter and Jordon (167) analyzed a relatively large number of traits and characteristics of college students who were recognized as leaders in campus activities at a Southern State University. They concluded that leaders were more self-sufficient, more dominant in face-to-face situations, and more aggressive but showed more doubt and uncertainty in the realm of religion.

STUDY OF VALUES

The **Study of Values** (1951) measures the relative prominence of six basic interests or motives in personality: the theoretical, economic, aesthetic, social, political, and religious. The classification is based directly on Eduard Spranger's **Types of Men**, which defends the view that the personalities of men are best known through a study of their values or evaluative attitudes. The scale is designed primarily for use with college students or with adults who have had some college work.

Spranger's Types

The Theoretical Man: The dominant interest of the theoretical man is the discovery of truth. In the pursuit of this goal, he characteristically takes a "cognitive" attitude, one that looks for identities and differences. His chief aim in life is to order and systematize his knowledge.

The Economic Man: The economic man is characteristically interested in what is useful. He is interested in the practical affairs of the business world, the production, marketing, and consumption of goods, the elaboration of credit, and the accumulation of tangible wealth. This type conforms well to the prevailing stereotype of the average American businessman.

The Aesthetic Man: The aesthetic man sees his highest value in form and harmony. Each single experience is judged from the standpoint of grace, symmetry, or fitness. He regards life as a succession of events; each single impression is enjoyed for its own sake.

The Social Man: The highest value for this type is love of people. It is the altruistic or philanthropic aspect of love that is measured. The social man prizes other persons as ends, and is therefore himself kind, sympathetic, and unselfish.

The Political Man: The political man is interested primarily in power. His activities are not necessarily within the narrow field of politics; but whatever his vocation, he has placed a high value on power. Since competition and struggle play a large part in all life, these men are strongly inclined toward possessing personal power, influence, and renown.

The Religious Man: The highest value of the religious man may be called unity. He is mystical, and seeks to comprehend the cosmos as a whole, to relate himself to its embracing totality.

The **Study of Values** was originally published in 1931. The revised form appeared in 1951 and provided improvement in fresh norms. The present norms for 2489 men found in 14 colleges are as follows:

	Theoretical	Economic	Aesthetic	Social	Political	Religious
Mean	43.75	42.78	35.09	37.09	42.94	38.20
SD	7.34	7.92	8.49	7.03	6.64	9.32

In addition to the general collegiate norms special norms have been developed for groups with special occupational commitments. These, however are based on much smaller numbers than the college sample. The manual for the third edition of the Allport-Vernon-Lindzey **Study of Values** carries differential means and standard deviations for the following student-major and occupational groups: Engineering, Business, Medicine, Education, Personnel and Guidance, Air Force Officers, Art and Design, and Clergymen.

An interesting development in the efficacy of the **Study of Values** has recently been reported in the Carnegie Corporation of New York **Quarterly** (45). At the University of California Institute of Personality Assessment and Research (IPAR) a six-year study on creativity with people who have *proved* that they are creative turned up some interesting correlates of such groups.

The creative "subjects" were studied by the method of personality assessment developed by the Office of Strategic Services during World War II. This method involves the administration of a number of different tests, questionnaires, personal interviews, and the eliciting of biographical information. It is possible in this way to learn a great deal about the attitudes, values, interests, preferences, and life histories of individuals. A composite picture of the "person as a whole" emerges. How do creative people look?

They are fairly intelligent, but although a certain amount of intelligence is required, beyond that point being more or less intelligent does not crucially determine the level of an individual's creativity.

What about special aptitudes? Early in life, creative individuals show the skills necessary to their ultimate careers: architects were good at drawing as children; mathematicians always had a talent for math. But many creative people come to their final careers late, because they have so many skills and aptitudes that they find it difficult to choose among them.

Clearly it takes more than intelligence and specialized skills for creativity, so that interests play an important role. All of them score high on interests which might lead them to be psychologists, architects, author-journalists. All of them score low on scales for purchasing agents, office workers, bankers, farmers, carpenters, policemen, and morticians.

From the decisive pattern of interests which distinguishes highly creative people, it is shown that creative talent is not very interested in small detail, in the practical and the concrete, but is more concerned with the meanings, implications, and symbolic equivalents of things and ideas. Not only do creative people show a strong congruence of interests, they also share the same values.

For all the creative types, the aesthetic and the theoretical values are the strongest; the economic tends to be the weakest. What is surprising is that the two values which are usually considered to be conflicting are so high and of so nearly the same strength for all creative groups.

Other findings support the hypothesis that creative individuals are more able than most to give expression to opposite sides of their nature, to achieve a reconciliation of the conscious and unconscious, reason and passion, rational and irrational, science and art. All the highly creative male groups studied scored high on a "feminity" test: more open in their feelings and emotions, more sensitively aware of themselves and others, and possessing wide-ranging interests—traits which in our culture are considered "feminine." On the other hand, most of them were not effeminate in manner or appearance, but instead assertive, dominant, and self-confident.

Another indication that creative people are more open to experience from within and without is that they seem to have a positive preference for complexity—even for what appears as disorder. When presented with a series of drawings of various types, they consistently choose those which are more abstract, perhaps chaotic; when offered an opportunity to make mosaic patterns using many or few colors, the highly creative tend to employ more colors, the less creative, fewer.

It seems that the less creative person has to impose order immediately, but the more creative sees the possibility of imposing a higher level or order having previously experienced more disorder.

So far all the creative types have been, with slight variations, much alike in interests, values, and preferences. It is when compared with the general population on Jung's scheme that startling differences occur. Most people show a consistent preference for one of two attitudes towards experience: preferring either to judge or to perceive. A judgmental type of person places emphasis upon the control and regulation or experience, while the perceptive type is inclined to be more open and more receptive to all experiences. He seeks to know as much as possible about life.

In Jung's scheme, the second preference is for one of two types of perception: sense-perception, which is a direct becoming aware of things by way of the senses; and intuitive-perception, which is indirect perception of the deeper meaning and possibilities inherent in things.

In the general population, three out of every four persons are sense perceptives. They concentrate on things presented to their five senses, and they focus their attention upon existing facts. The one out of four who perceives intuitively looks expectantly for a link between something present and something not yet thought of, focusing habitually upon possibilities. Highly creative people in all fields are overwhelmingly intuitive: 93 percent of the writers, 90 percent of the mathematicians, 100 percent of the most creative architects.

The creative person is a nonconformist. His nonconformity lies in the realm of ideas, not in the realm of behavior. Hence, he seldom fits the layman's stereotype of him. The IPAR has found that he is not the usually emotionally unstable, sloppy, loosely-jointed Bohemian. The truly creative person is simply independent. They are not well-rounded; they have sharp edges, (Carnegie Corporation, 45).

Stein (cited in Carnegie Corporation, 45) for many years, first at the University of Chicago and now at New York University, has been studying the characteristics of the creative process. He has made some interesting observations of the way in which creative individuals work. The creative man seems to know when to be disciplined (for discipline is essential to creativity) and when not. He is more likely to play, in a certain sense, with things and ideas. He is willing to allow all kinds of ideas and feelings to enter his mind; he can accept his own impulses.

It is often reported that people "attack" a problem, and that is precisely what many do. But Stein observed that highly creative persons are not so likely to try to force or pull out a solution; they tend to become part of the problem field, sensing its forces and following its leads, and thus to let the problem "solve itself."

Less creative workers seem more oriented toward quick achievement. The more creative work more slowly at first, marshalling resources. Then they move quickly, with an air of certainty, to a synthesis. The less creative person tries to achieve a synthesis earlier, but then keeps checking back, retracing steps. In the long run, they are not as efficient, and in working on their research problems they are not as likely to achieve creative solutions.

TABLE 8
Student Leader Scores: Study of Values

	Theoretical	Economic	Aesthetic	Social	Political	Religious
M	39.8	36.7	35.4	37.9	45.2	45.2
SD	6.7	10.4	8.0	7.2	6.7	6.7

A comparison of the means with the published means for 2489 men resulted in four significant differences being established. The normative group reported means that were significantly higher than the student leader group on the Theoretical and the Economic scales at the .01 level of significance. The student leader group mean for the Religious scale was significantly higher . . . at the .01 level . . . than that of the norm group, and significantly higher on the Political scale at the .05 level of significance.

In contrast to the findings of IPAR on Creativity, it appears that both the normative group of college students and the student leader groups at John Carroll University are not candidates for membership in the "Creative" classification, and that undergraduates in the 14 normative schools and the locale of this investigation have not developed the independence of thinking along with the "sharp edges" that characterized the truly creative group studied at IPAR.

Further examination of the published norms, using collegiate male samples in many types of institutions as well as various career groups, did not produce a single grouping that had a distribution of values that matched the student leader group. The major variation from most groups rests in the reversal of scores in the theoretical and religious areas. Whereas most of the samples had higher theoretical than religious scores, the student leader group at John Carroll University reversed the arrangement.

The manual reported intercorrelations for the six scales showing thirteen of the fifteen relationships to be negative. This was approximated by eleven of the fifteen student leader intercorrelations which were negative.

Significant correlations were noted between academic achievement and several personality variables. Unexpectedly, an r of .472 between GPA and the Allport-Religious Value, and an r of -.429 on the Economic Value were recorded.

In view of the college and post-college commitments of the student leader group (only one entered a religious order), the suggestion that undergraduate leadership is related to strong contemporary alignments, including material gain and dominance over others, was not borne out in this case. Allport, following Spranger, suggested that an attempt to secure a cosmic harmony was the factor underlying this Religious value orientation. The homogeneity of the sample on professed religious alignment and the Catholic foundation of the University were factors operating in this study and constituted influences that were not examined.

MINNESOTA MULTIPHASIC PERSONALITY INVENTORY

A major shift occurred in the area of paper-pencil, self-reporting personality testing with the construction of the Minnesota Multiphasic Personality Inventory, hereafter to be referred to as the MMPI. Partly owing to its clinical origins, and partly because of certain innovations of technique, this inventory has been received with much favorable attention. Since its appearance in 1940 and the publication of the first official manual in 1943, the MMPI has stimulated a flood of research and has been used in research designs for many purposes.

In sharp contrast to many inventories which concentrate upon individual differences among relatively normal persons, the MMPI deliberately sets out "to assay those traits that are commonly characteristic of disabling psychological abnormality" (Psych. Corporation, 1951). The inventory consists of 550 affirmative statements, which the subject is asked to answer in either a true or false manner insofar as the statement applies to him.

The MMPI items range widely in content, covering such areas as: health, psychosomatic symptoms, neurological disorders, and motor disturbances; sexual, religious, political and social attitudes; educational, occupational, family, and marital questions; and many well-known neurotic or psychotic behavior manifestations, such as obsessive and compulsive states, delusions, hallucinations, ideas of reference, phobias, sadistic and masochistic trends, and the like.

The MMPI provides scores on ten clinical scales and three validity scales. Each scale consists of items which differentiated between the corresponding clinical group and a normal control group of approximately 700 persons. The latter were all visitors at the University of Minnesota hospitals, and represented a fairly adequate cross section of the Minnesota population of both sexes between the ages of 16 and 55. The scales were thus developed empirically by "criterion keying" of items, the criterion being specific psychiatric diagnosis. By this method, the following scales were prepared (Manual, Psych. Corp., 1951).

Scale 1, Hs (Hypochondriasis)

The Hs scale is a measure of the amount of abnormal concern about bodily functions. Persons with high Hs scores are unduly worried over their health. They frequently complain of pains and disorders which are difficult to identify and for which there is no clear organic basis. It is characteristic of the hypochondriac that he is immature in his approach to adult problems, tending to fail to respond with adequate insight.

Scale 2, D (Depression)

The D scale measures the depth of the clinically recognized symptom or symptom complex, depression. A high D score indicates poor morale of the emotional type with a feeling of uselessness and inability to assume a normal optimism with regard to the future. A high score further suggests a characteristic personality background in that the person who reacts to stress with depression is characterized by lack of self-confidence, tendency to worry, narrowness of interests, and introversion. This scale, together with the Hs and Hy scales, will identify the greater proportion of those persons not under medical care who are called neurotic, as well as those so abnormal as to need psychiatric attention.

Scale 3, Hy (Hysteria)

The Hy scale measures the degree to which the subject is like patients who have developed conversion-type hysteria symptoms. Such symptoms may be general systemic complaints or more specific complaints such as paralyses, contractures, intestinal complaints or cardiac symptoms. Subjects with high Hy scores are also especially liable to episodic attacks of weakness, fainting, and are more immature psychologically than any other group.

Scale 4, Pd (Psychopathic Deviate)

The Pd scale measures the similarity of the subject to a group of persons whose main difficulty lies in their absence of deep emotional response, their inability to profit from experience, and their disregard of social mores. This scale tends to indicate an antagonism to authority when it appears in a male college student's profile.

Scale 5, Mf (Interest)

The Mf scale measures the tendency toward masculinity and feminity of interest pattern. Males with very high Mf scores have frequently been found to be either overt or repressed sexual inverts. However, homosexual abnormality must not be assumed on the basis of high scores without confirmatory evidence. The Mf score is often important in vocational choice. A high coding of this scale among men is particularly frequent in an educational setting.

Scale 6, (Paranoia)

Pa scale was derived by contrasting normal persons with a group of clinic patients who were characterized by suspiciousness-oversensitivity, and delusions of persecution, with or without egotism. When paired high with Pd, it differentiates the anxiety subgroup.

Scale 7, Pt(Psychasthenia)

The Pt scale measures the similarity of the subject to psychiatric patients who are troubled by phobias or compulsive behavior. The compulsive behavior may be expressed by excessive hand washing, vacillation, inability to escape useless thinking or obsessive ideas. The phobias include all types of unreasonable fears. Pt appears to be related to general anxiety states: tension, indecisiveness, confusion, disorganized thinking.

Scale 8, Sc (Schizophrenia)

The Sc scale measures the similarity of the subject's responses to those patients who are characterized by bizarre and unusual thoughts. In the college group, high scores in Sc indicated confusion, vagueness in goals, lack of knowledge or information, or lack of academic motivation, and disorganized thinking.

Scale 9, Ma (Hypomania)

The Ma scale measures the personality factor characteristic of persons with marked overproductivity in thought and action. The hypomanic patient is active and enthusiastic and may be somewhat depressed at times. His activities may interfere with other people through his attempts to reform social practice, his enthusiastic stirring up of projects in which he then may lose interest, or his disregard of social conventions. In the college group, high scores in Ma were associated with aggressiveness or belligerence, conflict in family situations, or mother conflict.

Scale 0, Si (Social introversion-extroversion)

High Si indicates introvertive characteristics, especially shyness, social insecurity, and social withdrawal.

With the exception of certain factorially derived inventories such as Cattell's Sixteen Personality Factor Questionnaire (Cattell & Stice, 1962), the MMPI has been subjected to more factor analytic investigation than any other test in wide-spread use. Wiggins (390), in a substantial review of the MMPI, observed that despite considerable interpretative controversy, a remarkable agreement exists as to the dimensionality of the instrument. When the intercorrelations of the MMPI are factored, two substantial factors emerge which account for the vast majority of common variance. These factors are consistently marked by Welsh (1956) A and R respectively. Recent studies tend to interpret these as "anxiety vs. integration" and "extraversion vs. introversion."

During the last decade, the foregoing substantive interpretations of the MMPI factors have been seriously challenged by investigators who maintain that response styles and sets vitiate or limit the credibility of substantive interpretations (see Rorer, 1965). Edward's insistence that a "social desirability" factor and Messick and Jackson's "acquiescense" factor in the MMPI raise questions about the interpretability of the scale. Block (1965) defends the substantive interpretation of the MMPI and calls into question the relevance of even the existence of response styles.

Cohen (55) noted that the MMPI was the most thoroughly researched clinical procedure extant. Moreover, this research has been marked by a high order of both statistical and clinical sophistication and hard-headed empiricism. On the other hand, it was originally developed by selecting items on the basis of their differentiation of each of a series of psychiatric diagnostic groups from hospital visitors, and that, as a result, the scores reflect surface rather than source traits.

Wiggins (390) summarized factorial analyses of the MMPI with the conclusion that in a college population, the first two factors noted by Welsh (1956), A and R, were present. These were designated as "anxiety-proneness versus ego resiliency" and "impulsivity versus control."

Kleinmuntz (193) prepared an annotated bibliography of MMPI research with college populations that summarized 179 articles.

That such an innovation in personality assessment as represented by the MMPI would attract much attention and be widely used is readily understandable. Its application in college settings will be briefly reviewed in order to demonstrate its use in the present study.

Goodstein (127) reported a study in which a comparison of the results of the MMPI administration to large groups of male undergraduates at eight different colleges and universities sought regional differences. When the mean scores were subjected to an analysis of variance, the results indicated that there were no significant regional differences.

Although there is a characteristic profile for the college male that differs little from college to college, it is markedly different from the characteristic profile of the non-college male and from the characteristic profile of the college female.

The consistency in the pattern of scores among the eight schools also seemed worthy of note. The peaks on Ma, Mf, Sc, Pt, Pd, and Hy suggest that there is a characteristic profile for college males. They appear to be more feminine in their interests, to be more active, less inhibited, but more worrying than the male population in general.

The use of the MMPI with college populations has been criticized on two points. First, college students tend to be more deviant than the general population in their MMPI responses, and second, local or regional norms are thought necessary for each college or geographical region. Goodstein (127) reported that in addition to his study on college males, Black collected from the literature MMPI data on a large group of college females, a total N of 5014, at fifteen colleges and universities. Although he did not use an overall test of significance, Black concluded, "These data suggest that there is a characteristic profile for college women which does not differ from college to college."

Bier (26) in a comparative study of five Catholic college groups using the MMPI, secured 1284 profiles from students in professional schools of medicine, dentistry, law, theology and from a college group. A significant feature of the distribution of scores is the consistent manner in which the means for the present group rise above the mean of the general population as established by the test norms. Inspection reveals that 89% of the group means on the MMPI scales are above 50.

In Bier's study, the observed frequency of scores above 70 is about one in sixteen. This difference is certainly significant and confirms very strikingly the unmistakable tendency of the subjects to score higher than the population at large upon which the MMPI was standardized. On purely statistical grounds it would be expected that about one in forty of the MMPI scales would have a standard score in excess of 70.

Williamson and Hoyt (393) administered the MMPI to student leaders for the purpose of testing two hypotheses: (1) That students holding positions in formal organizations would differ from students in leadership roles of informal groups, and (2) Fraternity and sorority leaders would differ significantly with respect to personality characteristics from "students in general."

The authors present two major findings which they feel may prove productive for other studies:

1. As groups, student leaders engaged in political activities, especially those of a "liberal" or "radical" cast are, characteristically, different in personality makeup

from student leaders engaged in other types of activities. This suggests that the motivation of such students could be termed "unstable" or "neurotic."

2. Fraternity and sorority leaders do not differ from other types of students in general (except on Mf—social and intellectual cultivation—where they approximate in stature the Heroic type of ancient Hellenistic thought and literature).

In an unpublished study (1961) the Counseling Center at John Carroll University set out to establish its own norms for the undergraduate population. Work bearing directly on this study was initiated during the Spring term of 1959 when the incoming freshmen of the class of 1959 were tested. Of the pilot group tested, 247 were given the MMPI instead of the **Bell Adjustment Inventory** which had been part of the test battery in the past. A comparison of the data obtained from this effort and that of the Goodstein study are presented in the table that follows:

TABLE 9

MMPI T Score Means, Standard Deviations of Incoming Freshmen at John Carroll University and a Group of Freshmen at Various Colleges

Group	Hs	D	Hy	Pd	Mf	Pa	Pt	Sc	Ma
*VC, M =	52.3	52.8	55.0	56.3	58.5	53.0	56.7	56.9	58.7
SD =	8.3	11.1	7.8	9.8	10.1	8.3	10.3	10.8	10.2
N = 5035									
JC, M =	52.3	52.0	56.3	59.9	59.3	53.4	58.6	59.8	58.2
SD =	8.7	11.4	8.2	9.9	12.0	8.8	11.2	13.0	10.6
N = 247									

*VC is used as the abbreviated form for the various colleges used in Goodstein's study.

Table 11 provides a statistical and inspectional basis for noting the characteristic distribution of scaled scores.

TABLE 10

T Score Means, Standard Deviations on the MMPI for Student Leaders

	L	F	K	Hs	D	Hy	Pd	Mf	Pa	Pt	Sc	Ma	Si
Mean	46.2	51.5	57.7	53.2	52.3	60.2	58.3	63.3	55.2	58.6	57.3	60.3	44.9
SC	6.5	6.5	7.6	9.0	13.1	7.9	7.7	10.0	8.2	11.5	11.2	10.1	7.9

It is singularly conspicuous to note that the findings reported by Williamson, Goodstein, Bier on the one hand and the freshmen and Student Leader group performances at John Carroll University on the other produce an MMPI profile that is almost uniformly located between the 50th and 65th T scores. In another unpublished study (1961) the MMPI profile for 35 students pursuing a master's program at John Carroll University was wholly between the 50th and 65th T score limits.

Very little support is given to the findings of Brower (35) who reported significant correlations at (.001) for r's of -.57, -.60 and -.65 between W-B IQ's and Pd, Hs, and Hy scales respectively. In the student leader study, comparable r's were 0.01, .01, and .19 with the WAIS Full Scale IQ. More support is accorded to the findings of Wexner (384) dealing with the relationship of intelligence and the nine scales of the MMPI, and that of Yeomans and Lundin (401) who found that college males in the top quarter of their classes had higher Mf scores and lower scores on the Pd and Ma than men in the lowest quarter.

In examining the correlations between the MMPI scales and the WAIS Full Scale IQ of the Student Leaders, not a single significant correlation was secured. In another instance, Clark (51) and Dahlstrom (62) point out that there do not appear to be any overriding personality correlates of job status. Since relationships have been demonstrated between intelligence and educational level, educational level and careers in an hierarchial fashion, but no direct relationship between personality variables and intelligence, it would be unexpected to find a statistically demonstrable relationship between personality variables and occupational levels.

TABLE 11
Intercorrelations Among MMPI Basic Scales
for College Freshman Males

	L	F	K	Hs	D	Hy	Pd	Mf	Pa	Pt	Sc	Ma
L		-03	35	-06	21	30	-05	01	16	-26	-23	-06
F			-42	52	38	09	47	28	32	53	68	32
K				-40	-17	35	-22	-16	00	-74	-67	-46
1-Hs					36	35	36	26	31	58	62	30
2-D						29	31	32	31	41	34	-07
3-Hy							19	19	38	-05	00	-12
4-Pd								12	26	39	46	37
5-Mf									39	34	33	00
6-Pa										28	34	05
7-Pt											80	43
8-Sc												50

In comparing the intercorrelations of the Bechtold and Dahlstrom (1953) Basic Group found in Table 12 with those of the Student Leader Group noted in the Correlation Matrix on page 225 several observations are pertinent. While no replication of the r's is found, the array of r's tended to be in the same direction; but the magnitude of the r's was not comparable. In other words, despite the fact that the profiles of the two student groups consistently followed the pattern of distribution between the 50th and 70th T Scores, the basic interplay of factors of the two groups was not identical. Some credence is given to the varying motives and dynamics that characterize the college freshman as distinguished from the college senior. Sanford (314) and Freedman (103) maintain that despite superficial similarities in surface features, greater distinctions are evident in basic personality dynamics of the two groups than is commonly recognized. The transformation is not an additive one, but appears to be a topological one.

Vaughn (368) described the personality characteristics of a sample of exceptionally high achieving college males. On the SAT scales, the Verbal Score was 598 and the mean Math score was 598. The mean total IQ on the CTMM for males was 128. Inasmuch as the University of San Francisco is a comparable institution under Jesuit administration, the MMPI findings for males is cogent. Table 12 presents these results and the John Carroll University findings.

TABLE 12

MMPI Means and SD's for Male Exceptional University Students
at the University of San Francisco and John Carroll University

Scales	U.S.F.		JCU	
	M	SD	M	SD
L	47.55	3.02	46.167	6.54
F	51.27	4.73	51.53	6.47
K	56.32	8.27	57.72	7.60
Hs	51.78	6.00	53.17	9.00
D	53.91	8.88	52.25	13.04
Hy	55.43	7.08	60.22	7.90
Pd	57.59	8.97	58.25	7.66
Mf	62.79	9.32	63.31	9.98
Pa	53.59	7.99	55.22	8.23
Pt	57.56	9.93	58.56	11.49
Sc	57.14	9.85	57.28	11.22
Ma	55.53	9.43	60.25	10.06
Si	51.99	9.55	44.92	7.90

Comparisons of the means point to ten scales showing no significant differences in the two samples drawn from different sections of the country, but having strong similarities in many aspects. Two of the significant differences were at .01 level for Hy and Si, and one difference at the .05 level for Ma. An explanation is afforded for these outcomes, in part, because the University of San Francisco sample was chosen on the basis of unusual academic achievement (GPA–3.50 or higher), and the John Carroll University sample (GPA–3.05) was drawn from students who had been chosen for leadership, demonstrated by membership in "Who's Who in American Colleges" and presidencies of student organizations. The higher scores on Hy, Ma, and the lower score on Si would be in the predicted direction because these three scales reflect personal involvement in social settings. The Honors group at San Francisco would be expected to manifest a greater detachment from group activities and a stronger inclination to literary and cultural pursuits.

Sanford (214), commenting on his research at Vassar College, stated that seniors, on the average, were more unstable or "upset"; more uncertain about themselves and about life than are freshmen. The typical entering freshman was idealistic, sociable, well-organized and well-behaved, and on standardized personality tests she scored as a pretty sound and healthy specimen. The typical senior's scores are higher in regard to disturbance. Seniors report more depression, more self-criticism, more anxiety and doubt, more consciousness of conflict, more hostile complaints against the environment, more unusual fantasies and behavior problems, more disturbances in physiological functioning. Disturbances of a truly serious and incapacitating nature are very rare; it is possible that the picture the seniors give is due to greater ability to report their difficulties.

Sanford (214) continued his characterization of seniors by adding that they were more informed of their cultural heritage, had more cultivated tastes with broader interests, and greater attachment to things of the mind. They were less authoritarian, less conventional and conforming, less fundamentalist in religious outlook, and showed more awareness and appreciation of the diversity of points of view and standards adopted by others. They showed more signs of trained intellects and were more "liberated."

Comparisons of MMPI profiles of the Student Leaders and the Beginning Freshmen on the thirteen scales (see correlation matrices on pages 225 and 229) did not point to any striking differences. Two slight variations occurred on the Si and Hy scales. The Student Leaders were more extroverted and prone to more conversion of physical symptoms.

Dahlstrom and Welsh, (62) addressing themselves to the screening and selection use of personality scales, emphasized that no test will perform equally well in all settings; the MMPI is no exception. Although the MMPI was originally advanced as an aid in psychiatric diagnosis and evaluation, it has been used in scores of settings against hundreds of different criteria. Caution is urged in transposing solutions from one setting to another, and that independent evaluation of solutions is called for when different samples or settings are investigated.

Many studies have attempted to evaluate the personological contributions to differential success in scholastic coursework. Most of the studies have used concurrent validational procedures but a few have obtained the personality measures before students entered a program of studies. Gough (1953a, 1953b,) has pointed out the significant shift in the psychological processes involved in academic success from high school, where conformity is given high weighting, to college or more clearly graduate school, where success through independence and originality is given increasingly greater emphasis.

Brozek (1955) contrasted two high ability groups differing in age by nearly thirty years (college students averaging twenty years and business and professional men averaging forty-nine years of age). He found the older men higher on scales Hs, D, Hy, Mf, and Si with only the difference on scale 3 (Hy) not reaching a statistically stable level. These older men were lower on scales Pt, Sc, and Ma to a significant degree.

There is no way from the existing studies in the literature to separate the effects of intellective differences per se from the results of differences in general socio-economic status that operate concurrently. The brighter subjects usually go further in school or achieve more easily and with less effort at any given level. Among the basic clinical scales the only consistently positive correlations with intelligence have been with scale 5 (Mf), but only with male subjects. (Dahlstrom and Welsh, 62).

RORSCHACH INK BLOT TEST

An enterprise dealing with the place of the Rorschach within the broader orbit of psychology would be incomplete without consideration of an issue that recently has aroused a vast amount of argumentation: the dependability and trustworthiness of the Rorschach method as a diagnostic tool. The problem itself is certainly a legitimate one, recognized by every serious psychologist with respect for scientific standards. The controversy centers not around the need for such demonstrations for worth, but around the question as to just what means of demonstration may be accepted as scientifically irreproachable. Rickers-Ovsiankina (298).

Psychometric practice, influenced by its basic philosophy and behavioristic tradition, relies for such purposes on the two time-honored indicators—reliability and validity. For the readily isolatable and accurately measurable variables of psychometric assessment, these indicators constitute an entirely appropriate means of establishing in correspondingly dissective and quantitative fashion the respectability of a test is a view of Rickers-Ovsiankina (298). As the reader realizes by now, the Rorschach, and for that matter any projective technique, having grown up in a distinctly different theoretical climate has very little in common with psychometric tests either in objectives or in actual test composition, or in underlying premises. It hardly can be surprising, therefore, that its organismically integrated configuration of variables does not yield smoothly to evaluation by the traditional procedures of reliability-validity probing.

To engage profitably in explorations of the theoretical and research potential of the Rorschach method, it is essential to keep in mind the psychological tenets inherent in this highly valued, yet inadequately understood, diagnostic procedure.

The most outstanding virtue of the Rorschach method is generally recognized to lie in its power for providing an integrated pattern of the total personality. Rorschach's primary interest was in getting at the nature of the basic modes of functioning, underlying all of an individual's psychic activity. He was quite explicit in emphasizing his goal was to uncover how, rather than what, the person experiences.

It was Rorschach's (304) conviction that a person's perceptual responses to the ink blots were capable of serving as clues to such basic tendencies so long as the responses were viewed consistently in the frame of this systematic orientation.

Besides Rorschach's choice of categories of analysis, his manner of employing these variables is of equal importance for a full appreciation of this instrument. He never interpreted any one of the categories by itself, but always as dependent upon the others, thus adhering to his basic principle of interaction among psychological functions right at the level of their correlates within the test data.

Rickers-Ovsiankina (298), in concluding her introduction to the psychological premises points out that unraveling the isomorphism of percept and personality is complicated by the fact that the correspondences do not constitute one-to-one equivalents. Every category of test performance taps more than one psychological function and, conversely, a psychological characteristic is derived from a combination of several test categories.

RORSCHACH TEST FACTORS: GENERAL PSYCHOLOGICAL VALUES

This section will present a brief description of the major Rorschach variables as held by Hertz in Rickers-Ovsiankina (298), a summary of the statistical findings by the group of student leaders, and pertinent findings from other investigators on the variable under discussion.

NUMBER OF RESPONSES (R)

Hertz (153) stated that *response* is not important in itself, although it may be qualitatively important. It shows degree and kind of productivity, ambition, interest in task, and ease or strain in novel situations.

The findings for the Student Leader group are as follows:

Mean	SD
30.0	9.8

These means fall within the range of 25-35 that Hertz presented for adult norms.

Rossi and Neuman's (308) comparative study of Rorschach norms for medical students reported a mean of 33.6. They reported that such a mean for responses is within the range of productivity expected from superior individuals in the natural sciences. For example, Roe (301) found the mean response to be within the 30-40 range for biologists, physical scientists, and faculty members. A mean R with the same range was obtained from 24 medical students by Shoemaker and Rohrer (in Rossi and Neuman, 308).

Klopfer (194) pointed out that the range of responses found most frequently in all large scale investigations of adults seems to be between twenty and forty.

Beck (17) maintained that the response total is one of the test's best indices of intelligence in liberation. His mean was 30.35 with a SD of 15.89.

REACTION TIMES

Deviations in terms of the individual's own average are highly significant. The initial reaction time (RT) and the total time (TT) throw light on the freedom of self-expression, extent of inhibition, fluctuation in productivity, and distortion in flow of ideas.

The times for the Student Leader group were:

	Mean	SD
Reaction Time	11.3	4.6
Total Time	74.6	11.3

Rorschach's statement, "It has not been found useful to fix a time limit to the responses," has been borne out by the experience of practically all experts (in Klopfer, 194).

Beck (17) reported the central tendency for all the cards to be around twenty seconds.

MENTAL APPROACH

The mode of approach to problems varies greatly from one individual to another. One person prefers meticulous observation of details and hesitates to draw general conclusions; another may start with a general survey of the situation before turning his attention to details; a third may be inclined to jump to conclusions. The element in the Rorschach reactions which reflects the manner of approach is the choice of location (Klopfer, 194).

Klopfer reported that a subject following completely the Gestalt qualities of the cards is expected to use a whole card in about one-quarter of the responses (W), the usual detail areas in about one-half to two-thirds of his responses (D), and only the remainder of his responses, usually not more than 10 percent, will be located in unusual detail areas (Dr) or in the white space.

THE WHOLE RESPONSE (W)

The whole response (W) represents the ability to combine, abstract, and generalize. Moreover, it is indicative of ability to search out broad connections. A relatively high number of W, according to the tradition of the Rorschach literature, represents an emphasis on the abstract forms of thinking and the higher forms of mental activity—as, for instance, the logical or constructive activities, philosophical or religious speculation, esthetic or ethical understanding. Klopfer (194), however, states that this tradition cannot be accepted unqualifiedly; not every W can be evaluated in this manner. The productions must be of high quality to satisfy the qualification.

The percentage of W's needs to be qualified in the light of the form accuracy level. The fact that a record contains a high number of W's which are neither simple nor evasive does not guarantee that they represent substantial achievements in the realm of higher mental activity.

The Student Leaders performances were as follows:

	WO	W	WP	W(S)	TOTAL W
Mean	.75	9.00	2.0	1.25	13.1
SD	.75	3.5	1.1	.67	

The percentage of W exceeded 50%. Hertz (153) and Klopfer (194) report that adult norms usually find from 20 to 30 percent of W responses. The absence of reported standard deviations precluded any calculation of the significance of percentages between the Student Leader group and normative data. It does appear to be considerably higher, and it is offered as a significant deviation upwards from expected performances for the normal population.

Rossi and Neuman (308) obtained a mean W for the medical group of 10.6, which is also quite similar to the mean W's reported by Roe for other superior groups by Molish, et al., for a group of fourth-year medical students. The percentage of W in the Rossi & Neuman study, where the R was 33.6, is 30%, a figure that appears considerably less than the 52% for the Student Leader group. Again, the absence of reported standard deviations precluded any calculation of a test of significance.

Beck (17) maintained that the number and quality of W is an index to a subject's present functioning intelligence. The qualifier "present" is important. The best Rorschach figures for yielding such an index are those of cards III, IX, X, which are of about equal difficulty; not far behind these come figures II and VIII. In these figures, only the most superior individuals, those who rank somewhere in the upper 5% of the population, produce W with any frequency.

NORMAL DETAILS

Two major categories are represented by this determinant in Rorschach analysis: the use of a segment of the card that is relatively large and seen frequently is described as a normal detail (D), and smaller segments used infrequently are described as rare details (Dr).

The D response, according to Hertz (154), represents analytic ability. It demonstrates the capacity to see that which is obvious and common but important and essential in a situation. It elicits the ability to note the concrete and the practical, is an index to the extent of contact with daily life, and may be construed as depending on common sense.

The Dr response represents the tendency to select details not generally seen by the average person; it is a tendency to be precise, observant, critical, pedantic, sensitive to detail, discriminating, as well as trifling, nagging, and excessively thorough.

Klopfer (194) stated that traditionally it was assumed that about two-thirds of all responses of an intelligent adult should be usual details. This is correct if D and Dr are considered together. An intelligent subject will not only locate half of his responses in the obvious areas of the cards, but he will place 5 to 15 percent of his responses in other portions which are not so obvious as D but are conspicuous enough to attract his attention. A lack of D's, especially in cases where they comprise less than one-third of R, indicates a definite lack of recognition of the problems of everyday life.

The medical students in the Rossi and Neuman (308) study produced means of 17.1 D's and 5.1 Dr's. This is a slightly higher mean D score than Roe's groups of biologists and physical scientists and a slightly lower mean Dr score than her groups. That the medical students would use more large details and less small details than either biologists or physical scientists is in accordance with expectation.

The Student Leader group performances on details follows:

	DO	D	DP	DR	DRO	TOTAL D
Mean	1.0	8.8	1.0	.95	.35	10.8

The percentages represented by the frequencies of D for the Student Leader group is 44%. Hertz (154) reported that D% for adults would fall between 60 and 70. Klopfer (194) maintained that D should represent from 45 to 55% of the record. The percentages achieved by the Student Leaders fall below both the Hertz and Klopfer figures. However, the absence of standard deviations precluded a statistical analysis of the magnitude of differences.

In the area of Dr percentages, the Student Leader group registered a 5% proportion. Klopfer's figures call for a 5 to 15% Dr productivity, and Hertz's classification for adult norms reports a range of 0 to 10% for Dr responses.

From these percentages it can be concluded that the Student Leaders are overproductive insofar as W responses are concerned, with a consequent reduction in detail awareness. This would be in support of claims and observations that leaders must be able to survey the challenge or problem in sweeping fashion, leaving the closer and more minute analysis for others to undertake.

ORGANIZATION

Rorschach did not refer directly to organizational activity as such in his original monograph. He considered it indirectly, however, in reference to the whole factor or W. This factor represented for Rorschach the capacity of the individual to combine, abstract, and generalize. It indicated a conscious or unconscious willing in the direction of achieving complicated performance Hertz (153).

According to Beck (17) the organization score is an index of the intellectual energy as such . . . the intellectual functioning per se. It is the index to thinking power, and it varies directly with intelligence.

An organization factor termed g (the g taken from the word "organization") was identified and developed at the Brush Foundation in conjunction with analyses of other Rorschach factors (1951). Hertz further reports that the organization score is utilized rather widely in the analysis of records in clinical practice. Unfortunately, comparatively little systematic work has been done to establish its scientific validity. For the most part, reliance has been placed on theoretical assumptions and on empirical findings with normal and pathological subjects.

Beck et al. (17) developed norms for Rorschach factors in their study, of the normal personality on the basis of 157 subjects, age range 17 to 69, all employees of the Spiegel Mail Order House in Chicago. They give norms for Z, for the group as a whole and for vocational categories.

In the Brush studies, the children of the superior group had a median of 10.5 sum g wt, children of the high Otis IQ group showed a median of 15.1; college women earned a median 13.0 according to Hertz.

STUDENT LEADER ORGANIZATION SCORES (g)

	Mean	SD
Who's Who	13.2	5.4

While direct comparison of Beck's Z scores with Hertz's g scores is not readily obtained, two studies by Hertz (153) (154) found correlations of .954 and .958 between her g and Beck's Z. With this prefatory note, the mean Z score for medical students in the Rossi and Neuman (308) study can be invoked. This mean of 29.4 for medical students is very close to the mean score of 28.6 reported by Beck for his group I subject (executives), and this is almost twice the mean score of 16.2 for his Group IV subjects (unskilled).

The organizational score for the Student Leaders appears to be where one would expect to find a superior group in terms of this variable.

WHITE SPACE RESPONSES (S)

The white space response is described as deriving from those answers in which white spaces are interpreted rather than the black or colored parts of the figure which surround them.

The personality correlates of primary S are variously interpreted. Rorschach's basic assumption was the "space responses always indicate some sort of oppositional trend." Later investigators, according to Fonda, are inclined to ascribe more positive values to S. It is now regarded as a manifestation of ego strength which finds itself revealed in active mastery of the environment and in efficient reality testing.

Rossi and Neuman (308) reported a mean of .76 for S responses in their study of 188 medical students. Hertz (154) concluded that the range of S's, primary and secondary, would be from 0 to 3 in adult norms. Fonda (in Rickers-Ovsiankina 298) held that the individual differences in 5% are remarkably stable and persistent, and the average rate among healthy and intelligent young adults may be taken as a reflection of optimal conditions in the sphere of autonomy and independence. When the rate is at the optimum, the presumption is that, at least with respect to achievement of active mastery, the ego is functioning adaptively. According to this rule of thumb, the optimum rate is about 4% or one in every 25 of all responses in the protocol. Actually, the average rate rises from 2% in 15 response records up to 6% in protocols having 60 or more responses. Departure from the optimum rate in either direction gives reason to believe that the ego is operating defensively in its efforts to ward off anxiety associated with the need for autonomy and achievement of active mastery.

The Student Leaders produced the following amount of S activity:

Mean	SD
1.75	1.2

Beck (17) held that in most healthy individuals a minimum number of S percepts—from two to four—will be found. They reflect an essential ingredient in personality, the holding to a purpose. More than the normal number of S evinces too much contrariness. In an apparently healthy subject, the excess would point to an undesirable restiveness; in a sick person, to an aggravation of the trait and of the illness.

From the citations of Rorschach authorities, the presence of S activity in the Student Leader groups constitutes both expected and essential components of achieving individuals.

DETERMINANTS

After the various possibilities offered by the answer to the question, *where* does the subject see what he sees, have been exhausted, the important question arises, *how* does the subject see what he sees; in other words, what formal elements other than location determine the formation of the concept which the subject has chosen.

In his first ingenious choice of the various determinants, Rorschach selected three main categories: kinesthetic or movement elements, form elements, and color elements. A few months before his death he discovered the fourth main area of determinants; viz., the shading elements. (Klopfer and Kelley, 194). The accumulated experiences of the last twenty years has led to many new differentiations and realignments in the description of the various categories of determinants.

FORM LEVEL (F+)

The aspect of behavior that is assessed by this determinant is the accuracy of form perception. Involved in this functioning are the power of observation, precision and definiteness in thinking, conscious attention to stimulus presented, hence capacity for concentration.

Korchin (in Rickers-Ovsiankina, 298) concluded that perceiving, whether highly structured objects or ink blots, always represents a joint interaction of the organism and the stimulus. The interpretation of form level in the Rorschach depends on the assumption that in neither case does perception consist simply of the passive reception of "what is there."

The term form perception is used in the present context as a shorthand designation of reality testing. According to Rorschach, a high % of F plus responses depends on the ability to concentrate, the availability of clear memory images (engrams), the ability to bring such memory images into consciousness, the ability to select from among these the most fitting to the stimulus. It assumes control of the perceptual and associational processes and their critical interpretation. For Rorschach, these abilities were the sine qua non of intelligence (Rickers-Ovsiankina, 298).

Beck (17) stated that empirically the fact is that the F plus finding varies regularly as two chief personality variables, namely, the intellectual endowment and affective state. The one sets an upper limit on F plus. The other can disrupt the potential for it or heighten it beyond the optimum, to a point of dysfunction. The more intelligent the individual, the higher his F plus percentage. But the highest F plus scores of all are found in the depressed, and when the very intelligent subject is emotionally disturbed or excited, or excessively elated, the F plus percentage decreases. The 60% point as a critical minimum for the healthy was originally set empirically. The statistical findings corroborated it. The mean for Beck's group is 83.91, the standard deviation 8.12. Thus the mean, minus three times the standard deviation, would come to just about 60 percent.

Korchin maintained that the healthy ego is not only able to maintain critical control but also is able to relax it as well. Creative behavior often depends on regression, which is, however, under control and "in the service of the ego." The fact that form level is not linearly related to the psychological health was recognized by Rorschach (304), who pointed out that optimum and maximum are not synonymous.

.... we find the best forms in the pedants and depressed subjects, especially in psychotic depressions. These subjects take the test very seriously. They search laboriously for good forms, bringing to bear all their attention and faculties of self-criticism so that they achieve an F plus percentage of almost 100, though the answers are extraordinarily stereotyped, showing a poor range of variation.

More recent writers have invariably pointed to the fact that the highest level of F plus is found in the individual with constrictive defenses who is neurotically unable to relax control.

Hertz (153) provided the range of 75 to 90% for F plus responses in her adult norms. This overlaps with the mean cited earlier by Beck.

The Student Leader performances in this determinant are as follows:

	F+	F-	%F+
Mean	13.5	3.95	77%
SD	5.4	2.20	

The obtained percentages of F plus responses conform with the expected from the normative studies by Hertz, Beck, and Klopfer and Kelley.

MOVEMENT (M)

The factor that is explored in this category is intra-psychic activity. It is the activity of the inner life in the realm of imagination or intuition. It represents the capacity for fantasy, productive, creative or original ability. It is an index to power of introversion.

Rorschach had but one movement response category. For him it tapped the fantasy of personality. Subsequent workers, however, in recognizing the variety of movement responses that were not associated with humans found it necessary to differentiate between human movement (M) from that of animal movement (FM) and inanimate motion or movement (m).

Klopfer views the FM as an indicator of instinctual forces which are near the conscious level and threaten to influence overt behavior, and if the FM are more numerous than the M, that it is indicative of immature psychological development. Piotrowski (in Rickers-Ovsiankina, 298), on the other hand, held that the FM are positively though not necessarily highly correlated with physical vigor.

The inanimate response (m) is presumed to represent wished-for-life roles which the individual feels to be beyond his ability to assume. It may also represent, according to Piotrowski, an underdevelopment or repression of inner life. Only a minority of subjects, practically all of them of at least average intelligence and with a well-developed habit of psychological self-observation produced m. In another sample of 40 normals, all with IQ's of over 115 and nearly all college-educated, m were found in 27 records; 14 subjects had more than one m.

The difference between restraint and absence of restraint in the action tendencies of genuine M is of universal importance. Its importance is independent of differences in intellectual level, in degree of social responsiveness and intensity of living. Business executives differ greatly from Army prisoners. Yet the main difference between executives who continued being successful despite increasing responsibilities and promotions, and those who had failed after they had reached the highest rungs on the managerial level, could be expressed in degrees of freedom of action shown in their M. Piotrowski analyzed 50 individual Rorschach records of successful and unsuccessful top business executives. The following types of M were found with significantly greater frequency in the successful group: self-assertive and confident postures, constructive cooperation for a common purpose, display of mutual respect, friendly or non-hostile facing of each other, and dancing.

Hertz held that a normal record should contain at least one good M, and that the ratio of M to FM should be 2:1 in adult cases. Klopfer reported that a mature well-adjusted person, of not more than average intelligence, usually does not produce more than three M, unless he has very strong introversive tendencies. An adult with superior capacities should show at least 5 M, regardless of whether he is more on the introversial or the extraversial side. The usually desirable relationship between M and FM in mature, intelligent adults is one in which M exceeds FM. Three or more m would certainly cast some doubt on the inner adjustment of any subject.

Rossi and Neuman obtained a mean M of 3.7 for the medical students, and this follows expectations for superior subjects. It is also close to means of 3.1 and 3.8 reported by Roe for her groups of biologists and physical scientists, respectively. However, when the mean M is compared to the mean FM, the medical students had slightly lower M balance. The FM mean was 3.9 to the M mean of 3.7.

The Student Leader mean movement scores are as follows:

M	FM	m
4.3	3.65	1.00

The means for the Student Leader group fall within the ranges that have been reported by Hertz, Beck, Piotrowski, and Klopfer and Kelley. The balance between the M and FM categories probably derives from the fact that the students have not reached the maturity that was cited by the authorities.

However, the alignment does square with the findings of the medical students in the Rossi and Neuman study.

COLOR

The practical Rorschach problem of the interpretive meaning of color response has not been a subject of much debate among clinical Rorschach workers. It is safe to say that not many would disagree with, in essence, Rorschach's (304) own original formulation:

> The C and the CF answers express the more ego-centric affective responsiveness, while the more adaptive effective responsiveness is expressed in the number of FC's.

Color perception as such is a more immediate and passive experience than form perception, requiring less in the way of perceptual tools or organizing capacity. It is associated with a passive perceptual mode in that it becomes more dominant, more compelling in quality, and perhaps even antagonistic to form articulation in conditions in which active perceptual organizing capacity is impaired or is only rudimentary; at the same time, under optimal conditions, color becomes integrated with form perception, is itself modified in subjective experience, and acquires new functions of economy and enrichment. Shapiro (in Roe, 301)

Response to color, in the Rorschach test, presents information as to the individual's sensitivity to events known to be exciting to the healthy persons of his cultural group generally. The undiluted color reaction, (C), is the test's equivalent of the uninhibited feeling experience. The color-form (CF) is characteristic for a less impulsive but still highly labile reactivity. The form-color (FC) association is one in which form dominates the experience. The FC demonstrates emotional adaptability, in which emotional rapport is present with the environment.

Rossi and Neuman found the following mean values for color responses for medical students: FC–2.7, CF–1.2, C–.47.

The Student Leader group in the present investigation produced the following color means:

FC	CF
3.8	.95

The clearly indicated preference for FC responses gives support to the view that the group of leaders had developed clear perception of form dimensions, while remaining in harmony with environmental contacts. This group would lend support to Beck's view that the FC response bespeaks the level of the grown person, who has more fully introjected the outside world. He reacts with emotions, but these are tempered by his regard for how the other feels.

CHIAROSCURO (FCh and ChF)

The work of Binder (in Rickers-Ovsiankina, 298) has been the major contribution to this Rorschach response. The FCh is a rather rare category of response, and is scored when the following condition has been met:

> Within the selected blot area, the subject, from among all the conspicuous shadings, *picks out each individual one,* primarily emphasizing the delimiting forms of the individual shadings, and only secondarily their chiaroscuro values.

The subject in FCh responses maintains control over central mood reactions; he has anxiety with self-consciousness; he is aware of what is going on within oneself and maintains a careful attitude toward promptings from within. In the ChF responses the individual is subject to central mood (dysphoric) reactions.

The infrequency of Ch responses is pointed up in the mean values for this determinant by Rossi and Neuman in which the mean for medical students was found to be .53 for Ch and FCh responses combined.

In the Student Leader group the mean responses for the categories of FCh and ChF or Ch were:

FCh	ChF
.75	.05

ERLEBNISTYPUS

The concept of experience type emerges as one of Rorschach's most important contributions. That people with differing life experiences should see different things in ambiguous ink blots was almost a truism in Rorschach's day, and that a specific type of response determinant—human movement or color—could measure long-standing and important personality characteristics. The M: sum C relationship apparently reflected a deeply ingrained life style most likely constitutional in origin, although modifiable to some extent by mood swings, aging, extreme situational disturbance, or psychotherapy.

The ratio for a given individual derived from his protocol indicated a pattern that could be observed in day-to-day behavior, but which went beyond this readily observable level and suggested potentialities as well.

For the moment, it must be concluded that almost nothing of a systematic nature is known concerning the physiological or constitutional correlates of the M: Sum C ratio.

Combining the requisite scores into an experience-type formula for the Student Leader group resulted in the following relationship: 4.3:4.75.

If the Rorschach assumption holds, then it is readily noted that the experience balance is on the extratensive side, and that the group was drawn more strongly to dealing with forces outside of themselves than they are in deep and frequent reflection and introspection. The fact that high M values were obtained does reveal that the groups are capable of and do resort to some inner living and scrutinizing.

CONTENT

According to Beck (17) the Rorschach projects personality both as neutral psychic structure and, though less fully, as social trend. The one tells the psychologic composition of the individual, the factors so far described—intelligence potential, fantasy life, affective experience . . . i.e., the abilities. It does not tell for what end they are being used, or what the personal needs and interests of the subject are. That is, the psychic structure tells what the subject can do, but not whither he is heading.

For some clue, usually not in full perspective, as to personal needs, attention is focused on associational content. Evaluation of content takes account of breadth, or the number of different categories into which the content is distributed; of the richness or originality; of quantity of human (H) and part human (Hd) percepts; or quantity of animal (A) themes, and many other categories as will be revealed in subsequent pages.

Breadth varies directly as functioning intelligence, as even a brief experience with the test demonstrates. In the most superior, those who had had opportunity for cultivation, breadth of associational content is not only one index of potential, but also of the degree of its actual development through formal schooling, contact with the arts, travel, and many life experiences. Conversely, the fewer the content categories, the less intelligent or the less intelligently functioning, the individual is—i.e., he is of low endowment, or anxious or depressed, or habitually rigid and inhibited.

Table 13 presents the mean scores for the Student Leader group in terms of the content variety in responses.

The range of content categories revealed in Table 13 is such that a great deal of versatility can be ascribed to the interests and preoccupations of the Student Leaders.

TABLE 13
Means for Rorschach Content Categories
for Student Leaders

Category	
Humans (H)	4.5
Human Details (Hd)	1.15
Animals (A)	12.35
Animal Details (Ad)	.95
Anatomy	1.70
Blood	.00
Botany	.85
Clouds	.45
Fire	.75
Geology	.35
Scenery	.85
Apparel	.45
Architecture	.65
Art	2.15
Emblems	.15
Household	.20
Maps	1.00
Food	.15
Weapons & Mechanics	.35

The %A according to Hertz (152) is an index to the degree of sterotype in thought and action as opposed to adaptivity. the %H reveals the degree of interest in human beings and human problems.

If Hertz's observation holds, the significantly greater %A over that of %H for the student leaders provides almost a reversal in the type of content that should be the major concern of leaders. This development may be a function of the lack of maturity that undergraduates have attained, even though discharging leadership responsibilities. Developmental theory provides some support to the view that more concern is generated about personal attainment than a genuine concern for the welfare of others.

MMPI vs. RORSCHACH

The difficulty in translating the results from one type of psychological measure to another is recognized by all workers in the field. Despite this widely accepted fact, the findings of the two most widely acclaimed personality tests were transformed into z scores for the purpose of direct comparison.

In order to arrive at some measure of deviation from the group norm on the MMPI, the mean of the ten test categories was calculated, and from this measure the mean of each student's T scores for 10 scales was calculated. Subtracting each student's mean from the group T mean provided a numerical basis for establishing the individual's magnitude of deviation in either direction from the group profile.

Converting the Rorschach protocols to a numerical system posed a far greater problem and is offered as a conservative estimate of the individual adjustment or personality complexity of the students. As a measure of the student's resourcefulness in handling the task, a score was obtained that was based on the summation of the organization score (g), the number of movement (M) responses, and the number of form-color (FC) and color-form (CF) responses. It was duly recognized that the g score would contribute most heavily to the final score of the Rorschach index. It was pointed out in an earlier section that the group mean for g was 13.2, that the group mean for M was 4.3, and the mean for the FC plus CF was 4.75. Yet, it is acknowledged that the g score is a measure of mental approach to problem solving that may be more pervasive than single measures of inner living and affect integration.

When the z scores for the MMPI and the Rorschach were correlated, the resulting r was found to be .15 for the 36 students in the sample. Such a low degree of relationship between many samples on the same two variables would occur frequently by chance. Consequently, it must be concluded that the two most widely used tests of personality are not tapping the same levels of functioning. The very distinctive rationales that undergird the two scales are not interchangeable insofar as the performances of a select group of young male subjects are concerned.

The disposition of many investigators to ascribe special values to specific techniques or procedures should be tempered by an observation from Harris (142). It cannot be repeated too often that prediction of complex criteria such as psychiatric diagnoses or success in an occupation should not be regarded as a fair indication of the general validity of a psychological instrument, unless the instrument was constructed to mirror the complexity of the criterion. Batteries of tests, have on occasion, been assembled for industry or for the military organization with just such a purpose in mind, but the Rorschach test was not designed, and cannot be properly employed alone, for the prediction of such complex criteria.

One more excursion into the literature (Bass, 11) provided the following summation:

Surveying 15 studies reporting 101 results concerning leadership and empathy, Mann observed 74% of the results were positive and concluded that while researchers have been unable to obtain positive results which are statistically significant they have obtained positive results with impressive consistency. Likewise, Chowdry and Newcomb found that leaders tend to be able to judge group opinion better than non-leaders or isolates. But the superiority of leaders over non-leaders was restricted mainly to issues relevant to the specific groups in which they were leaders. When matters concerned groups in which they were not leaders, their superiority tended to disappear.

There are a number of traits frequently found with some consistency among successful leaders in a variety of groups and situations, such as persistence, consistency, self-confidence, sociability, need for achievement, and dependability.

Study of the correlation matrix, page 225, with reference to the five Rorschach variables (W, D, M, FC, and g) resulted in the following conclusions:

1. No variable on the Rorschach was highly related to the GPA.
2. No significant correlation was noted with the EEG-R score.
3. Non significant relationships were noted with the intellectual measures, although W+ reached an r of .317 with the WAIS FS.
4. In terms of relationships with the MMPI, significant correlations were approached or achieved between the Rorschach M and the MMPI-k, R-W and MMPI-Hy, R-g and MMPI-Hy, R-M and MMPI-Ma, and a surprising r = -.39 between the R-M and the MMPI-Si. In this last instance, it would generally be suggested that introversive tendencies as noted on the Si scale would be correlated with intellectualizing as represented by the movement score on the Rorschach.

Examining the relationships between the Rorschach variables and the **Study of Values** scales produced the following:

1. Significant correlation is noted between the W+ and the Theoretical value. This indicates the power to engage in looking at wholes and a preference to engage in such activities to be related.
2. An r = -.318 between Rorschach-D and the Economic Scale is somewhat unexpected because the common sense view would hold that attention to details and practicality would be positively related.
   The similar relationship of Rorschach-D to Political values (r = -.314) in a Student Leader group would not be hypothesized.
3. The r = .430 between the Rorschach D and the Allport-Social, and Rorschach-D and Allport-Religious of r = .352 were significant. The ability to attend to and to assess accurately the details in perception are related to valuing humanity and cosmic forces.

Intracorrelations among the Rorschach variables resulted in several significant relationships. The most notable one was an r = .936 between the W+ and the g+ scores. The heavy influence of the W response in the organization score is not surprising; it may suggest that one merely reflects the role of the other.

In view of the 165 intercorrelations that appear between the Rorschach variables and the other 31 variables, the presence of only 12 significant correlations or nearly significant correlations at the .05 level adds credence to the claim that the Rorschach does not assess personality factors in the same fashion that other scales do.

ELECTROENCEPHALOGRAPHY

The electroencephalograph provides as rich, as varied, and as informative a set of data as the neuropathologist's microscope, the neurologist's examining kit, the psychiatrist's interview, or the psychologist's tests. All of these means of examining the brain supplement one another and are more or less complementary: none is exclusive. Electroencephalography is a missing link between morphological neurology and dynamic psychiatry. (Gibbs, 1964)

If as it has been claimed that "tools fashion the thinking of the age" (Doty, in Brazier, 1958), then any comprehensive exploration of behavior will require probing into the apparatus that is instrumental in behavior.

A search of published data on EEG variables and leadership since the historic work of Berger which led to the acceptance of such a clinical procedure failed to turn up a single study to provide a basis for replication. Although there have been studies relating intelligence, personality, maturation, and emotionality to neurological factors, tremendous effort has been expended on studying more circumscribed processes and structures in the brain. Moreover, the primary uses of the EEG have been for medical purposes rather than personality assessment.

Despite the short history, dating back to 1929, that represents the life span of EEG findings, a voluminous literature has developed. In preparation for the study under consideration, the literature and bibliographies for the period were reviewed with special attention paid to references dealing with psychological or educational correlates to EEG phenomena.

LITERATURE

Glaser (118) noted that the "normal" electroencephalogram is really a statistical concept based on its empirical correlations with physiologically and structurally normal nervous systems in presumably normal subjects. The EEG records the electrical activity mainly from neuronal units in the outer cortical mantle. Their activity is, at least in part, under control by the lower nuclear systems, particularly those of the reticular activating system. The present dominant concept concerning the major basis of the EEG is that it represents the electrical activity of the dendrites in which massed synaptic potentials of apical dendrites, mainly of pyramidal cells, become synchronous and oscillating as fields of maximal amplitude.

The electrical activity of the cortex, like life itself, is a series of events, some of which are cyclical and some of which are transient. Rhythmic activity ranges from below one to above 100 cycles per second, and the voltage range is from below one microvolt to 1,000 microvolts (1 millivolt). Among adults the range of the dominant frequency is from 8 to 13 per second, and with electrodes on the scalp the voltage is usually between 5 and 50 microvolts. Voltage and frequency are, in general, inversely related (Knott and Travis 199), but at resonant frequencies (for example, 10 per second) voltage is usually high, and at non-resonant frequencies (for example five per second) it is low (Gibbs, 114).

The electrical activity of the cortex starts during intrauterine life (Lindsley, 211). It is slow at birth, increases in frequency with increasing age, slows with senility, and stops with death. The most dramatic rhythmic alteration is that which occurs in the approximately 12-hour cycle of sleeping and waking, for during sleep the electrical activity of the cortex commonly becomes as slow as in intrauterine life.

It is taken as a working assumption that the EEG tracing is correlated with neural activity but no assumption is made as to the origin of the activity recorded by the EEG. It is not possible from the EEG tracing to state whether the origin of activity is cortical or subcortical. (Johnson et al., 178)

Gibbs and Gibbs (114), in one of several atlases on electroencephalography, state that EEG has been recorded in almost every condition of health and disease. They state that the five major parameters that have been established as closely related to EEG's are: (1) brain metabolism; (2) age; (3) level of consciousness; (4) clinical symptomatology of epilepsy and related brain disorders; (5) the pharmacological action of stimulants, sedatives, and anti-epileptic substances.

Many types of injury slow the electrical activity of the cortex; for example, trauma, infection, anoxia, hypoglycemia, chemical poisoning. The brain's reaction to injury is much the same regardless of the etiological agent (Gibbs, 114).

Although attention, age and sleep are the major modifiers of the normal EEG, Lindsley (212) pointed out that changes occur in the electrical activity of the cortex with emotionally disturbing stimuli, but that these are indistinguishable from those that occur with attention.

The Davises (66) made extensive use of the alpha (or percent time alpha) rhythm. This expression is obtained by calculating the percentage of the elapsed time during which countable alpha waves are present. The aspect of the electrical activity of the cortex that correlated best with changes in the central nervous system function is its general frequency. When groups of 100 persons were studied, the percentage of slightly abnormal electroencephalograms ranged from 6 percent to 24 percent abnormal (Gibbs, 114).

Ulett and Johnson (369), studying a young male adult group, reported on the pattern and stability of EEG activity in the following manner:

> It has appeared to us that alpha pattern is not merely an occipital phenomenon, but that it usually dominates the whole EEG and that when present it produces a predictable stability of EEG response over time and seems to lock into place the activity from all areas of the cortex. It also seems to matter little whether one records from two scalp areas or from scalp to "indifferent ear." In those persons who lack alpha, the records fluctuate not only from time to time but also from scalp area to scalp area. Although from inception of the science of electroencephalography to the present time alpha has been closely linked to visual activity, from these results it would seem that it must play some more basic role in brain organization. Recent research regarding the reticular activating system and the concepts of alerting attention and awareness must fit prominently into the picture. The clearly shown quantitative differences in amount of alpha between the first and later recordings in the subjects studied here would indicate some function of alpha that is other than solely visual in nature. This shifting in alpha activity may also account for the low reliability over time of most present classification systems which usually depend heavily upon alpha activity. Such shifts in amount of alpha may also account for some of the conflicting results when alpha activity is related to personality and physiological variables.

In 1944 Lindsley (212), reviewing the first fifteen years of studies involving the EEG, observed:

> Berger's discovery that the human brain during a relative state of rest, in the absence of specific stimulation, has an electrical beat or rhythm of its own was surprising indeed, so much so that his results were looked upon with considerable skepticism until confirmed by others.
>
> For most clinical purposes, the experienced electroencephalographer familiar with normal and abnormal variations of the EEG can readily detect the pathological features of the record. However, for more detailed study and analysis for experimental purposes there are several, quite precise, quantitative measures of the different characteristics of the record which may be made. Among these may be mentioned frequency or the average voltage in terms of microvolts, and percent time or the amount of time that certain waves are found in the record. The latter measure is frequently applied to alpha waves for the alpha index.
>
> Whereas interindividual variability among normal subjects is clearly apparent, intraindividual variability tends to be small. Moreover, clearly distinguished patterns are noted in tracings taken from the developmental cycle, birth to adulthood.
>
> Relatively little investigation of the relationship between intelligence and the EEG has been carried out with populations of normal subjects.
>
> From the foregoing account of the use of the EEG in the study of neurologic and psychiatric conditions it is evident that the most important applications have been in the field of the former. With further refinement of the technique and better standards of classification of EEG data in terms of the range of characteristics observed in the records of normal individuals there is a possibility that the more subtle personality and behavior distortions observed in psychiatric disorders may be illuminated by analysis of the EEG.

Jasper (174), in the first presidential address to the American Electroencephalographic Society in 1948, summarized some of the major developments in the field with such statements:

Much of the concern about physical correlates of the EEG does not touch the problem of their functional significance. Walter made the intriguing proposal that the basic mechanism of brain waves represents a perceptual scanning system that oscillates rhythmically when undisturbed by patterns of centripetal impulses.

Adrian confirmed the close relationship which we have all observed between the alpha rhythm and concentration of attention or to certain types of generalized "tension state." The low voltage, fast, asynchronous waves which are recorded from the attentive or alerted cortex, the regular alpha rhythm from cortex in wakeful repose, and the very slow waves which characterize the cortex in sleep or coma should give a clue to the functional significance of this constant electrical activity.

Attempts have been made to formulate a mathematical basis for the complex interrelationships involved. It is too early to evaluate properly the scope and significance of these developments. Before us lies a new attack on some of the most important problems of human behavior, the neuronal mechanisms underlying processes of awareness, thought, and action.

Penfield (276), in presenting the Fifth Sherrington Lecture at the University of Liverpool, prefaced his formal discussion with the observation that "the work of Sherrington, Pavlov, or any other scientist has not yet proven the complete identity of brain and mind or demonstrated how brain action is converted into thought and thought into brain activity. I have done this also as a preamble to the following discussion of the motor, sensory and psychical phenomena produced by cortical stimulation." He concluded this formal paper stating:

Reconsideration of the results of stimulation of sensory, motor, and the interpretive cortex of the main brain, when patients are conscious, shows how striking are the basic differences in function of these areas. The evidence of difference however rests upon the difference in the connections of these areas.

Dromic conduction from the motor cortex leads to movement of muscle. No signal of stimulation enters consciousness. The patient is only aware of movement and believes that he did not will movement.

Dromic conduction from the various sensory cortical areas obviously leads into the organizing circuits which are subcortical and central. The patient is then conscious of the most elementary sensation of the type served by the area of cortex which the electrode has touched.

Finally, conduction of current from the interpretive cortex which lies on the superior and lateral surfaces of the temporal lobes (and possibly also the inferior and mesial surface) may have two different effects. First, a signal is caused to appear in consciousness, one signal from a small group of possible signals. The signals are interpretations of present experience such as feelings of familiarity, strangeness, fear, position, direction of movement, etc. Under normal conditions such signals are familiar to everyone, but they can only be accurate if preceded by subconscious comparison of present experience with past similar experiences.

The second effect of temporal stimulation is the recall of experience from the past. This seems to be sequential reactivation of those things of which the patient was aware during a previous period of time.

EEG AND INTELLIGENCE

Historically, the teacher, counselor, and psychologist have been preoccupied with external behavioral responses. Answering questions, composing answers, making choices and understanding motives are examples of responses that were analyzed. With the growing realization that neurological forces were present in all behavior, attention has increasingly been focused on underlying mechanisms of behavior. What a person did was not comprehensible without some awareness of why he did it, or how it was accomplished. With such increasing sophistication in explaining behavior, explorations into historical developments and into current physiological determinants have become the style or research into learning processes.

In education the chief explanation of success and failure is closely tied in with recourse to intellectual ability as the chief determinant. In view of this historical and current emphasis, this section will be devoted to an examination of studies conducted over the past thirty years to find EEG correlates in intellectual functioning.

Mundy-Castle (256), using 72 European adults, mostly University students, in a study on the EEG and mental activity, reported:

> results of statistical analysis confirm the view originally expressed by Adrian and Mathews that the alpha rhythm is very much concerned with visual processes. There is no doubt, however, that the alpha rhythm may be fully blocked without conscious involvement or visual activities, and most of the evidence suggests that this is attributed to an attention or alerting factor, as also originally invoked by Adrian and Mathews as a requisite for alpha blocking.

Knott (197), in evaluating the whole problem of the relation between the EEG and intelligence, stated:

> There seems to be at least three factors that have operated against the discovery of any correlation in normal subjects: First, the records have not been taken under conditions involving intelligent behavior. Second, techniques of analysis that are limited to certain characteristics of the alpha rhythm do not provide a complete analysis of the EEG. Third, there is the very real possibility that the EEG technique is incapable of providing an adequate and detailed picture of critical function. This incapacity of the technique, however, has not yet been demonstrated.

Evidence concerning psychological correlates of the alpha rhythm is conflicting. Golla, Hutton, and Walter (126) classified alpha records into M, R, and P types, and found that subjects with M types of record used mainly visual imagery in thinking, P types used auditory-kinaesthetic imagery, and with the R's, either type of imagery might predominate. In M or Minus records Alpha activity is minimal; in P or Persistent records Alpha activity is prominent, and in R or Reactive records, the mental activity paces the EEG responses.

Slatter (332) reported an investigation into the EEG correlates of mental imagery in a group of 60 medical and dental students in an attempt to understand how the various divergences of opinion might have arisen.

The results leave little doubt that visual imagery is associated with reduction in alpha rhythms, whereas verbal imagery is associated with their persistence.

Moreover, the findings suggest that the alpha rhythm bears an inverse relationship to the degree to which visual imagery is easily and naturally used in thought. Habitual visualizers therefore tend to have records showing lower alpha amplitudes than habitual verbalizers. The predominant verbalizers have relatively high amplitude records.

The great complexity of related phenomena which constitute even the simplest of thought processes are all being accompanied by the change in a simple wave form, and it is not necessarily contradictory therefore that correlations have been made between different aspects of personality and changes in alpha rhythms. The various factors involved in personality may be so closely associated together that there is a common effect on the alpha rhythms.

In 1956, Ellingson (82) undertook to review the period since Lindsley's 1944 review. He reported:

> Studies of relationships between EEG variables and intelligence have been relatively few. Lindsley reviewed the literature up to 1944 and concluded that "it appears doubtful that there is any very high degree of relationship between intelligence as measured by tests and the EEG." Ostrow drew a similar conclusion in 1950. Only three references to the EEG and intelligence have appeared since Ostrow's review.

Shortly after the Ellingson review, Mundy-Castle (259, 260) reported findings from a series of studies. Investigation into the relationship of tapping speed and alpha rhythm, using a group made up primarily of college students (mean age 20.16), produced the following results:

> Mean alpha amplitude: 35.65, SD 15.42. In alpha range and alpha index no significant correlation was found, but there was a significant negative correlation between alpha index and alpha frequency where r equaled -.66, p less than .005.
>
> The findings support our growing belief that differences in results of comparable yet independent searches for psychological correlates of EEG variables may be partly due to sampling influences. A clue as to the nature of one such sampling factor may lie in the significantly greater amplitude and the greater alpha index of the predominantly student group, since both of these measures are known to be related to level of arousal (see Lindsley, 1944). Statistics on the EEG recordings for the older staff and the younger student group, while not significantly different at the .05 level, are in the expected direction.

Alpha Amplitude:	Staff Mean	25.00	SD	11
	Student Mean	30.00	SD	13
Alpha Index:	Staff Mean	45.00	SD	32
	Student Mean	65.00	SD	21

Concerning himself with relationships of the EEG and mental activity in whites and Negroes Mundy-Castle (260) concluded:

The results of the statistical analysis confirm the view originally expressed by Adrian and Matthews that the alpha rhythm is very much concerned with visual processes. With reference to the theta rhythm the consistent trend in the history of EEG relating theta rhythm with emotional lability and cortical immaturity is maintained by the present study.

Differences in the main characteristics between the EEG's of normal Europeans and normal Africans have been discussed in detail elsewhere. There are no gross differences, and those which are present appear to be related to environmental and cultural rather than genetic factors. The present results suggest that insofar as the electrophysiological mechanisms of the brain are concerned, there is also little difference between these racial groups.

Mundy-Castle (256), reporting on the electrophysiological correlates of intelligence, presented findings which previously had not been noted. Increased sophistication in statistical treatment and research designs by himself and other investigators is claimed. The article reported:

Reuning found significant positive correlations between critical flicker fusion frequency and alpha frequency, while a joint investigation by Biesheuvel and Pitt and Mundy-Castle reported significant intercorrelations between ratings of the temperament variable primary-secondary function, scores derived from perceptual and motor speed tests, and alpha frequency in the EEG. The differentiation of primary and secondary functions of the nervous system was first made by Gross in 1902. The "primary function" (PF) refers to the tendency of the process to continue for varying periods of time after cessation of the stimulus. Secondary function is believed to influence all subsequent associations, tending to limit them to the "thema" of the primary function. The general effect of SF is to give continuity and integration to mental events, since it favors persistence of attention and rate of work, relative stability of moods and interests, and action in the light of past experience.

Before proceeding it should be noted that previous studies of the EEG and intelligence have produced largely negative results although in no instance has the Wechsler-Bellevue test been used. Moreover, in appraising the results, it should be remembered that the EEG and intelligence scores in this study were obtained quite independently and by different persons without any contact.

Our first finding was confirmation of the hypothesis that alpha frequency would be significantly correlated with Vocabulary. It was also significantly correlated with Verbal IQ, Practical IQ, and General IQ. The relevant conclusion for the present context is that the amount of alpha rhythm present in an EEG is in part related to the extent to which visual imagery is used during thought, and that persons who think predominantly in visual images tend to possess "minus" type (low voltage, low index) alpha rhythms, whereas those who think predominantly by verbal-motor imagery tend to possess "persistent" (medium to high voltage, high index) alpha rhythms.

The relevant conclusion from Mundy-Castle's study, which examined relationships between EEG findings and Wechsler-Bellevue scores (factored), was that the amount of alpha rhythm present in an EEG is in part related to the extent to which visual imagery is used during thought, and that persons who think predominantly in visual images tend to possess "minus" type (low voltage, low index) alpha rhythms, whereas those who think predominantly by verbal-motor imagery tend to possess "persistent" (medium to high voltage, high index) alpha rhythms.

In a study involving the staff at the South African National Institute of Personnel Research (N = 34, mean age 24.0, 20 of the sample were college graduates), the above proposition appears well supported by a factor analysis. The visual-concrete factor A contained a fairly substantial positive loading of alpha frequency and a negative loading of alpha index, whereas the verbal-abstract factor B had its second greatest saturation in alpha index with alpha frequency showing a very slight negative loading. If we assume, as seems justified, that these two factors are related to intelligence, then we can conclude that . . . differences in habitual mental imagery, which are reflected in the characteristics of the alpha rhythm, may also contribute to differences in verbal as opposed to practical intelligence.

In view of the conception of intelligence as proposed by Wechsler (375), and considering that there have been only two attempts at correlating intelligence with EEG phenomena (in both instances using only alpha frequency) among normal adults, it would appear that the general assumption that there is no such relationship rests on inadequate experimentation (Mundy-Castle, 256).

In a critical review of the relationship between EEG and test intelligence, Vogel and Broverman (373) summarized their findings in the following manner:

Evidence for the relationship between these two variables seems strongest for samples of children, institutionalized geriatric patients, mental deficients, and brain-injured persons; and weakest for samples of normal adults. However, criticism must be directed at some of the previous research procedures and methodological considerations.

Vogel and Broverman and other researchers expect EEG indices to be related to higher mental processes. There is no reason to assume that the bioelectrochemical events which produce alpha in the insect, in the sympathetic nervous system of the cat, and on the cortex of man have the same significance for mental functioning. It may be that EEG waves have different neural implications depending upon the kind of nervous cell in which they appear.

Six studies have reported on the relationships between alpha frequency and intelligence in adults. Three found no significant relationships (Beisheuvel & Pitt, 1955; Gastaut, 111; Shagass, 1946); two studies (Mundy-Castle, 259, Mundy-Castle & Nelson, 261) reported positive, significant correlations; and one study (Sugarman, 352) reported a significant negative relationship (Vogel & Broverman, 373).

Following the publication of the Vogel and Broverman (373) article which affirmed that some relationships can be shown to exist between intelligence and EEG phenomena, Ellingson (83) rebutted the position in the following manner:

1. Evidence concerning relationships between normal brain phenomena and IQ in children and in mental retarded individuals is contradictory and inconclusive.
2. The weight of available evidence suggests that there is no relationship in normal adults.

3. EEG abnormality and decreased intellectual capacity are both effects of organic brain disorders, and hence tend to be related to one another.

Ellingson went on to cite the long unchallenged observation of Henry (1944): "In view of the disconcerting manner in which such correlations shift about at different ages, discretion prompts the more conservative conclusion that there is no demonstrated relationship."

A rejoinder from Vogel and Broverman (374) disputed Ellingson's position with the assertion that his commentary on their work is based essentially upon mistakes in regard to facts and faulty assessment of the data they presented and the many studies cited.

Continuing with their efforts to demonstrate relationships between EEG findings and intelligence, Vogel and Broverman (375) reported in the following manner:

The consensual opinion that EEG and intellectual functioning are unrelated is based largely on the assumption that "since both alpha and beta activity appear to be quite primitive functions of neural tissue,,," the EEG should not be expected to relate to "complex and phylogenetically recent" mental functions (Ellingson, 82, 83). This assumption has been challenged by Vogel and Broverman (373, 374), who have maintained that the scarcity of evidence linking the EEG to complex mental behaviors is due less to a failure to find relationships than it is to a failure to initiate research.

The few investigations of EEG-intelligence relationships that have been conducted have been hampered by a rigid adherence to traditional methodological approaches. For instance, previous studies have typically compared intelligence estimates to EEG measures obtained during rest, whereas Vogel and Broverman (373) have argued that EEG measures obtained during periods of active intellectual effort would more likely be related to cognitive measures.

Also at issue is the question of which is more likely to be related to EEG measures: general intellectual ability, or particular aspects of intellectual ability? Vogel and Broverman (373) have argued that since numerous independent factors of intelligence are known, it is more meaningful to investigate relation of EEG to particular mental abilities than to some composite index of general intelligence. However, most previous work has focused upon the relationship between EEG and general level of intellectual ability. No studies have been reported of the relationship of EEG to cognitive style, which may be defined as commonly occurring patterns of particular mental abilities.

Finally, it would seem appropriate to broaden the almost exclusive concern of the EEG-intelligence studies with occipital alpha frequency by investigating relationships between intelligence and EEG measures other than alpha, obtained from other than occipital leads.

Reviews of previous work (Vogel and Broverman 373, 374) suggest that a high-level of general intellectual ability is likely to be associated with (1) an absence of slow wave activity (delta and theta); and (2) the presence of fast alpha frequencies. No literature exists on the relationship of general intellectual ability to EEG frequencies faster than those within the alpha range, or on the relationship of any EEG phenomena to cognitive styles in general.

In studies conducted on superior college and secondary youth, strong relationships were found between slow wave index and good task performance (repetitive work). These findings are relevant to the findings of Mundy-Castle (256) and Arellano and Schwab (1950), who reported increments in slow wave activity during periods of mental efforts. Slow waves in such instances have been interpreted as inhibition of attention or even drowsiness. It is difficult to understand, however, why EEG signs of sleep or relaxation should be associated with effective mental performance. Without surrendering the idea that slow waves represent inhibitory phenomena, it would seem logical to postulate the existence of two kinds of behavioral inhibition, both of which are represented by slow waves. "Class I inhibition" would refer to a gross inactivation of an entire excitatory process which results in the induction of a relaxed, less active behavioral state, as in sleep or in the inhibition of previously learned behavioral acts. "Class II inhibition" would refer to a selective inactivation of particular responses so that a continuing excitatory state becomes directed or patterned, as in the facilitation through practice of a behavior act to the point that the act becomes overlearned or automated. Thus, while Class I inhibition suppresses entire response systems, Class II inhibition suppresses inappropriate response tendencies within an activated response system.

The suggestion that alpha activity has an inhibitory function was advanced by Darrow (1947) who argued that alpha represented "an inhibitory process involving the discharge of subcortical and sympathetic impulses back into the cortex, thereby moderating or terminating the cortical excitation." He later argued that this "termination of cortical excitation was associated with the 'automation' or 'habituation' of learned behaviors, and with the subsequent shift from 'cortical to subcortical control' over behavior."

Darrow (1957) and Sokolov (1963) have both argued that beta represents a process of cortical activation, called by Sokolov the "orienting response," such that beta appears when stimuli are perceived as novel, and disappears with habituation or problem solution.

In the college and secondary school samples, the correlations between automatization and prorated Wechsler IQ's were respectively -0.38, df 34, P ⟨ 0.05; and -0.57, df 23, P ⟨ 0.01; i.e., the weak automatizers had higher IQ's in both samples.

A conceptual problem remains in that slow alpha frequencies, which we have found to be associated with strong automatization and superior task performance, have also been reported to characterize mental retardates as contrasted with normals, children as contrasted with adults, and brain-injured as contrasted with normal persons (Vogel and Broverman, 373).

The tendency of mental retardates, children, and the brain injured to have relatively slow alpha frequencies may reflect Class I inhibition, rather than Class II inhibition. The interpretation of EEG slow waves, in a specific situation, would seem to be contingent upon their behavioral correlates (Vogel and Broverman, 374).

Hughes (166) summarized the published reports on electroencephalography and learning from which the following findings were extracted:

In the investigation of learning disabilities, a difficult problem has been the lack of clear definition of terminology. It now appears that there are various types of learning deficits, and attempts to summarize the data within the entire field must deal with studies on different types of populations (Hughes, 166).

In human studies dealing with electrophysiological changes during learning, the desynchronization of the alpha activity has been commonly noted, in addition to an increase in the alpha asymmetry from the two hemispheres. Some studies have also emphasized that synchronization may occur between cerebral regions. The evoked potentials to the conditioned stimulus may become more similar in different brain regions, suggestive that learning is likely a state involving interacting patterns in extensive neural regions. Phase relationships between these regions may also play an important role. In the category of a DC type of change, the "contingent negative variation" will likely prove to be the first reproducible, specific electrophysiological kappa waves on the temporal areas apparently are not the extension of alpha activity from the occipital areas, and these waves seem to appear in individuals during the process of thinking and other mental acts. As a further means of implicating the temporal areas, direct electrical stimulation of only this lobe can elicit memories or recollections.

Perhaps the major value of this review will be to show that a relatively large number of correlations have been found between the results of electroencephalography and various psychological tests; encouragement, therefore, can be given to investigators interested in pursuing studies in this general area.

This was found to be the case when multivariant techniques were adopted but not with univariant analyses, suggesting that the interaction of these variables must be considered in any type of correlational analysis.

EEG AND PERSONALITY

The utilization of EEG recordings to investigate personality development was not long delayed after the establishment of the scientific worth of the findings of electrical recordings from the cerebral cortex.

In normal persons Gottlober (129) studied certain personality traits in relation to the EEG. He concluded that individuals showing a high degree of extraversion tend to show a "dominant-subdominant" alpha rhythm, but indicated that it could not yet be stated that introverts show predominantly a "mixed rare" type of alpha. Henry and Knott (148), repeating Gottlober's study, were unable to verify these results.

A psychoanalytic approach was utilized by Saul, et al., in search for correlates of the individuality of the EEG pattern. They concluded that two opposing trends correlated with low and high alpha indices. A low alpha index was said to go with a trend toward activity and a high alpha index with a trend toward passivity or inhibition. The latter (high alpha) group is made up of individuals who are described as solid citizens, patient workers and planners. The low alpha index group is associated with trends toward aggressiveness, leadership in social affairs, doing rather than intellectual sublimation. It is pointed out, however, that these "active" and "passive" types are not entirely unmixed.

Rubin and Bowman (311), following up the approach of Saul and collaborators, studied a group of 100 peptic ulcer patients. They concluded that there is a relationship between peptic ulcer and a passive, receptive personality structure. In support of this they offer their personality data, which they believe indicates that peptic ulcer patients are in general a dependent, mother-identifying group as children and adolescents. On approaching maturity the high and low alpha groups develop differently, the former continues to be dependent on a mother surrogate, but the latter manages to achieve independence, through a strong "reaction-formation" to an underlying passivity. It was claimed that more of the higher "dominant" alpha group held their jobs over a prolonged period and more of them were passive toward their mates.

Gallagher et al., (108), discussing cortical activity and personality development, concluded in this vein:

as in clinical cases there is no one-to-one relationship between electrical activity of the cortex and an individual's behavior. Nevertheless, if electrical activity of the cortex falls within certain normal limits, the chances that the personality will be either good or poor are increased. The deviation from the norm encountered in electroencephalograms of boys with poor and good personalities are in many cases identical, but in general cortical activity which is unusually slow is likely to be associated with poor personality and cortical activity which is unusually fast with good personality. Like many other bodily attributes, the pattern of the EEG is an inherited constitutional characteristic which changes systematically with age and is grossly and permanently altered only by diseases, trauma, and nutritional disturbances. The findings of Gibbs, Lemere, and Davis all tend to emphasize the importance of organic factors rather than psychological experiences as |determinants of personality. Furthermore, the findings of the above investigators are in agreement with those of Jasper et al., Lindsley and Cutts, for their reports state that children whose general behavior is in a social sense bad have as a group more slow activity in the EEG's than normal children.

Saul, et al., (320) reported further on the psychological correlations with the EEG for 136 subjects in psychoanalysis. Their findings were:

All showed patterns within the normal limits, but these fell into three groups: High alpha; Low voltage, fast: M-mixed (including MF-mixed fast and MS-mixed slow).

EEG classifications remained stable from year to year. (The group had significantly more women than men). These were the following consistent psychological correlations with type of EEG: 1. Very passive individuals have "high alpha" EEG's (a much higher percentage of men than women). 2. Women with strong masculine trends have low voltage-fast or at least low alpha patterns; (This was less definite); women with very active maternal drives have low alpha patterns; 3. Frustrated, demanding, impatient, aggressive, hostile women have mixed fast or mixed type EEG's. (Only two men had clear "mixed fast" type records, and they were of this kind of personality.

In a discussion of this report, Dr. Liberson mentioned his study of the EEG and vocational aptitudes in a group of railway engineers. Two EEG groups showed significant correlations: 1. High alpha and superiority in vocational and psychological aptitudes; 2. "Mixed" and bad test performance and bad vocational records. He concluded however that the correlation was between "EEG and test attitude, not between EEG and specific ability."

Lindsley (213) reviewed the literature pertaining to emotion and EEG, and concluded that:

under conditions involving some degree of emotional arousal, as in apprehension, unexpected sensory stimulation, and anxiety states, two principal kinds of changes are reflected in the EEG. (1) a reduction or suppression of the alpha activity, and (2) an increase in the amount of beta-like fast activity. These changes will by now be recognized as constituting part of the activation response of Magoun.

Palmer and Rock (275), investigating the high alpha incidence in the EEG and personality patterning for twenty white males in a penal institution, noted that the sample had EEG records showing high alpha incidence throughout the cortex. At the time of the recording or near it, there was one striking similarity in their personal histories ... all showed "inadequate father identification relationships with a consequent inability to act out the masculine role ... this deficiency is considered as 'constitutional' in terms of a lack of crystallized experience in the form of lack of maleness.."

Kennard et al., (189) reported that the overall distribution of frequency patterns of groups of individuals having different personality characteristics showed significant differences, and that, furthermore, these EEG patterns could be correlated with specific personality attributes. Thus, the number of individuals in penal institutions who showed a high peak of EEG alpha activity was significantly high as compared to that of a normal group, and almost no schizophrenic patients in a mental institution produced such pure alpha activity.

Mundy-Castle (156) reported that the consistent trend in the history of EEG relating theta rhythm (slow waves) with emotional lability and cortical immaturity is maintained by the present results concerning significant associations between age, reports of emotional instability, and the incidence of theta rhythm.

Mundy-Castle (260) maintained that persons rated as more primary functioning (quick, impulsive, variable, stimulable) possessed higher alpha frequencies than persons rated as more secondary functioning (SF) (slow, cautious, steady, hypo-reactive).

Ruch (312) presenting a conspectus of the neurophysiology of emotion and motivation at the Vineland Conference in 1958, especially of research activity in this area, cited the experiments of Stennett (341) in which Stennett established an inverted U relationship between performance and arousal, a relationship which Hebb (1955) predicted on theoretical grounds. This relationship means that for a given task there is optimal degree of motivation; below this, performance is less and if this optimal arousal is exceeded, the performance suffers. One of the major implications of such a finding that it is imperative to establish distinctions in capacity and motivation in order to achieve the objective for a given stress not "what a man can do but what he will do." Too frequently, the assessment of motivation has been derived from the performance, in which high performance is ascribed to high motivation. It is demonstrable that height of motivation can interfere with performance, just as too little arousal can result in low productivity.

Ellingson (82) commented on EEG correlates and Rorschach productivity as follows:

> There have been some attempts to relate Rorschach scoring categories to the alpha index. Travis and Bennett compared two groups of normals with alpha indices over and under 50. They found that the high index group gave significantly more whole responses but was significantly lower than the low index group with respect to

R, Dd, plus S%, sum C, and W, and took significantly more time. Brudo and Darrow found significant rank order correlations between M and alpha index of .532 for 11 normal children, .636 for 10 behavior problem children with possible brain damage, and .619 for the groups combined.

Sisson and Ellingson after discussing limitations in using the Rorschach test in this manner to investigate relationships between personality and other variables, concluded that "no study has been done conclusively showing a relationship between any feature of the normal adult EEG recorded under standard conditions and any personality trait or variable.... Since alpha and beta activity appear to be quite primitive functions of neural tissue, we find it difficult to believe that any of their measures will be found to correlate with any of the dimensions of so complex and phylogenetically recent an entity as the human personality.

It must be clear from this review that activity in the field of Neurophysiology since World War II has been prodigious. Each new discovery seems to reveal the brain as an even more versatile organ than was previously appreciated. It will be recognized that while the body of confirmed and established facts relating EEG phenomena and psychological processes has been considerably increased since Lindsley's review of 1944, the body of unconfirmed data has likewise increased

Rabinovitch (291) has pointed out the lack of agreement among those who have tried to correlate brain wave patterns with personality and psychological disorders. In a study involving psychiatric patients, inmates of penal institutions, and a group of controls he found that in 140 comparisons made between EEG profile characteristics and 14 Rorschach variables only two indicated significant relationships: (1) Those subjects with no M on the Rorschach had a significantly greater incidence of electrical activity in the fast range of 16-20 than those who had 3 or more M responses. (2) The subjects with no Space responses had a significantly lower incidence of well-organized graph profiles than those subjects with 2 or more Space responses. However, chance factors would account for 7 significant relationships at the .05 level. Thus it would be safe to conclude that there is no relationship between any single Rorschach scoring category and the EEG relationship.

In the same study the comparison of EEG data from psychiatric patients with those of normals indicated a strong tendency for the patients' EEG's to show more activity in the theta and fast frequency ranges and less interrelatedness of activity between the various cortical areas. These findings conform the observations of previous workers that gross differences in personality adjustment, in the absence of any neurological dysfunction, are related to EEG patterns.

The Rabinovitch study suggested that anxious persons and psychiatric patients show less interrelatedness of activity between cortical areas. Moreover, those subjects whose Rorschach scores point strongly to introversive personality trends show well organized EEG's with a relatively large incidence of high alpha. This finding is contrary to that of Henry and Knott (148), who found no difference between introverted and extroverted subjects. However, Saul (320) pointed out relations between passive personality trends and high alpha indices which would tend to support the present findings.

Gastaut et al., (111) confirmed the existence of posteriorly-situated slow-waves in young adults since they found them in 30 percent of a series of pilots and candidates otherwise normal; from the psychological point of view they found these slow waves were associated with immaturity of affect, which is expressed in a particular way, namely, in the aggressiveness found in this group.

Henry (149), participating in a conference to review the literature since 1948, addressed himself to the topic of **Electroencephalographic Correlates with Personality**. The cogency of his work in terms of the dimension under discussion assisted materially in bringing focus to this topic. Significant points cited:

Papers on electroencephalography and personality have been appearing in the EEG literature from the earliest years yet. . . . the quantity has remained small, and the quality has often been less than outstanding.

The first firm hint of possible relationships between the EEG and personality appeared in the Cold Spring Harbor Symposium for 1936. It was here that Davis (1936) mentioned and subsequently reported the broad relationship between the EEG and personality. "A high alpha index is characteristically associated with a passive, dependent, receptive attitude toward other persons, provided this attitude is freely accepted and not thwarted or inhibited internally. . . . . A person with a high alpha index may work to satisfy his desires but usually under protest, by force of circumstances, or by conscious effort. . . . . Low alpha indices are usually associated with a consistent, well-directed, freely indulged drive to activity.

From the early period of EEG studies and personality, it was generally agreed that no obvious characteristic differences in the EEG differentiated the normal individual from his non-deteriorated brethren with psychiatric disorder, although as a group the latter showed a somewhat high titre of deviant or abnormal record.

Gottlober (129) reported that an organismic pattern in which a dominant-sub-dominant rhythm appears accompanied by an extroverted personality is more common than one in which it appears accompanied by an introverted personality. A critical analysis of the Gottlober data by Henry and Knott (148) concluded that there is an equal proportion of extroverts in both high and low alpha groups.

More recent studies by Ulett et al., (369) contain a sobering commentary on the surprising variability of reactions on repeated follow-up examinations—as many as 9 over a 3 year study of 182 normal young adults. Cases with deviant or disorganized spontaneous activity had no clinically apparent deficit, nor was there evidence of such even during EEG disruption induced by photic stimulation. . . . . We appear to be a long way from the confident use of the EEG in the prediction of relative performance within a group of individuals without pathology.

No review of this area of investigation would be complete if it failed to comment on the massive interdisciplinary effort in which "Report on relations between electroencephalographic variables and those expressing the personality and sensori-motor functions of 511 recruits, aged 20" was included. Gastaut concluded . . .
. . . No relation exists between the EEG variables and those of the Rosenzweig tests and the intelligence tests. . . . . From this it appears that the primitive bioelectric function of the brain, simple and similar in the different stages of phylogenesis, cannot be connected to immediate modes of apprehension of an entity as complex and phylogenetically recent as the human personality. Far from abandoning the problem of correlations between the EEG and personality, our future task must

therefore be the transformation obtained from each one of them, in order to render them comparable.

STUDENT LEADERS EEG'S

After the recommendation of Gibbs (114) standard monopolar leads were placed so as to secure cortical potentials from all the lobes. Amplification was set to produce a deflection of 5mm when 50 microvolts was applied to the input grids, and the paper speed was set at 3 cm = 1 second.

TABLE 14
Distribution of EEG Frequencies, Amplitudes (voltage) and Alpha Index for Student Leaders

	Mean	SD	N
Frequency	10.43	1.08	36
Amplitude	33.6	15.0	36
Alpha Index	63.06	26.06	36

The amplitude mean and the alpha index approach very closely those same indices as reported by Mundy-Castle (1958) in his study of college students. His figures for amplitude mean of 30.00 SD 13, and alpha index mean of 65.00, SD 21, show that the two samples are drawn from the "same" population.

In addition to the typical evaluation of records for frequency, amplitude, and alpha index, a five-point rating scale was devised.* Such a scale permitted the statistical analysis of findings from different assessment procedures. Ratings were made by an Electroencephalographer and not this investigator.

The Student Leaders' means and SD's on the two values were as follows:

EEG-R   Mean = 1.72   SD =   .91
EEG-Alpha Index   Mean = 63.06   SD = 26.06

The magnitude of the SD's forces the conclusion that no precise interpretation can be made of the statistics secured in this instance. The overriding homogeneity of the sample of students precluded finding a specific finding.

Many conditions which cause slowing of the electrical activity of the cortex predispose to a big build-up with hyperventilation. This suggests that the basic frequency of cortical activity is an important determinant of the response to

---

*Medical Writing Associates, Willoughby Hills, Ohio.

hyperventilation. Any deviation from the normal waking pattern is likely to be associated with big build-up. (Gibbs, et al.,114). Slow activity is somewhat more commonly associated with such a variation than is fast activity.

As part of the routine examination of the Student Leaders a period of three minutes of hyperventilation with about 50 deep breaths per minute was included because in susceptible persons this procedure commonly precipitates seizure discharges or some form of build-up.

A Five-Point Rating Scale

1. Within Normal Limits.
    a. Good, stable background rhythms awake and/or asleep;
    b. Good bilateral symmetry under all conditions;
    c. Normal photic driving;
    d. No more than slight slowing with good hyperventilation.

2. No Definite Abnormality.
    a. Rare or poor or asymmetric alpha rhythm;
    b. Poor bilateral symmetry, awake or asleep;
    c. Scattered, non-focal limited theta activity;
    d. Appreciable slowing with hyperventilation;
    e. Excess fast activity;
    f. Suggestion of positive spikes not verified due to poor technique.

3. Borderline.
    a. Poor bilateral symmetry, awake and asleep and with photic stiumlation;
    b. Pronounced hyperventilation effect;
    c. Some excess, diffuse slowing in theta band;
    d. Any limited focal slowing;
    e. Positive spikes, even in otherwise normal record.

4. Abnormal.
    a. Seizure activity in any stage (positive spikes not rated as seizure discharges);
    b. Excess delta activity, with or without theta, focal or diffuse;
    c. Severe slowing on hyperventilation with poor recovery as accentuation of spontaneous slowing.

5. Grossly Abnormal.
    a. Much seizure activity in any stage;
    b. Much generalized or focal slowing.

Gibbs (114), in studying the amount of build-up between normal control subjects and epileptic patients, reported a big build-up for 10% of the normals and a 45% build-up for epileptics in the age range 21-25.

Ulett, et al., (370) in a comprehensive investigation of pattern, stability and relationship among activation techniques with a total freshman class of a seminary (N was 182, mean age 20.2) arrived at the conclusion that most subjects showed no activation response during hyperventilation, while a small percentage, 14.0, showed an extreme cortical response. The mean recovery time for the mild activation group was 25 seconds, the mean time for the moderate activation group was 30 seconds, and the mean time for the extreme activators was 35 seconds. Thus as expected, the more disturbed the EEG record, the longer the recovery period.

Examination of the records of the 36 Student Leaders showed 5 records in which build-up was present. This compares almost exactly with the 14% figure cited by Ulett above. Of the five Student Leaders showing significant build-up, four showed rapid recovery within one minute. The one record with a build-up and slow recovery was also characterized by a generalized dysrhythmia in the resting state.

In an interesting departure that concerned itself with cortical activity and cognitive functioning, Johnson et al., (178) investigated the effects of photically induced EEG disruption and cognitive activity. [This study was prompted by a former study of Hovey and Kooi, 1954.] They used 21 patients with varying types of seizures of differing etiology and of varying age and IQ levels, and studied the performance on subtests of the Wechsler Adult Intelligence Scale during spontaneous paroxysmal discharges. They reported that disturbances in the higher integrative mental processes were significantly associated with paroxysmal cerebral activity, and these were usually manifested by non-answer responses or, to a lesser extent, by don't-know responses and requests for repetition of the question. These disturbances occurred in the absence of overt seizure.

The Johnson (178) study used 28 male subjects; fourteen of these had shown EEG activation and 14 had failed to activate during several previous exposures to intermittent photic stimulation.

The results of his study indicate that the cognitive function involved in learning, retention, and recall as shown by the tests here utilized are not necessarily impaired by disruption of the usual patterns of neural activity as shown by the EEG. Though the degree of EEG disruption was not extreme, the fact remains that no impairment in cognitive functioning was found despite sudden and considerable change from the usual resting pattern of brain wave activity. Other research to date has consistently used a patient population and primarily persons with convulsive disorders.

Further evidence that a well organized and synchronously discharging cortex is not necessary for effective functioning is provided by the results of earlier work from this laboratory. In a quantitative study of pattern and stability of EEG activity, comparison of the profile of activity over 24 frequencies, 3-33 c/sec., in the occipital, parietal, and frontal areas revealed four definite groups with respect to cortical organization. There was a dominant occipital well-organized cortical pattern, a well-organized pattern but one in which occipital alpha was not dominant, slow activity with a disorganized cortical pattern, and a pattern with general disorganization and with multipeaks of activity. While 71 per cent of 46 subjects had well-organized cortical patterns with alpha activity in the occipital area being the dominant or nearly dominant EEG activity, 29 per cent had dominant slow activity or multipeaks of activity with general disorganization of the pattern of activity or multipeaks of activity over the three cortical areas. All of these subjects were graduate students successfully pursuing their demanding intellectual tasks.

Despite the finding that all of the subjects' alpha rhythms, best formed in the occipital lobe areas, fell well within the normal limits of 8 to 13 per second waves, six questionable and two marginal records were obtained. Table 15 provides a summary treatment of these records.

TABLE 15

Nature of EEG Pathological Features

Generalized dysrhythmia (unspecific)	3
Epileptic features	2
Focal qualities	1
Low voltage tense records	2

Although no clinical seizure manifestations had been reported in the histories of the six subjects, further neurological examinations were made available for preventative purposes and additional study.

The percentage of abnormal records (17%) compares with those percentages cited by Gibbs (114) in which he found the range to be between 12 and 16 percent, depending on the size of samples studied. His percentages are based on individuals whose frequencies fall below 8 per second or above 13 per second. In the present study, the application of the term abnormal was for reasons other than frequency.

An examination of the correlation matrix, page 225, focused on the EEG findings and the other 34 variables, permits the following observations to be made:

1. Although personality and intellectual factors have been found to be negatively and positively correlated respectively with achievement, every comparison of EEG ratings with intellectual outcomes was positive. However, only two of the ten such relationships (r = .370 for EEG-R and CMT, and r = .322 for EEG-R and SCAT-Q) were significant. Chance would lead one to expect one such relationship.

2. The absence of significant correlations between the EEG and the many personality variables (only two of 24 r's reached significance at the .05 level) gives support to positions taken by Ellingson, Gastaut, and Henry that data secured from various levels of human functioning cannot be expected to act isomorphically, i.e., activity in a cell, organ or system does not equate to behavior on a higher level.

Wells (385), reviewing the extensive investigations pursued during the recent past, and attempting to correlate electroencephalographic actitity with behavior, stated that such investigations have broadened only slightly our concepts of how the central nervous system actually works to effect normal behavior. These studies have been a disappointment by failing to provide new concepts of central neural function and by failing to provide either a firm scientific basis for the comprehension of behavior or a firm basis upon which a therapeutic approach to central nervous system dysfunction could be constructed.

With widespread changes in electrical activity occurring throughout the nervous system, it is human to hope that one particular structure might be most important in promoting normal function and to hope that within one structure the "neural trace" of memory might be found. Detailed study, though, of electrographic activity in the intact animal, as well as of the changes produced by hyperactivity and ablation, suggests that, so far as conditioned reflexes are concerned, there is no "head" ganglion. Investigations by Russian and Western workers have put to flight the fancies that there might somewhere within the nervous system be a locus for the engram. The position, long held by many workers, has been reemphasized that neural function is a result of complex interrelationships between diverse parts, the function of the whole being infinitely more subtle than the function of any one of its component parts (Wells, 385).

While these investigations (Wells, 385) have emphasized the involvement of multiple structures within the nervous system in even the simplest sensory associations, they have as yet been unable to associate changes in the electrical activity of the brain with overt behavioral manifestations. Almost no one has asserted that the electroencephalographic changes observed with juxtaposed stimuli bear any direct relation to the behavioral activity of the animal. We are still faced with the overriding problem of relating changes in the brain's electrical activity to the subject's behavior.

Necessary or useful differences in observational viewpoint make difficult an acceptable translation of findings from one level of complexity to another. Any technique that has been applied with success to a simpler level of organization is applicable to more complex systems of the same general type. The reverse is not true.

Several findings in the Leader study do not support those reported by Saul, Gallagher, Rubin and Bowman, and Rabinovitch. On the other hand, views reported by Mundy-Castle, Ellingson, Slatter, and Liberson, Gastaut, Henry, and Vogel and Broverman are supported by this investigation.

Specifically, contrary findings were noted in these instances:

1. Saul's finding that a low alpha index tends to go with a trend toward activity and a high alpha index with a trend toward passivity or inhibition is not borne out with the Student Leaders.

    Saul's low alpha index group was associated with trends toward aggressiveness, leadership in social affairs, doing rather than intellectual sublimation. Almost the same description could be ascribed to the high alpha index group in the present study.

2. Rubin and Bowman reported that in a group of 100 peptic ulcer patients that the high alpha group tends to be dependent on a mother surrogate, that the high or dominant alpha groups held their jobs over a prolonged period and more of them were passive toward their mates. In the present study the one aspect that was comparable concerned the dependency of the Student Leader group on mother surrogates, and the consequent passivity to females. In no matter as elicited by the personality scales did this characteristic emerge although the high alpha index was characteristic.

3. Gallagher contended that, in general, cortical activity which is unusually slow is likely to be associated with poor personality and cortical activity which is relatively fast with good personality. This conclusion would have to be revised insofar as the "good personality" and EEG correlates are concerned. The Student Leader group maintained an unusually stable pattern of alpha activity rather than much Beta (fast) activity.

4. Rabinovitch observed that those subjects whose Rorschach scores point strongly to introversive personality trends show well organized EEG's with a relatively large incidence of high alpha. In the present investigation, the consistently high alpha indices with extroversive signs were noted. It may well be that Henry and Knott's observation that no difference in such functioning can distinguish introversive and extroversive subjects so singularly.

Specifically, supporting data were noted for these studies:

1. Mundy-Castle reported that the amount of alpha rhythm present in an EEG is in part related to the extent to which visual imagery is used in thought processes, and that persons who think predominantly in visual images tend to produce "minus" type (low voltage, low index) alpha rhythms, whereas those who think predominantly by verbal-motor imagery tend to possess "persistent" (medium to high voltage, high index) alpha rhythms. The Student Leader group, which was extremely apt verbally and obviously active, produced a high alpha index mean of 63.

2. Slatter reported that alpha rhythm bears an inverse relationship to the degree which visual imagery is used in thought. Habitual visualizers tend to have records showing lower alpha amplitudes than do habitual verbalizers. The predominant verbalizers have relatively high amplitude records. Again, the Student Leader groups were predominantly verbalizers with high alpha indices.

3. Liberson commented on Saul's findings with the observation that in his studies on the relationship of EEG and vocational aptitudes in a group of railway engineers that a significant correlation obtained between high alpha and superiority in vocational and psychological aptitudes. The correspondence between superior aptitudes, achievement, and personality integration on the one hand and the high alpha index on the other cannot be discounted as coincidental.

    Some cogency can be granted to the position outlined by Vogel and Broverman (375) that a resting EEG does not tell a sufficient story in terms of what the client does in an active intellectual interlude. Analogously, the "idle of a motor" does not fully predict the power that it generates when it is accelerated. On the other hand, significant clues can be secured about the overall performance possibilities from the EEG in terms of humans and from the "idle" for engines.

In view of this position, there is a reconcilable ground for the Ellingson and Vogel and Broverman polarities.

4. Ellingson, Gastaut and Henry observed that no study has been done conclusively showing a relationship between any feature of the normal adult EEG recorded under standard conditions and any personality trait or variable. Since alpha and beta activity appear to be quite primitive functions of neural tissue, it is difficult to believe that any of their measures will be found to correlate with any dimensions of so complex and phylogenetically recent an entity as the human personality. Repeated attempts to correlate EEG findings with intelligence, achievement, personality, and scholastic aptitudes for a group of student leaders failed to produce a single significant coefficient of correlation. By appropriate norms for each measure, the scores were consistently found to be better or higher than those of peer groups. It may well be that Ellingson's view of the lack of statistical correspondence for functions from different levels of human functioning is warranted . . . not because there is no relationship, but because the techniques and procedures for showing such relationships have not been developed. In terms of the types of assessment that have found support from the present investigation, it is noteworthy that agreement was readily established in those instances where intelligence and perceptual processes were investigated, but that personality and EEG findings were less readily reconciled.

5. Recently published studies by Hughes (166) and Vogel and Broverman (375) somewhat challenge the views reported in the previous point. The plea from both investigators insists that improved methodological considerations should be attempted before broad generalizations can be made about the relationships of EEG outcomes and psychological processes or traits.

Using multivariate procedures, Hughes was able to establish a large number of correlations between EEG results and various psychological tests. Vogel and Broverman advance an interesting interpretation to account for discrepancies in previous research findings. They argue for two types of inhibition as explanatory bases for slow alpha activity. The traditional explanation maintains that explosion of intellectualizing is correlated with such activity. However, Vogel and Broverman demonstrate that slow alpha activity can be related to habituated or overlearned responses.

This latter development may account in part for the greater incidence of alpha activity in the Leader group than in the Failure sample. The habituation or relaxed performance of the Leaders may have been a major factor in the lessened hyperactivity (also found in the MMPI) and the greater academic productivity.

Penfield's preface to his Sherrington lecture in which he stated that relationships between structure and function are not easily deciphered is in line with this investigator's convictions that explanations for human behavior will require a unifying principle. This assertion does not deny that modes of expression can be studied and understanding achieved of the role of constitutional, learning, and situational forces operating in all behavior. Gardner Murphy's address on new vistas in personality research enjoined investigators to recognize that control of the simpler processes may be the command of more complex processes.

FIVE-YEAR FOLLOW UP OF STUDENT LEADERS

A limited amount of work has been carried on in the follow-up of college graduates in terms of the amount of knowledge that is retained, the direction in which personality and value dimensions move, and in the replication of findings secured as undergraduates.

Webster et al., (378) observed that:

> Undoubtedly it is no surprise to the majority of educators that a great many students pass through college without experiencing significant changes in basic values, or without even becoming much involved in problems that interest teachers. The vast enterprise that is American higher education today cherishes traditional cultural values, including vocational training, rewards for hard work, and social adjustment; these have prevailed, often to the exclusion of an interest in the intellectual and aesthetic problems with which scientists and artists are preoccupied.

A very comprehensive longitudinal study of political, social and economic outlook was carried out by Nelson (1954). In 1936, Nelson tested 3,758 students in a variety of colleges, and in 1950 he repeated the testing with 901 of his original subjects. He discovered a postcollege trend toward "slightly more liberalism" over the 14 year period, but for the most part, the results indicated that the original positions were maintained with a considerable degree of consistency. In 1950, Nelson tested undergraduates at one of the colleges involved in the study and found them to be more liberal than their predecessors in 1936 and concluded "that liberalism does not seem to be a function of the age of the individuals or of what they are taught in college." Rather it is a "product of the times."

Beardslee and O'Doud (Sanford, 315) addressed themselves to what is known about the vocational aspirations of entering college students. It should be noted that virtually all studies of occupational preferences among high school and college students reveal an unrealistically high selection of professional careers.

The career orientations of men change during their four years of college under the impact of the differential demands of alternative academic programs, financial barriers to graduate training, changing interests, and other pressures. These changes suggest that many young men must alter their goals to more modest levels and that they must form an identity around different images and models. This is of necessity a painful but often maturing process for many of the most highly talented members of our society.

To the overview of the flow of career choices in relation to the images of occupations, it is necessary to comment on the distribution of college graduates in the occupational world. Havemann & West (146) gathered information on the jobs held by recent college graduates, men and women under 30 at the time of their study. The people questioned were a sample of alumni from approximately

1,100 colleges and universities. Men divide about equally between business and the professions.

In a penetrating study of the values and beliefs of college students, Gillespie and Allport (1955) stated: "The best way to generalize his goals seems to be in terms of the search for a rich, full life." One of the keys to his future is the occupational role that fulfills the promise of a college education. They note that the contemporary student is not concerned with the political and social problems that surround him. Indeed, he is not even concerned with philosophical or religious issues. In a sense, he is involved with himself and his future.

Rieman and Jencks (1962) stated that college is the initiation rite for the middle class and that most of the earlier longitudinal investigations of changes in student values and attitudes revealed small but significant changes in one or a few kinds of attitudes. Except for minor discrepancies, the differences observed would still be described today as changes in the direction of a more liberal attitude on social issues and a more tolerant attitude toward persons.

Recent studies, particularly that of Jacobs (173), hold that there is a profile of values which holds for 75-80% of all American college students. The current student generation are "gloriously contented" in their present activity and in their outlook toward the future. They are "unabashedly self-centered," aspiring above all for material gratifications for themselves and their families. A need for religion is generally recognized, but students do not expect religious beliefs to govern daily decisions. Rather, they expect that these decisions will be socially determined. Jacob's book has been criticized from a number of views. Rieman (1958) commented that the qualities of studies were not differentiated; that findings did not distinguish between men and women; and that the Jacob's view is overly censorious. Comparisons of alumnae (a representative sample) with senior scores on the MMPI are available for Vassar graduates of 1955 tested four years later. The chief finding is that the alumnae are lower on all of the clinical scores. This indicates that the alumnae, as compared to their state as seniors, reveal less evidence of emotional difficulty, anxiety, or psychological unease and more evidence of physical and psychological well-being. (Freedman, 1962)

The original sample of thirty-six selected Student Leaders at John Carroll University in the academic year, 1960-1961, was used in this follow-up study. At the time of the original study, all of the Student Leaders agreed to furnish information pertaining to health, schooling, vocational strivings, marital adjustments, and other areas of development. A questionnaire was devised by Duber (1965) to cover the above categories. Also, several of the original psychological tests used initially were included in the packet sent to each individual in the sample. The first mailing left John Carroll University in October, 1965. A reminder was dispatched on December 17, 1965. All of the replies included in this study were returned by January 31, 1966.

In the original 1960 study, there was a total of thirty-six subjects. It was impossible to locate one of these subjects either through mailings to former addresses or through the efforts of the Alumni Affairs Office at John Carroll University. It was also further discovered that one of the men was killed in an air crash early in 1965. Therefore the total sample available for this study was thirty-four. Of this sample, twenty-eight men completed the questionnaire and tests.

TABLE 16
Career Preferences of Student Leaders
at the Point of Entry To College and Five Years Following Graduation

	1957	1965	% of Shift
Business	11	10	-9%
Law	5	7	+40%
Science & Medicine	10	2	-800%
Teaching & Psychology	8	5	-38%
Clergy	0	1	+100%
Journalism	0	3	+300%
In Military Service		6	
Undecided	2		

It is interesting to note that 97 percent of the group indicated in their senior year at John Carroll University that they intended to continue in graduate studies. Of the twenty-eight respondents, 76 percent indicated that they had either received graduate degrees or were actively engaged in graduate studies.

TABLE 17
Graduate Degrees Awarded to Leaders

Master of Arts	9
Master of Science	2
Ph.D.	1
Law Degree	5
MBA	2
Total	19
Fashion Design	1
Total	20

There were ten men pursuing either their first or second graduate degrees at the point of the five year follow-up.

Sixty-eight percent, or nineteen, of the group of twenty-eight respondents were married. From the nineteen marriages, there were nineteen children.

There has been no change in religious preference in the group. However, several respondents indicated a more questioning attitude toward their traditional beliefs. An equal number also indicated a deeper involvement in their religion than they experienced in college days.

Interest in the world about themselves, and involvement with clubs and activities, seemed to characterize this group in their college years. The

TABLE 18
Self-Rated Physical Conditions by Leaders

Condition	1957	1965
1. scarlet fever	3	3
2. indigestion	5	8
3. frequent colds	7	7
4. sleeplessness	2	5
5. headaches	6	13
6. mumps	8	9
7. nervous breakdown	–	1
8. heart trouble	–	1
9. backaches	3	4
10. speech defects	–	1
11. dizziness	1	1
12. measles	16	17
13. easily exhausted	4	2
14. gas in abdomen	1	11
15. chicken pox	9	12
16. shaking spells	1	–
17. excessive sweating	2	3
18. unpleasant dreams	4	4
19. influenza	6	15
20. fainting spells	–	–
21. eye strain	5	7
22. glandular trouble	1	1
23. cont. tired feeling	5	7
24. muscles twitches	3	2
25. whooping cough	7	7
26. anemia	1	1

post-college period found a considerable decrease in club and organization affiliations. Less than fifty percent reported belonging to a single organization or club.

On the 1957 questionnaire, the subjects were asked to rate themselves on a list of twenty-six physical conditions and twenty-six personality traits. This request was exactly duplicated on the 1965 questionnaire.

The total number of physical conditions noted in 1957 was 112.

The total number of physical conditions noted in 1965 was 148.

TABLE 19

Self-Rated Personality Traits of Student Leaders

Trait	1957	1965
1. friendly	25	27
2. reserved	6	12
3. stubborn	7	7
4. self-confident	8	16
5. irritable	1	4
6. cheerful	16	16
7. tactful	9	15
8. worrisome	4	6
9. anxious	4	7
10. capable	14	23
11. nervous	5	4
12. depressed	--	1
13. quick-tempered	3	5
14. unhappy	--	--
15. social	14	14
16. tolerant	14	15
17. pessimistic	3	2
18. cynical	4	3
19. impetuous	1	8
20. self-conscious	8	10
21. average poise	22	21
22. aggressive	5	9
23. meek	2	--
24. bashful	1	1
25. inferior	2	1
26. conscientious	15	20

There are several observations on the material gathered in the questionnaire that should be noted. The most obvious one is that this sample of a leader group is extremely stable both in its goals and self-evaluations. This five-year period seemed to be one of growth and establishment. The pursuit of academic degrees, advanced professional training, and the establishment of the family unit, seemed to be paramount. This attention to self-development necessarily brought about the exclusion of involvement in activities not pertinent to these goals.

The higher ratio of referral to both physical conditions and personality traits presented an interesting picture. On the one hand, the physical conditions which show the greatest percent of increase are clearly those traditionally thought to be a result of pressure: indigestion, headaches, and gas in the abdomen. On the other hand, the personality traits showing the greatest increases are not so clearly defined. One grouping reflects the pressures of life; irritable, reserved, worrisome, anxious and impetuous. The other grouping reflects the attitudes of men who feel that they "have arrived": self-confident, capable and aggressive. Not one of the subjects considered himself to be unhappy.

Two standardized inventories used in the 1960 assessment of the student leaders were administered in the five-year follow-up. The findings on the Allport-Vernon-Lindzey **Study of Values** and the MMPI will be summarized in this section. In view of the absence of six respondents from the original grouping, the statistical work was limited to those students who were present for both assessments.

TABLE 20
Means and SD's for Student Leaders on the
Study of Values in 1960 and 1965

| | 1960 | | 1965 | |
Value	M	SD	M	SD
Theoretical	39.9	6.2	40.2	6.0
Economic	35.6	10.5	37.3	9.6
Aesthetic	34.0	6.2	35.4	8.3
Social	39.2	6.9	37.6	7.4
Political	45.5	6.6	46.0	6.9
Religious	46.3	7.3	43.6	8.8

No significant changes occurred in the value orientations of the student leaders in the five-year period. Slight decreases were noted in the social and religious areas and similarly slight increases in the economic and aesthetic scales.

TABLE 21
Means and SD's for the T Scores on the Thirteen Scales
on the MMPI for Student Leaders Administered in 1960 and 1965

Scale	1960		1965	
	M	SD	M	SD
L	46.2	6.5	46.9	6.3
F	51.5	6.5	50.8	6.1
K	57.7	7.6	58.3	7.2
Hs	53.5	9.2	54.4	8.1
D	51.6	12.0	55.1	11.4
Hy	59.8	13.2	61.1	5.7
Pd	57.7	6.0	59.0	7.9
Mf	64.2	10.2	63.1	9.2
Pa	54.8	8.5	55.9	6.1
Pt	57.6	8.5	58.2	9.9
Sc	57.5	10.0	55.3	10.4
Ma	60.1	10.3	58.4	9.7
Si	41.1	6.8	44.6	7.1

No significant differences were found in those instances where numerical differences were noted.

CONCLUSIONS—LEADERSHIP

Beginning with the extensive search of the literature for pertinent studies dealing with measured psychological characteristics of leaders, followed by comprehensive testing of a sample of 36 Student Leaders, to the examination of test findings dispelled any notion that a clear delineation of the phenomenon could or would be achieved.

The many definitions of the concept, the wide variety of procedures with varying rationales for its measurement, and the unresolved matter of how leadership *develops* will continue to interfere with an early and widely accepted analysis of leadership. Despite such obstacles and complications as noted above, the search for understanding will continue because so much importance is attached to this type of human behavior.

It is the fond hope of all investigators to be able to advance the amount of knowledge that bears on some topic, or better still, to solve the mystery of some psychological delimma. Until the grand scheme is laid bare, it becomes the grubbing task of many to investigate segments in the hope that the "big picture" will emerge.

What can be reported in summary fashion about leadership in this context?

First: Much has been written on the topic; most of the writing has been exhortatory and programmatic. The term has been invoked for describing the direction of or the management of leadership types of activity. Leadership will continue to be a phenomenon or term that many claim to understand, a condition that almost as many believe they could exercise if but given the opportunity, but still too elusive to handle unless the particular variety or situation is spelled out.

Second: Even though investigators have studied intensively leaders in various settings and have produced profiles and other graphic representations, much less is known about how it develops, or what the crucial experiences are that propel or guide the individual along the course to a leadership role. In the absence of critical data to guide the training or development of leaders, the shotgun or scatter approach is followed rather than a highly definitive approach. In the former approach, the parent, the counselor, and the teacher resort to providing a wide variety of experiences, skills, and opportunities in the hope that something will eventuate from the process. Not entirely acknowledged is the amount of waste motion and even sidetracking that occurs in what is essentially a trial-and-error procedure with some refinements.

Third: More and more studies are reported on characteristics of leaders in education, in industry, in government, and in the armed forces. Sufficient agreement is emerging to point up that leaders are above average in intelligence, have demonstrated significant traits at times prior to the period under investigation, are generally well-adjusted, disposed to labor beyond job requirements, enjoyed relatively happy childhoods in stable homes, have blueprints for their lives and not fantasies, are reasonably self-confident though not without some anxiety about the manner in which they are discharging their assignments, tend to be self-critical but not perfectionistic in demands on themselves and associates, and are apt verbally but not drawn to pedantic jargon. They are somewhat militant individuals who do not take readily to committee leadership or strain after conformity; they are usually in good health and find respite in physical or sports outlets.

With reference to hypotheses entertained at the outset of the study, several can be examined with reasonable assurance.

The expectation that Student Leaders would produce low amplitude, fast waves (Beta) was not supported by the findings. Rather than presenting a picture of restiveness and vigilance, pretty much the opposite picture emerged. The leader group was noteworthy in producing EEG records that represent very stable pictures. The substrate for outstanding performances in personality, intellectuality, and productivity is a sound neurological integration as revealed by EEG patterns taken during a waking but resting state.

Concerning another hypothesis that has been generally found tenable, viz., that the laws of nature are correlative rather than compensatory, considerable support can be marshalled to support such a generalization. The Student Leader scores were significantly above the average norms for men on those measures where ranking represents a continuum from high to low of some trait or ability. In such aspects as intelligence, achievement, scholastic aptitude, positive adjustment, clearly defined values, and self-criticalness, the Student Leaders surpassed their normal peers.

CHAPTER 8

Profiles of Student Failures

Carrying through on the convictions espoused in the introduction, the second phase of longitudinal studies on the college male focused on the failing student. In contrast to the interest generated about student leadership, the concern for the poorly achieving student is growing rapidly, albeit belatedly. A sample of the literature on this topic will be reviewed in the next section of this chapter.

The failing group of students herein studied consisted of a random sample of failing students in the freshman class of John Carroll University. This class numbered 680 men who enrolled in the fall term of the 1962-1963 school year. At the conclusion of the first semester of college work, 140 males were found who failed to maintain a C average in that period. A random sample of 42 students was secured to undergo intensive psychological testing in the same fashion that had previously been carried out with Student Leaders.

In addition to the comprehensive testing that was carried on by the techniques noted under Instrumentation at the conclusion of the first semester's studies, the progress of the sample was kept under scrutiny for five years. The performances of the survivors were then compared with the complete dropouts who had failed to achieve academic respectability.

INSTRUMENTATION

Wechsler Adult Intelligence Scale, The Psychological Corporation, New York, 1955.

Rorschach Ink Blot Test, Grune and Stratton, New York.

Minnesota Multiphasic Personality Inventory, The Psychological Corporation, New York, 1951.

Allport, Vernon, Lindzey, **Study of Values**, Houghton-Mifflin Company, New York, 1951.

Grass Eight Channel Electroencephalograph, Model IV, Grass Instrument Company, Quincy, Massachusetts.

LITERATURE ON UNDERACHIEVERS

Summerskill (Sanford, 315), under a grant from the Ford Foundation, undertook a study that summarized the literature on attrition or dropouts from college. He observed that the problem has been of continuing concern for at least 40 years, but the literature fails to yield adequate or conclusive answers. The knowledge on the attrition process is surprisingly meager. Scores of pertinent-investigations have been conducted, including thoughtful and well-designed studies at various colleges, and two major surveys have been undertaken by agencies of the federal government (Iffert,168; McNeeley, 246).

Previous research arose chiefly in institutional or administrative concerns, and only rarely has the process of attrition been analyzed in psychological or sociological terms. The colleges' interest in attrition directly, and underachievement indirectly, has at least three origins. First, there is a persistent underlying concept that the American college is organized as a training center rather than as an intellectual center. Colleges are supposed to qualify young people for entrance to careers in business or industry, science or technology, medicine or law, homemaking or community service. Secondly, interest has derived from the marked increase in size and complexity of colleges, and these large institutions give rise to concerns about efficiency and costing. The third reason is both less subtle and less talked about: dollars leave the income side of the budget when students leave the college. Such research efforts have not been adequate in gaining better understanding of the problem, nor has it succeeded in substantially reducing high attrition rates. (Summerskill, 353)

Summerskill reviewed 35 different studies that cited attrition rates for classes entering hundreds of varied colleges and universities from 1913 to 1962. Median values were computed for the aggregate of these studies with results as follows: median loss in four years—50%; median percent graduated in four years—37%. The attrition rate has not changed appreciably in the past forty years. The variability in attrition rates among colleges is great, ranging from 12% to 82% in the 35 studies reviewed.

The largest number of dropouts involves motivational forces—goals, interests, and satisfactions relative to college and other facets of student life. From existing data there is no way to determine accurately the percentage of dropouts for whom such motivational factors are of crucial importance.

It is estimated that 10 to 15% of dropouts report that personal adjustment problems are involved in their leaving school. Many clinicians believe that these problems are much more prevalent, but it is difficult to prove that the large dropout population is, in fact, different from the large graduate population with regard to the incidence of personal or social maladjustment at college.

Financial difficulty is an important cause of college attrition. Iffert (169) noted that it was ranked third by men and women for leaving college.

Summerskill found it to be one of the three most important reasons in 16 of 21 studies reviewed.

Factors associated with dropping out of college included:

1. The general conclusion to be drawn from the literature is that age per se does not affect attrition although older undergraduates may encounter more obstacles to graduation.
2. Studies do not show any significant difference in the rates of attrition for men and women.
3. Open to much needed research is the question of socioeconomic factors in relation to persistence in college. While there is an inclination to ascribe positive weighting to higher socioeconomic factors, the research findings are equivocal. (Summerskill, 353)

Summerskill (353) continued with the view that secondary school grades are the best existing predictors of college grades. In ten of eleven studies the dropouts had lower averages in secondary school than did the graduates. In at least 19 investigations of scholastic aptitude in relation to attrition, the average scores for dropouts were lower than graduates in 16 investigations.

Poor or failing grades at the beginning of the college career are highly predictive of dropouts. For example, samples of poor students at three different colleges had attrition rates of *78, 86,* and *91%* respectively (Dressel, 1943; Pope, 287; Potthoff, 1931).

Recognizing that up to one-third of the college dropouts are due to poor grades and academic failure, *it is equally important to realize that the majority of students leave college for nonacademic reasons.* In general, the attrition problems that predominate in the colleges involve the students' failure to meet the psychological, sociological, or economic demands rather than strictly academic demands of the college environment. (Summerskill, 353)

Summerskill concludes his review of the literature with suggestions for future research on the problem. He quotes Craven (1951) who maintained that students "have been classified, rather than understood," and Sanford (1956) who asked, "How can one discuss attrition without recognition of the goals of the institution?"

Bridgman (1960) undertook a study for the National Science Foundation to establish the extent to which the country's talented youth carry through their formal education to the point of graduation from college. He found that of the top 30% of high school graduates in terms of ability, only about 45% of the boys graduated from college.

Iffert (168), in the most comprehensive study of retention in recent years, estimated that although only 40 percent graduated from the original institution in 4 years, 50 percent would graduate from the original or from some other institution in that period, and 60 percent would do so ultimately.

Any attempt to ascertain the reasons that students with good ability do not continue their education makes clear the difficulty of identifying the real reasons accurately. The principal evidence secured concerning reasons for dropouts of able students comes from the Iffert study. From detailed information obtained from students, he concluded that, for boys from the top or second fifths of their high school classes, entry into military service, lack of interest in study, and financial need, in that order were the major reasons for drop-outs. It must be noted here that the Iffert study was conducted during the Korean crisis. (Bridgman, 1960)

The Iffert (168) report did not identify directly dissatisfaction with college facilities and services as an important cause of withdrawal; he examined student reactions to these functions of both students who withdrew and those who graduated. A high proportion of both groups expressed dissatisfaction with counseling, guidance, and orientation functions of the colleges. A significant number of able students, particularly in large institutions, were critical of the quality of teaching and size of classes. He concluded that very frequently students withdraw because of inability or unwillingness to endure the dissatisfactions they felt.

In response to a survey made in 1958, and addressed to college authorities rather than students, Bridgman (1958) noted that Deans of Engineering schools rated the students' lack of effective work habits or of adequate motivation as by far the greatest reasons for dropping out in the freshman year.

Wellington and Wellington (384), summarizing many studies on the characteristics of underachievers, observed:

> There is, then, some agreement from study to study about the characteristics of underachievers: low motivation, low self-confidence, low capacity to function under pressure, low seriousness of purpose, low concern for others, low sense of responsibility, and low dominance.

A corroboration of some of these ideas may be found in a study by McKenzie (1964). The subjects were male college students at the University of Buffalo who had taken the MMPI before beginning college work. Underachievers, normal achievers, and overachievers were compared on the clinical and validity scales. Both deviant groups were found to be more anxious than normal achievers, with underachievers externalizing their conflicts. They were characterized as impulsive, dependent, and also hostile.

Bloomberg (1954) found that college students showing high academic performance were somewhat more introverted than students with lower performance. Kerns (1957) in Lavin (204) found that underachievers derive their greatest pleasure in college from social activities while overachievers derive their pleasure from academic activities.

A number of investigations have studied the relationship between adjustment and academic performance, using the MMPI as the measure of adjustment. Hackett (1960) analyzed the items and indicated that low achievers were emotionally labile, defensive about revealing weakness, admired strength and power, and lacked warmth and acceptance of others. Lavin (204) concluded that more often than not studies find the MMPI to be unrelated to academic performance. However, the study by Hoyt and Norman (1954) suggests that the presence of some type of maladjustment is likely to be associated with differences in achievement when ability levels are held constant. The role of the personality may be one of a mediating condition.

Lavin (204) summarized the studies in which the Rorschach Test was used as a predictor of academic achievement with the conclusion that the test does not serve well as such a predictor. However, some of the findings suggest that it might be useful for predicting criteria other than grades. In single variable studies the relation between personality variables and achievement is still so tentative that it cannot be used confidently for practical purposes, such as for college admissions.

One hundred randomly selected four year institutions with very low freshman dropout rates were compared with a comparable group of institutions that had freshman attrition rates that were not "low" in order to determine whether the two types of institutions differed in respect to 22 selected variables. Nelson (1960) found that colleges with low freshman dropout rates did differ significantly from the comparison group on 15 of the 22 characteristics analyzed. Ten of the fifteen variables were personal (i.e., they related to student characteristics), whereas the remaining five were nonpersonal (e.g.. the size of the institution and the cost of attending it). He concluded that many of the differentiating variables pertain to the sex composition and academic caliber of the student body. Thus the present investigation does not support the speculation that research on environmental determinants of attrition might "obtain evidence that the dropout phenomenon had less to do with factors in the student than with a certain condition in the college itself" as suggested by Sanford, (1956).

Marsh (224) reviewed the literature for the past ten years with specific references to the dropout problem of colleges and universities. He concluded:

> Ability and achievement ratings seem to be useful primarily for spotting only those students on the low end of the scale who will clearly drop out due to academic failure alone.
>
> The hope for one or two neatly packaged single predictors is quite unlikely, and the need for greater precision and more research on the multidimensional level has become obvious. Since the dropout seems to be quite similar to the returnee in many ways such as background, intentions, and abilities, there may be some underlying structures of personality and patterns of thought for which adequate tests have yet to be developed.
>
> The conflicting results of some of the descriptive studies indicate variation among colleges, as well as likelihood of change from year to year within one campus.

Despite the current scramble of students to obtain a college degree, the rate of attrition at colleges and universities, public and private, has been rising alarmingly. Goetz and Beach (120) investigated reasons for large withdrawal rates at the University of New Mexico by questionnaire seeking to establish what attitudes distinguish those who voluntarily leave as opposed to those students who continue. Interestingly, the attitudes of the two groups were essentially alike with slightly more negative attitudes being shown by the continuers. The finding that continuers have virtually the same problems as withdrawees casts some doubt on past research and poses many problems for future research.

Kaufman (184), in an incisive commentary on the student relationship in college, noted:

> One cannot generalize about "student" or even "higher education," for the diversity and pluralism inherent in post-secondary education in the United States are obvious to even the most casual observer. Nevertheless, there are broad trends, differing in speed of development, that are evident and that apply to the majority of students and institutions of higher education.
>
> Increased pressure for university attendance, the rapid expansion of physical plant, the increasing multiple and even conflicting commitments which the university has to government, industry, and research—all serve to diminish the once-central role of the undergraduate student in the university and college.
>
> We know all too well that those students who are regarded (or regard themselves) as faceless, anonymous human beings are not the best hope for our society or for the future health and support of higher education. There will probably always be small colleges, but the direction of expansion is clear. Mayhew predicts that by 1975 three-fourths of all students enrolled in institutions of higher education will be in five hundred institutions.
>
> Added to the above considerations, Clark Kerr has pointed out in his **Uses of the University** the students' resentment to the lessening contact with faculty. The revolt that used to be against the faculty in *loco parentis* is now against the *faculty in absentia.*
>
> There are some who would maintain that the increasing reliance of students on legalistic definitions of student rights is in direct proportion to their perception that they have been "rejected" by their teachers and their institutions and that they will demand a relationship, even it must be legally determined.

It is interesting to note the problem of students in high quality liberal arts institutions who drop out (many return later). Often good students, they are portrayed as non-vocational in orientation, constantly challenging the "unreality" of the college to the issues and tensions of the "real world." (Kaufman, 184). On the other hand, a committee of the Engineering Manpower Commission stated in 1963 that the attrition rate in most engineering colleges is "far greater than that necessary to weed out the incompetent." The report points out that the problem is as much a human problem as an academic one and that the high attrition "casts the spell of gloom" over the entire engineering program. (Engineers' Joint Council, 1963)

Panos and Astin (1967), in a paper read at the American Educational Research Association Meeting, observed:

Factors related to the completion of four years of college within four years of enrollment were examined in a study of 36,405 students entering 246 colleges and universities as freshmen in 1961. By 1965, 65 percent had completed four or more years. Sex and persistence were unrelated. Students who had not completed four years of college were from lower socioeconomic backgrounds, had lower grades in high school, lower initial levels of educational aspiration, and aspired to practically-oriented occupations. Students were less likely to have completed four years where academic competition is high, where student participation in college activities is limited, where grading practices are severe, and where enrollments are large. Students were more likely to have completed four years where there were friendly, cooperative relationships among students, where students were involved in college life, and where concern for individual students were apparent. The results supported the notion that both student characteristics and environmental contexts affect educational outcomes.

Preliminary findings of a study of 1154 students who dropped out of Harvard University in the years 1955-1960 have been released by Dr. Armand Nicholi, psychiatrist of the University Health Services. Dr. Nicholi (267), who followed up on the dropouts for ten years, reported:

1. Approximately 24% of each entering class dropped out over a four-year period. Slightly less than half of these returned and graduated from Harvard. About one-fourth attended and graduated from some other college.
2. Over the last ten years, the dropout rate has remained constant, despite rising college board scores and the draft.
3. If a dropout has not returned to college within one year, he has only a 50% chance of ever returning.
4. The percentage of students who seek psychiatric help is four times greater among dropouts than among the general undergraduate population.

Any systematic review of the literature on underachievement points to a multiplicity of explanations and characteristics of maladjustment among the victims. Weider (1967) outlined 47 characteristics as having been proposed by various investigators for the condition. He goes on to state that a closer and more penetrating examination of typical academic underachievers reveal psychodynamics common to all. The basic insecurity engendered at home transfers to the school experience. The student becomes overly introspective. He develops a self concept based on lack of confidence and a weakened ego-ideal. These characteristics are associated with an unconscious need to fail through diminished motivation to study, and a seeking of parental rejection and punishment with the usual secondary gains of incipient neuroses.

AS FRESHMEN

At the time of admission to the University several varieties of biographical information were secured on the freshman sample. This information will be presented along with the comparable data secured on the Student Leaders when they were freshmen.

Family Relationships	Failures	Leaders
Number of Children:	3.4	3.2
Parental educational backgrounds:		
Elementary	11%	10%
High School	53%	47%
Some College	14%	22%
College Graduate	22%	21%
High School		
Origin:		
Private	87%	83%
Public	13%	17%
Activities		
Mean number engaged in:	1.65	2.75
Career Plans		
None	12%	5%
Law	6%	14%
Teaching	19%	22%
Science-Medicine	38%	28%
Business	22%	33%
Future Plans What do you plan to be doing 10-15 years hence?		
Vague	40%	14%
Specific	53%	86%
Wishful	7%	0%
Residence		
Commuter	47%	25%
Boarder	53%	75%
Self-checked personality traits		
Friendly	72%	95%
Reserved	44%	20%
Stubborn	19%	27%
Self-confident	31%	33%
Irritable	16%	1%
Cheerful	57%	55%
Tactful	31%	40%

Self-checked personality traits: (Cont'd)	*Failures*	*Leaders*
Capable	34%	50%
Anxious	19%	14%
Nervous	28%	14%
Quick-tempered	19%	14%
Social	38%	50%
Tolerant	53%	50%
Pessimistic	9%	11%
Cynical	6%	8%
Self-conscious	41%	27%
Aggressive	22%	21%
Average Amount of Poise	44%	89%
Conscientious	41%	50%

Self-checked conditions—
symptoms present in last six months

Indigestion	13%	8%
Sleeplessness	22%	5%
Headaches	31%	14%
Dizziness	16%	0%
Easily exhausted	9%	8%
Excessive sweating	9%	0%
Eye strain	22%	5%
Continuous tired feeling	19%	8%
Muscle twitches	19%	0%
Surgical procedure	38%	22%

A review of the self-recorded and checked items of the student leaders and student failures, both secured at the time of entrance to the university, permits the following conclusions:

1. Despite the equal representation of commuters and residents in the student population as a whole, the proportion of student leaders is overwhelmingly drawn from the resident students, but the student failures are representative of the student population as a whole.
2. Self-descriptions by the two groups of students found no major differences on many items. However, striking differences in self-descriptions were noted in which more negativity was found in student failures in terms of personality traits as well as a greater reactivity in physical symptomatology. The pattern of adjustment and consequent self-concepts that were being established over the previous eighteen years were influencing the productivity at the point of a new educational departure.
3. No major variations were noted insofar as the type of high school previously attended, the extent of parental schooling, the size of family group, church affiliation, and some personality traits.

4. Both in immediate career planning and in long-range aspirations, the failure group appeared to be less realistic and vaguer in its outlooks.

INTELLECTUALITY—FAILURES

This phenomenon will be limited to measures of functioning as represented by the Wechsler Adult Intelligence Scale, the School and College Ability Test, the Cooperative Reading and Mathematics Tests, and the Grade Point Average. In the continued and progressive buildup of comparisons, the findings on student leaders and student failures will be presented simultaneously.

The correlation matrix with its accompanying key represents the total assessment activity carried on with the student failure sample. Foldout appendix 2 will be the basis for discussion in subsequent sections on personality and electroencephalography.

Key to variables in correlation matrix:

1. GPA   -   Grade Point Average
2. EEG-R   -   Electroencephalogram Rating (see p. 227)
3. Alpha Index -   EEG rating in terms of % of 8-13 frequency
4. WAIS-V   -   Verbal Scale IQ of the Wechsler Adult Intelligence Scale
5. WAIS-P   -   Performance Scale IQ of Wechsler Adult Intelligence Scale
6. WAIS   -   Full Scale IQ of the Wechsler Adult Intelligence Scale
7. SCAT-V   -   Verbal Scale of the School and College Ability Test, Form 1A
8. SCAT-Q   -   Quantitative Scale of the SCAT, Form 1A
9. SCAT-T   -   Full Scale of the SCAT, Form 1A
10. Coop. Rdg. -   Cooperative Reading Test, Form T, C2
11. Coop. Math. -   Cooperative Mathematics Test, Form XX
12. MMPI-L   -   Minnesota Multiphasic Personality Inventory-Lie Score
13. MMPI-F   -   MMPI Validity Score
14. MMPI-K   -   MMPI Correction Score
15. MMPI-Hs   -   MMPI Hypochondriasis Scale
16. MMPI-D   -   MMPI Depression Scale
17. MMPI-Hy   -   MMPI Hysteria Scale
18. MMPI-Pd   -   MMPI Psychopathic Deviate Scale
19. MMPI-Mf   -   MMPI Masculinity-Feminity Interest Scale
20. MMPI-Pa   -   MMPI Paranoia Scale
21. MMPI-Pt   -   MMPI Psychasthenia Scale
22. MMPI-Sc   -   MMPI Schizophrenia Scale

Key to variables in correlation matrix: (Cont'd)
23. MMPI-Ma - MMPI Hypomania Scale
24. MMPI-Si - MMPI Social Introversion Scale
25. A-Th   - Allport-Vernon-Lindzey **Study of Values**—Theoretical
26. A-Ec   - Allport-Vernon-Lindzey **Study of Values**—Economic
27. A-Ae   - Allport-Vernon-Lindzey **Study of Values**—Aesthetic
28. A-Soc.   - Allport-Vernon-Lindzey **Study of Values**—Social
29. A-Pol.   - Allport-Vernon-Lindzey **Study of Values**—Political
30. A-Rel.   - Allport-Vernon-Lindzey **Study of Values**—Religious
31. R-W+   - Rorschach Whole Response Total
32. R-D   - Rorschach Major Detail Responses
33. R-M+   - Rorschach Movement Responses
34. R-FC+   - Rorschach Form-Color Responses
35. R-g   - Rorschach Organization Score

Scholastic aptitudes as represented by the SCAT are strikingly similar in terms of mean scores for the two samples under investigation. On the other hand an examination of the reading proficiency of the two groups produced a significant difference in the mean scores at the .05 level. A reversal of the just reported conclusion occurred in the comparison of the mathematics performance for the leaders versus the underachievers. In this case the low academic group posted significantly higher scores.

Both samples are significantly higher than published norms for liberal arts college students in terms of scholastic aptitudes and mathematics scores.

An examination of the correlation matrix in which grade point average is the predicted variable points out that not a single positive relationship was established with any of the other 34 variables. The only significant r was between the Rorschach M and GPA at -.352. However, the chance factor would produce at least one such significant relationship.

Turning to other relationships among the intellectual variables produced outcomes in the expected directions. That is, reasonably high intercorrelations within segments of the same instrument (SCAT,WAIS) and expected relationships between measures of scholastic aptitude and intelligence on the one hand and reading and mathematics abilities on the other.

Comparisons of the correlations for student leaders and student failures in terms of GPA and measures of intellectuality present strikingly different results. The magnitude and direction of the r's for leaders were in the expected direction and comparable to other investigations, but the student failures' array was in no way consistent with levels of abilities. The conclusion is compelling that student failures were performing in a manner that could not be predicted from standard measures of academic proficiency. The answers for why such an erratic picture emerged will not be available by any search of the matrix in which intellectual variables are summarized.

TABLE 22
Subtest and Total Weighted Scores of Student Leaders
and Failures on the Wechsler Adult Intelligence Scale

Test	Leaders		Failures	
	Mean	SD	Mean	SD
Information	14.5	1.9	13.5	1.7
Comprehension	15.4	2.4	16.2	2.6
Arithmetic	12.0	2.3	11.9	2.4
Similarities	15.0	1.9	13.0	1.4
Digit Span	12.9	3.2	11.6	3.3
Vocabulary	15.7	1.7	14.2	1.4
Digit Symbol	12.8	1.9	11.9	2.2
Picture Completion	13.1	2.4	11.4	2.0
Block Design	12.6	2.2	12.3	2.8
Picture Arrangement	10.7	2.4	11.6	2.4
Object Assembly	11.8	2.7	10.6	3.0
Verbal Scale IQ	127.4	7.8	122.2	7.2
Performance Scale IQ	113.8	9.3	110.3	11.1
Full Scale IQ	122.9	7.8	118.3	7.0

A comparison of the means for the two samples produced a t score of 2.51. The conclusion is not tenable that both samples are drawn from the same universe in terms of intelligence. A comparison with published norms finds both samples significantly different from the general population norms for their ages.

This statistically significant difference between Student Leaders and Student Failures should not obscure the fact that both groups are drawn from populations that are superior to the general population of their peers.

TABLE 23
Percentile Means, SD's for Scholastic Aptitude, Reading Proficiency,
and Mathematics Knowledge for Student Leaders and Failures

	Leaders		Failures	
	Mean	SD	Mean	SD
School and College Ability Test (SCAT):				
Verbal	75.0	18.3	72.2	16.7
Quantitative	83.5	16.4	75.1	16.0
Total	83.9	15.2	78.5	15.0
Cooperative Reading Test, C2, Form T	57.3	21.8	43.4	21.7
Cooperative Mathematics Test, Form XX	72.0	21.3	89.5	11.6

In addition to the correlations reported in Table 23, several other patterns of relationships were studied by multiple correlations. The major variables in the first instance were:

Variable X_1	Grade Point Average (GPA)
Variable X_2	EEG-R
Variable X_3	Cooperative Reading Percentile
Variable X_4	MMPI-D
Variable X_5	MMPI-Pt
Variable X_6	Rorschach-M

Table 24 provides a summary of the intercorrelations for the six variables mentioned in the preceding discussion.

TABLE 24
Intercorrelations for Five Independent Variables
and the Criterion Variable: Grade Point Average

	r_2	r_3	r_4	r_5	r_6
X_1 GPA	.21	-.25	.27	.23	-.35
X_2 EEG		.06	.19	.16	-.38
X_3 Coop. Reading			-.44	-.45	.18
X_4 MMPI-D				.77	-.16
X_5 MMPI-Pt					-.28

$R_{1.23456}$ * = .458 (Significant at .01 level for 30 df)

$R^2_{1.23456}$ indicates the proportion of variance of the dependent (predicted variable) which is explained or accounted for by the independent variables. Hence, the total variance of GPA may be analyzed or accounted for as follows:

.25% by correlation with EEG-R
1.21% by correlation with Cooperative Reading
23.04% by correlation with MMPI-D
8.41% by correlation with MMPI-Pt
9.61% by correlation with Rorschach-M
*-21.58% by dampening effect or interference due to negative correlation.
79.06% by variables other than above.

*(unusually large but this is due to both major contributors having -B coefficients. This would suggest that improved predicability by dropping either Cooperative Reading or MMPI-Pt or both could be achieved)

Another combination of variables was extracted for the purpose of securing a multiple correlation. The variables were as follows:

X_1 GPA
X_2 EEG-R
X_3 MMPI-Pd
X_4 MMPI-Mf
X_5 Allport-Ae
X_6 Rorschach g

TABLE 25
Intercorrelations for Five Independent Variables
and the Criterion Variable: Grade Point Average

	r_2	r_3	r_4	r_5	r_6
Variable X_1	.21	-.07	.20	-.24	-.14
Variable X_2		-.08	.18	.01	-.16
Variable X_3			-.28	-.06	.34
Variable X_4				.06	-.22
Variable X_5					.42

$R_{1.23456}$ = .3735 (significant at .05 level for 30 df)

$R^2_{1.23456}$ indicates the proportion of variance of the dependent variable (GPA) which is explained or accounted for by the independent or predictor variables. The total variance of GPA may be accounted for as follows:

3.61% by correlation with EEG-R
.16% by correlation with MMPI-Pd
3.61% by correlation with MMPI-Mf
7.84% by correlation with Allport-Ae
.36% by correlation with Rorschach g
-1.63% by dampening effect or interference due to negative correlations
86.05% by correlation with variables other than the above

PERSONALITY

The inability of intellectual variables to explain academic failure understandably pushed the search for explanations into other realms where the psychologist had developed instruments for the purpose of assessing non-intellective functions.

Before any major step is undertaken in this section to explore beyond the usual domains, it is necessary to enter a disclaimer. For purposes of investigation and perhaps of manipulation, the use of labels or categories specifying one test as intellective and another as personality must be heuristic. No support can be secured for treating the data as discrete, nor can the assumption of specificity of talents be defended.

The Allport-Vernon-Lindzey **Study of Values** scale resulted in the scores noted in Table 26.

TABLE 26
Means and SD's for Student Leaders and Student Failures
on the Study of Values

	Leaders		Failures	
	Mean	SD	Mean	SD
Theoretical	39.8	6.7	40.9	6.6
Economic	36.6	10.4	43.8	8.3
Aesthetic	35.4	8.0	36.3	7.7
Social	37.9	7.2	35.4	5.8
Political	45.2	6.7	42.3	6.5
Religious	45.1	7.8	39.9	7.5

Statistically significant differences were noted in two areas at .05 level. The Student Leader group posted higher scores on the Religious Scale, whereas the underachieving group placed a higher comparative value on the Economic Scale.

Neither group had the configuration that McKinnon (1961) found to be characteristic of creative groups who had elevated scores on the Theoretical and Aesthetic Scales.

The applicability of the MMPI has been investigated in many ways since its publication. Drake (76) established that there is a profile pattern which identifies the student who lacks academic motivation and is thereby more likely to fall into the group of underachievers even though his scholastic aptitude is high.

Drake noted that even though actuarial tables based on rank in high school class and the college ability test indicate that 70 percent of the entering students with ratings comparable to a centile rank of 85 on a college ability test should obtain a C average or better and 30 percent receive an average below C during their first semester at college, the chances are that predication will be reversed if the students obtain a particular pattern on the MMPI. The pattern reveals scales Ma and Sc among the three highest scales, Mf not high, and Si among the low. Drake claims that this particular pattern has been found to differentiate male counselees judged to be lacking in academic motivation. Furthermore, Drake noted that expectancy tables developed from his studies with the MMPI indicate that 67 percent of male students showing this pattern failed to obtain a C average during their first semester and only 33 percent obtained C or better. (This is a reversal of expectancy indicated on actuarial tables.) Hence, Drake suggests that counselors refrain from drawing conclusions based solely on data obtained from actuarial tables which point to satisfactory academic achievement.

The John Carroll University Counseling Center (1959) found that 12 of the 247 MMPI profiles included in the study conducted at John Carroll followed the pattern indicated by Drake as that of students lacking academic motivation. Even though SCAT percentiles of these 12 freshmen ranged from 79 to 90, 7 of the students failed to earn a C average. Of these 7, three were dropped from school. The quality point averages of the 5 who earned a C average ranged from 2.15 to 2.81. Two of this group ranked in the 90% ile in academic aptitude.

Another investigation to ascertain the efficacy of the MMPI in predicting academic progress was undertaken by Hackett (139).

Hackett's study grew out of an attempt to determine if MMPI scale scores would discriminate between groups of high and low achievers in a college group. Success in his first attempt led Hackett to investigate the various items of the MMPI in order to determine whether they might prove to be consistent discriminators.

Using the entire entering class of a midwestern land-grant college, Hackett obtained the following information:

1. High and low-achieving male students tend to make different self-reports about themselves on a questionnaire such as the MMPI.
2. Self-reports can be used to predict future academic achievement of male students.
3. Certain trends seem to exist in the identified items which permit analysis and tentative hypothesis formation regarding the personalities of low and high achievers.
4. The high-achieving group appeared to be men who were more interested in verbal activities. They seemed to project less, discriminate better, and to be emotionally less easily aroused. They appear to tolerate tension much better and to live at a more relaxed, confident tempo.
5. The low-achievers were emotionally responsive to their environment and were compelled to do something about dispelling their tensions. The tempo of their lives seemed to be faster than that of the high-achievers, although their activity was not necessarily productively oriented. Projection seemed to be a defense mechanism of great usefulness to this group. Strength and power seem to be important to these people. There appear to be many similarities between this group and the "authoritarian personality."

Studies reporting relationships between successful and unsuccessful progress in academic work were conducted by Kahn and Singer (179), who reported that the only differentiating scale was Sc, by Morgan (254), who noted that non-achievers had profile elevations on the Pd scale and low points on the Pa scale, by Quinn (290) who failed to find differentiating scales on the MMPI and maintained that differences in achievement were due to intelligence. Yeomans and Lundin (401) found that freshmen and seniors in the bottom quarters of their classes scored significantly higher on the Pd and Ma scales, and men in both top quarters scored significantly higher on Mf. Barger and Hall (1964) using an entering class of freshmen and sophomores at the University of Florida, found that high scores on Mf for males were related to continuation in studies, and that high Ma scores, which reflect activity or energy level, were more frequent than expected for males who drop out of college and who earn lower scholastic averages.

High scores on either Pd or Ma, especially when both scales have high ranks in the profile, are often indicative of nonconformity, rebelliousness, and high activity level. These traits are not conducive to high achievement in most academic settings (Dahlstrom and Welsh, 62).

In comparing the intercorrelations of the Failure group with those reported on the Basic Group of College Males reported in Dahlstrom (62), and presented on page 105, it is readily noted that the direction and magnitude of the r's are intermediate in position to those found between the Leaders and the Beginners to be reported on in the next chapter.

TABLE 27
MMPI T Scores and SD's for Student
Leaders and Failures on the Validity and Clinical Scales

Scale	Leaders		Failures		Sig.
	Mean	SD	Mean	SD	
L	46.2	6.5	45.9	7.3	
F	51.5	6.5	57.3	8.6	.01
K	57.7	7.6	54.4	9.7	
Hs	53.2	9.0	55.3	10.6	
D	52.3	13.1	58.8	12.0	.05
Hy	60.2	7.9	60.6	8.6	
Pd	58.3	7.7	63.8	8.9	.05
Mf	63.3	10.0	57.6	7.9	.05
Pa	55.2	8.2	56.8	9.5	
Pt	58.6	11.5	63.0	10.4	
Sc	57.3	11.2	62.6	12.5	
Ma	60.3	10.1	60.3	12.5	
Si	44.9	7.9	50.8	11.3	.05

Significant differences at the .05 level were obtained on the Depression, Psychopathic Deviate, Paranoia, and Social Introversion Scales, and at the .01

level on the Validity (K) scale. In four of the five differences the Failure sample scored higher, indicating a greater proneness to depression and pessimism suspiciousness, withdrawing from social contacts, and resistance to authority. On the other hand, the Student Leader group scored higher on the Mf scale, permitting the conclusion that despite demonstrated dominance and recognition in peer relations, the leaders were not aggressively masculine nor prone to challenge the constituted authorities.

The overall profile secured from both groups places them well within the expected limits for college males as reported in studies by Bier (26) and Goodstein (127).

Studies by Drake (76) and Hackett (139) which showed some agreement in what was described as a low achievement configuration (syndrome) were in part supported by these findings on the Failure or Underachievement sample.

RORSCHACH TEST

The Rorschach Test, a projective instrument used most frequently in clinical work, provides a method of inferring underlying personality dynamics from the assessment of a number of dimensions of perceptual behavior. These dimensions have sometimes been used for predicting academic performance Lavin (204).

All of the research to be cited has been carried out at the college level. In his review of the research Travers (366) states that some Rorschach dimensions are related to academic performance. However, more recent research does not indicate that Rorschach is a useful measure. The studies by Burgess & Clark (40) Cooper (1955), Rust and Ryan (1953), and Sopchak (1958) all find that the test predicts either poorly or not at all.

While statistically significant differences occurred on several sub-categories, the major conclusion derived from an examination of the protocols and the scoring summaries in general points to a similarity in the response patterns of the two student groups. Lavin's (204) conclusion that the Rorschach Test is a poor instrument for the prediction of academic performance is supported by the correlations found between Rorschach variables and GPA for underachieving students in this investigation. See Table 28.

ELECTROENCEPHALOGRAPHY

Three procedures were adopted to summarize recordings on the EEG. The first method was in terms of frequencies, amplitudes, and Alpha Index. These data are presented in Table 29. The second procedure was derived from an inspectional technique which produced a qualitative rating, and this is found in

TABLE 28
Summary of Rorschach Factors for the Leaders and Failing Students
at John Carroll University

Category		Student Leaders	Underachievers
Number of Responses		30	32
Whole Responses			
WO		.75	2.1
W		9.0	5.1
WP		2.0	2.2
W(S)		1.25	.53
Total W		13.1	9.9
Normal Details:			
DO		1.0	1.3
D		8.8	8.2
DP		1.0	1.20
Dr		.95	1.70
Dro		.35	.19
Total D		10.8	10.7
Space Responses:			
S		1.8	.66
Determinants:			
Form Level	(F)		
F+		13.5	13.2
F-		3.95	4.7
%F+		77%	75%
Movement:	(M)		
M		4.3	2.4
FM		3.7	3.8
m		1.0	1.4
Color	(C)		
FC		3.8	2.6
CF		.95	.81
Chiaroscuro	(Ch)		
Fch		.75	1.5
ChF		.05	.22
Erlebnistypus: M:Sum C			
Experience-Balance		4.3:4.75	2.4:3.41
Content:			
Human:			
H		4.5	2.9
Hd		1.2	1.3
Animal:			
A		12.4	8.96
Ad		.95	3.5
Anatomy		1.7	1.4
Blood		.00	.15
Botany		.85	1.6
Fire		.75	.37
Geology		.35	.65
Art		2.2	.34
Weapons		.35	.07
Organization Score:			
g		13.2	10.6

Table 30. The third method was based on rating scale, ranging from 1 to 5, presented below.

TABLE 29
Distribution of EEG Frequencies, Amplitudes (Voltage) and Alpha Index for Student Leaders and Underachievers

	Frequency		Amplitude		Alpha Index	
	Mean	SD	Mean	SD	Mean	SD
Leaders	10.43	1.08	36.6	15.0	63.06	26.10
Underachievers	10.3	1.7	35.2	17.0	63.75	26.1

An inspection of Table 29 points out the striking similarity of the two groups in terms of the frequency, amplitude, and Alpha Index for the Leaders and Failures.

TABLE 30
A Five-Point Rating Scale for EEG Records

1. Within Normal Limits, Awake and Asleep.
   a. Good, stable background rhythms awake and/or asleep;
   b. Good bilateral symmetry under all conditions;
   c. Normal photic driving;
   d. No more than slight slowing with good hyperventilation.
2. No Definite Abnormality, but
   a. Rare or poor or asymmetric alpha rhythm;
   b. Poor bilateral symmetry, awake or asleep;
   c. Scattered, non-focal limited theta activity;
   d. Appreciable slowing with hyperventilation;
   e. Excess fast activity;
   f. Suggestion of positive spikes not verified due to poor technique.
3. Borderline.
   a. Poor bilateral symmetry, awake and asleep and with photic stimulation;
   b. Pronounced hyperventilation effect;
   c. Some excess, diffuse slowing in the theta band;
   d. Any limited focal slowing;
   e. Positive spikes, even in otherwise normal record.
4. Abnormal.
   a. Seizure activity in any stage (positive spikes not rated as seizure discharges);
   b. Excess delta activity, with or without theta, focal or diffuse;
   c. Severe slowing on hyperventilation with poor recovery as accentuation of spontaneous slowing.
5. Grossly Abnormal.
   a. Much seizure activity in any stage;
   b. Much generalized or focal slowing.

TABLE 31
Nature of Pathological or Questionable EEG Features

Category	Leaders	Underachievers
Generalized Dysrhythmia and		
Paroxysmal Tracings	3	7
Epileptic Features	2	1
Focal Qualities	1	0
	6	8
Low Voltage Tense Records	2	6

The major conclusion to be drawn from Table 31 is that the Leader group produced six abnormal records to eight for the Underachieving group, and the respective percentages would be 16 and 25 of the total samples involved. Moreover, the incidence of low voltage (tense) records for the Underachievers was 19% as opposed to 5% of such records with the Leader sample. Lindsley (210) and Ellingsonn (82) noted that changes in the electrical activity of the cortex occur with emotionally disturbing stimuli and attention-concentration factors. The plausibility of the Underachieving group being under considerable duress following a poor semester of academic effort is easily defended.

An examination of the correlation matrix, page 227, relating the EEG-R variable with the various intellectual variables, found the coefficients following the same course as they did for the Leaders sample. Greater variations occurred when the personality variables (MMPI, Allport, and Rorschach) were correlated with the EEG-R for the two groups. No consistent pattern emerged that permits a generalization to be made on the relationship of the two types of phenomena.

FAILURES-FIVE YEARS LATER

The students in this phase of the investigation were admitted to the University in the Fall of 1962, and following a regular program of studies they would have graduated in June of 1966. To establish survival rates for students who had run into academic difficulties at the outset of their college work, a five-year record follow-up was made of the sample.

Of the 140 students who were initially designated as being below acceptable academic levels (less than 2.00 GPA), 42 were randomly chosen to participate in that intensive assessment. Thirty-two completed the total testing and are the subjects of the present chapter.

A check of University records one year after the normal expectancy for completion of studies produced the following outcomes:

TABLE 32
Graduation Rates for Failing Students

	Completed Studies		Failed-Dismissed	
	Number	%	Number	%
In 4 years	5	12		
In 5 years	7	17		
Transferred	3	7		
Total	15	36%	27	64%
	GPA = 2.20		GPA = 1.56	
	SD = .24		SD = .28	

Comparative figures for a random sample of freshmen who began studies in 1965 at John Carroll University and checked two years later are as follows:

	Number	%
In good standing	33	70
Failed-dismissed	9	20
Transferred	5	10
(Total Good Standing)		80

In examining the records for the total freshman class of 1962, it was noted that 21% of that group was deficient academically at the close of its first semester of college studies. A random sample of that underachieving group produced the figures cited above. The striking conclusion is—that of those who experience academic difficulties at the very outset of college work, only 1/3 recover to go on to completion of studies in the future.

Table 33 summarizes the pertinent test findings for the two groups of students who were designated as underachievers at the outset of studies.

The significant differences between underachievers who recover and those who eventually fail or are dismissed are on three of the 28 variables examined. The MMPI secured differences on the Pa and Ma scales. The traits are designated as suspicious-oversensitivity, and overproductivity in thought and/or action. The Ae scale on the Allport was the third significant variable between the two groups of underachievers. Suggested here is the greater disposition of the failing group to see life as a procession of events, each impression to be enjoyed for its own sake and to place form and harmony ahead of truth and utility. The triad of traits supports the findings of Hackett (139), who found a similar constellation in other samples of poorly achieving students.

While not reaching statistical significance, several other variables produced substantial differences between the two samples extracted from the underachiev-

TABLE 33

Means and SD's for Underachievers Who Recover Academically
and Those Dismissed for Academic Failure

Variable	Completed Studies		Dismissed		Significance
	Mean	SD	Mean	SD	
GPA	2.20	.24	1.56	.28	
EEG-R	1.75	1.0	2.4	1.25	
WAIS-FS	120.0	7.05	118.4	6.5	
SCAT-T	80.0	14.1	78.0	16.5	
Coop. Rdg.	37.5	19.7	48.0	21.6	
Coop. Math	91.2	7.6	89.0	12.2	
MMPI-L	48.3	7.8	45.5	5.7	
MMPI-F	55.3	6.4	59.2	9.6	
MMPI-K	54.5	8.7	53.5	11.05	
MMPI-Hs	54.9	12.5	55.3	9.2	
MMPI-D	60.8	10.3	57.5	13.0	
MMPI-Hy	59.5	11.3	60.5	6.5	
MMPI-Pd	62.4	10.5	64.8	8.1	
MMPI-Mf	57.8	6.5	57.3	8.0	
MMPI-Pa	54.5	11.0	63.0	8.2	.05
MMPI-Pt	64.3	10.8	62.8	10.5	
MMPI-Sc	57.8	9.3	65.0	12.6	
MMPI-Ma	56.6	7.5	64.5	13.6	.05
MMPI-Si	52.0	9.4	50.3	11.1	
Allport-Th	40.3	6.8	40.0	7.1	
Allport-Ec	46.2	9.2	42.6	8.5	
Allport-Ae	32.4	4.8	38.5	9.1	.05
Allport-Soc.	34.5	6.1	31.3	10.5	
Allport-Pol.	42.8	5.4	42.3	7.2	
Allport-Rel.	43.1	8.8	38.5	6.7	
Rorschach-W	5.2	2.3	5.8	2.1	
Rorschach-D	10.5	3.9	8.1	4.9	
Rorschach-M	1.75	1.3	2.7	1.9	
Rorschach-FC	2.57	1.8	2.5	1.7	

ing group. These were the EEG-R scores in which the successful group earned a
higher rating in terms of overall evaluation of records; the Allport-Religious scale
of the successful group was considerably higher than the failing group; the
MMPI-Sc scale which found the successful group more in contact with its
environment, and the MMPI-F scale which found the losers persisting in being
nonconformers than eventual achievers.

On all measures of intellectuality, the two groups were essentially alike insofar as functioning abilities were concerned. Interestingly, the poorer reader (not statistically) group was found in the eventually successful sample.

CHAPTER 9

Profiles of Beginners

The third phase in the study of college males was undertaken to secure data dealing with beginning students that could be used for comparative purposes with Leaders and Failures.

Two samples of students were randomly drawn from the entering class of 1965. The experimental sample, initially numbered sixty, and 47 men completed the extensive testing. The control group numbered fifty.

All of the assessment procedures were carried out according to specifications of the technique by trained workers, and the principle of "confidentiality" was invoked. The participants were apprised of the testing outcomes after the completion of the first year of studies. They were, moreover, assured that the findings would be available subsequently for any use they might wish to make of the results.

The implications of testing the Student Leaders and Failures "after the fact" of such designations were not lost on this investigator. The complexity of distinguishing what effects such roles played in the testing outcomes could not be ascertained. In the present investigation considerable caution was invoked in order to deal with questions and developments before they emerged in the study. For this reason the inclusion of a control group, chosen randomly at the same time that the experimental group was formed, was deemed necessary. Table 34 presents the precollege measures of scholastic abilities and achievement of the two samples.

TABLE 34

Means and SD's for Beginning Freshmen on the SAT
and High School GPA

Sample	SAT				H.S. GPA	N
	V		M			
	Mean	SD	Mean	SD		
Control	498	76	524	82.1	2.50	48
Experimental	514	79	543	84.2	2.58	47

Statistical analyses of differences between the two samples of freshmen who enrolled at John Carroll University in the Fall of 1965 provided no significant differences. It can, therefore, be concluded that both samples were drawn from the same population.

At the conclusion of two years of college work, a follow-up check of the records of the control and experimental group resulted in the findings presented in Table 35.

TABLE 35

Means and SD's for Two Samples of College Freshmen on GPA and Rates of Dismissal Failure, Transfer, and Honors Achievement

Sample	GPA		Dismissed-Failing	Transferred	Honors
	First Year	Second Year	%	%	%
Control	2.48	2.356	27%	15%	21%
Experimental	2.38	2.521	23%	10%	13%

The array of data found in Table 35 supports the claim that both the experimental and control groups were drawn from the same population in terms of abilities and previous high school achievement, but further support is marshalled for the conclusion that both samples continued to perform in a commensurate fashion through two years of college. The "Hawthorne effect" did not operate to give the experimental group any noticeable gain in motivation or achievement.

Since it has been shown that the experimental group is representative of the freshman class of 1965, and this freshman class is representative of classes enrolled at John Carroll University over the past five years through studies reported in a **Decade of Studies on John Carroll University Students,** (Nosal, 1963), it was deemed important to tease out many relationships for the evidence that might serve administrative, instructional, and counseling functions in the University. Hopefully, the information might be generalized to other college university settings where comparable student populations are found.

Several changes occurred in the adoption of assessment procedures from those used in the studies on Leaders and Failures. These included the substitution of a recently devised assessment procedure by Magda Arnold, **Story Sequence Analysis,** for the Rorschach Test, the substitution of the SAT for the SCAT, and the installation of the Grass VI-B Electroencephalograph in the EEG Laboratory. Discussion on these topics will be reserved for the appropriate section dealing with the technique.

INSTRUMENTATION

Scholastic Aptitude Test (SAT), College Entrance Examination Board, Princeton, N.J.

Wechsler Adult Intelligence Scale, (WAIS), the Psychological Corporation, New York.

Cooperative Reading Test, C2, Form T, Educational Testing Service, Princeton, N.J.

Story Sequence Analysis (SSA), Columbia University Press, N.Y.

Minnesota Multiphasic Personality Inventory, The Psychological Corporation, N.Y.

Allport, Vernon, Lindzey, **Study of Values**, Houghton-Mifflin Company, Boston.

Grass Electroencephalograph, Model VI-B, Quincy, Massachusetts.

Biographical information on the entering freshman experimental sample is summarized as follows:

Parental Schooling	
Elementary Education	7%
Some High School	7%
High School Graduate	46%
Some College	12%
College Graduates	28%

These percentages approximate those found on the samples of student leaders and failures treated in previous chapters.

High School Origin	
Private	83%
Public	17%

The percentages reported here are consistent with the historical pattern at John Carroll University, but there is a slight increase in public school graduates enrolling.

College Housing		GPA-at end of First Year
Commuters	55%	2.233
Residents	45%	2.524

The slightly larger proportion of commuters to dormitory residents is in line with student origins in the past. What is more interesting is that the residents posted a better GPA for the first year than did the commuters. While the difference did not reach statistical significance, the direction of the change in spite of comparable abilities and the previously noted disproportionate resident origins of student leaders support the contention of Sanford that students should attend college away from home.

In keeping with the convictions and assumptions outlined in Chapter 6, particularly the efficacy of multivariate analysis, the correlation charts on pages 225 and 229 will be the main source of information that will be expanded into discussions on topics in subsequent sections. (See foldout appendix 3, p. 229.)

INTELLECTUALITY -- BEGINNERS

By the practice established in the previous chapters, the findings in this section will be primarily restricted to measures of grade point average, the Wechsler Adult Intelligence Scale, the SAT, and the Cooperative Reading Test.

The substitution of the SAT in the present sample for the SCAT which was used with the Leader and Failure groups resulted from a change in University policy to require all entering students to submit the SAT scores before admission as distinguished from the earlier practice of administering the SCAT at the beginning of the fall semester.

Table 36 presents the results of the WAIS testing.

TABLE 36
Means and SD's for the WAIS Scaled
Scores Subtests and Major Sections of the Scale
for Beginning College Males

	Mean	SD
Information	13.7	
Comprehension	14.5	
Arithmetic	12.2	
Similarities	12.7	
Digit Span	12.1	
Vocabulary	13.5	
Digit Symbol	12.2	
Picture Completion	11.8	
Picture Arrangement	12.0	
Block Design	11.2	
Object Assembly	11.5	
Verbal Scale IQ	121.0	8.14
Performance Scale IQ	112.0	9.57
Full Scale IQ	119.0	7.47

A comparison of the WAIS Full Scale IQ found no difference in the means of the Beginners and the Failures, but there was a significant difference between the Beginners and the Leaders at the .05 level. The slight statistical difference should not obscure the matter of greater importance, viz., that all three groups surpass 90 percent of their age peers in terms of general intelligence.

In reviewing the intercorrelations found between the many measures of intellectuality and the criterion variable, GPA, for the Beginners sample, only one r was found to be statistically significant. The SAT-V and GPA r of .32 was found. This contrasts with six significant r's for the intellectual variables and GPA in the Student Leader sample, and not a single such relationship was found in the Failure group.

In attempting to translate the SAT scores secured on the 1965 freshman sample into SCAT equivalents, some assistance is available from a study conducted on the 1960 entering freshman class on whom both SCAT and SAT results were available. The SCAT total percentile of 72 was equivalent to a mean SAT score of 500. From such a transposition it can be concluded that a slight improvement in the caliber of the freshman class of 1965 was not significantly different from the class of 1962 that produced the Failure sample in these studies.

PERSONALITY

Two familiar measures of personality used in previous assessment of Student Leaders and Failures were continued. These were the MMPI and the **Study of Values**. The major change occurred in the substitution of the SSA projective procedure for the Rorschach Test. The reason for this change was prompted by the consistently low relationships found between Rorschach variables and the other criteria adopted in this study, and the widespread interest generated in achievement motivation by McClelland and associates who used TAT materials for their investigations.

The appearance of the **Story Sequence Analysis** (Arnold, 1962) a new method of measuring motivation and predicting achievement, prompted the substitution. Arnold (7) maintained:

> In reviewing literature on the TAT, it was noted that too much attention was being focused on the theme of each individual story and that as a result the story with its plot and outcome was disregarded. If it were possible to score WHAT THE STORY is saying and include ALL THERE IS TO THE STORY, one would discover a new dimension in the TAT which might allow very different correlations with behavior.

With this in mind Arnold set up a method of story analysis in which each story was condensed into an import. The import leaves out incidental details but preserves the kernel or meat of the story. When the imports are read in sequence, a picture of the individual emerges that portrays his attitudes, his intentions for action. Every story makes a point, expresses a conviction. In every case emotions may influence the action, but the outcome is primarily an expression of the storyteller's convictions, garnered from experience and reflection. The plot sets the problem, the outcome solves it. Both the type of problem, and the outcome are characteristic for the storyteller himself.

Through extensive research involving several hundred records, Arnold and a group of graduate students found that it was possible to score the story imports objectively and to arrive at a final score which indicates a man's positive or negative motivation. Positive motivation was found among high achieving elementary, secondary, and college students, effective teachers, competent executives and well-adjusted Navy men. Negative motivation was found among low achievers, ineffective teachers, and naval offenders. The group developed a scoring system for assessing positive or negative motivation. The system was derived empirically from records of matched pairs of high and low achievers and was cross-validated on other samples. By means of linear transformation a Motivation Index was obtained. Arnold and her group prepared two tables which make it possible to find the Motivation Index (M.I.) for any final or consistency score derived from sequences of 10, 11, 12, 13, 14, 15, 16 and 20 stories. Further research on the M.I. is being carried on at the present time.

To help obtain significant diagnostic data in this study, Arnold's method was used with the experimental group. The thirteen TAT pictures (1, 2, 3BM, 4MF, 6BM, 7BM, 8BM, 10, 11, 13MF, 14, 16, and 20) which Arnold and her colleagues found most satisfactory were shown in the order listed. Students were instructed to tell a story with a plot and outcome. Seven minutes was allowed for each story. Imports for each story were prepared and an M.I. was obtained for each examinee. A correlation of .37 was obtained between M.I. and the GPA. The relationship is significant at the .05 level.

The SSA-Mi produced a higher correlation with GPA than all of the intellectual variables. It was exceeded by only the Allport-Religious scale which resulted in an r = .41 with GPA. Support is marshalled for the claims of McClelland, Arnold, and others, that when holding the ability variable constant, then the motivation index can be a major discriminator in predicting academic outcomes. That this variable was assessing some factor other than those dealt with by the other scales is given credence by the fact that only one significant correlation was obtained between the Mi scale and the other 27 variables. Some of the implications of this development were discussed in Chapter 2.

Table 37 continues the pattern demonstrated between the value orientations of the Student Leaders and Student Failures outlined in the previous chapter. What is of special note here is that although the Student Failures and Beginners

TABLE 37
Means and SD's for Student Leaders, Failures, and Beginners
on the Study of Values

Value	Leaders		Sig.	Failures		Sig.	Beginners	
	Mean	SD		Mean	SD		Mean	SD
Theoretical	39.8	6.7		40.9	6.6		41.8	7.5
Economic	36.6	10.4	.01	43.8	8.3	.05	38.0	6.9
Aesthetic	35.4	8.0		36.3	7.7	.01	31.3	7.0
Social	37.9	7.2		35.4	5.8	.01	41.0	7.7
Political	45.2	6.7		42.3	6.5		44.2	7.1
Religious	45.1	7.8	.01	39.9	7.5	.01	44.3	6.4

were at comparable stages in college studies when the **Study of Values** was administered, the Beginners posted higher scores on Social and Religious values, significant at the .01 level, and conversely, the Failure group secured significantly higher scores on the Economic and Aesthetic scales. It would appear that the failures were interested in contradictory movements. To be practically oriented and conscious of material rewards is not consistent with emphasizing the importance of aesthetic experience. The confusion of values may have produced some of the malaise which was present in the Failure group. The need to postpone sense fulfillment and other gratifications or the cultivation of a "frustration tolerance" did not appear to be well-developed in the Failure group.

MMPI

Table 38 presents the T score Means, SD's, and significance ratios for the three samples investigated in this study.

Previously, it was shown that the Leaders differed from the Failures in a statistically significant manner on the F, D, Pd, Mf, Pt, Sc, and Si scales. In comparing the Leaders and Beginners, only one significant difference was obtained, and that was on the Hy scale.

Differences between the mean T scores for Failures and Beginners were found on the F, D, and Hy scales. Despite the presence of reported differences it must be pointed out that the frequency of agreements is greater than differences. Moreover, on all the validity and clinical scales, the three samples fall within the generally found limits for college males.

In examining the intercorrelations of the MMPI scales as reported by Dahlstrom (62), the Beginner sample more closely approaches the magnitude and direction of the relationships with the Basic group than did either the Leader or Failure sample. There is some suggestion here that freshman college males in different institutional settings are more alike than freshmen and seniors in the same setting. The views of Sanford (317) and Friedman (103) are given support by such findings.

Nichols and Holland (1963), in a comprehensive study of first year college performance of high aptitude students in a National Merit follow-up, stated:

> The non-intellective predictors of college grades that were significant for both sexes seem to form two major clusters of traits: (a) perseverance and motivation to achieve, and (b) conformity and socialization.

The description above is more applicable to the Leader and Beginner samples than to the Failure group.

TABLE 38
Means, SD's and Significance Ratios for the Validity and Clinical
Scales on the MMPI for Leaders, Failures, and Beginners

Scale	Leaders Mean	SD	Sig.	Failures Mean	SD	Beginners Mean	SD	Sig.
L	42.6	6.5		45.9	7.3	46.2	6.5	
F	51.5	6.5		57.3	8.6	51.2	7.1	.01
K	57.7	7.6		54.4	9.7	54.7	7.8	
Hs	53.2	9.0		55.3	10.6	51.9	8.3	
D	52.3	13.1		58.8	11.9	51.8	12.4	.05
Hy	60.2	7.9	.05	60.6	8.6	55.5	9.4	.05
Pd	58.3	7.7		63.8	8.9	60.1	9.6	
Mf	63.3	10.0		57.6	7.7	59.7	9.7	
Pa	55.2	8.2		56.8	9.5	53.4	10.4	
Pt	58.6	11.5		63.0	10.4	58.1	12.8	
Sc	57.3	11.2		62.6	12.5	57.9	12.2	
Ma	60.3	10.1		60.3	12.5	58.8	10.4	
Si	44.9	7.9		50.8	11.3	49.5	11.1	

ELECTROENCEPHALOGRAPHY

Several changes occurred in the conduct of this phase of the study from earlier recordings which were carried on with Leader and Failure samples. Whereas resting but awake records were secured in the earlier examinations by the procedure recommended by Gibbs (114), the current assessment included

TABLE 39

Intercorrelations, Means, SD's for Eleven Variables from GPA, WAIS, SAT, SSA, MMPI, Allport, and EEG for Beginners

		GPA	WAIS FS	SAT V	SSA Mi	MMPI Hy	MMPI Pd	MMPI Mf	MMPI Ma	A- Ae	Rel.	EEG
	MEANS	2.42	119.25	514.68	79.93	55.49	60.11	59.70	58.83	31.28	44.26	1.79
	SD	.62	7.58	79.90	36.76	9.36	9.74	9.66	10.43	6.97	6.38	.91
WAIS	2	.18										
SAT-V	3	.17	.35									
MMPI-Mi	4	.37	.09	.08								
MMPI-Hy	5	-.02	.15	.13	.16							
MMPI-Pd	6	-.31	.12	+.06	-.22	.29						
MMPI-Mf	7	.26	-.20	.12	.18	.16	-.07					
MMPI-Ma	8	-.34	-.08	-.14	-.18	-.15	.24	-.12				
Allport-Ae	9	-.38	-.05	.18	-.18	+.01	.34	.28	+.04			
Allport-Rel.	10	.39	-.13	-.14	.23	+.01	-.23	.28	-.36	-.25		
EEG	11	+.24	+.17	+.14	-.12	+.11	+.02	+.07	+.08	+.04	+.04	

both a waking and a sleep record according to electrode placement recommended by the International Federation EEG Societies (the 10-20 system). Another change was in the improved instrumentation afforded by the Grass 6-8 Electroencephalograph, and the montage or mapping procedure outlined by Henry and built into the selector switch. To induce sleep, 2000 mg of dormisone were routinely administered under medical supervision.

The recourse to adding a sleep record derives largely from the recommendations of Gibbs (114, 1964) and Henry (151), who maintained that greater information can be secured from such recordings. The phenomenon of 14 to 6 per second positive spiking is difficult to obtain in waking records, but can be seen in sleep. The stage of late adolescent development for most college freshmen suggested that such a characteristic might be detected and subsequently related to academic performances. Unfortunately, technician ineptness precluded securing the sought-for type of runs, and no opportunity presented itself to comment on the relationship of this much debated phenomenon and its presence and role in college males.

Table 39 presents the major intercorrelations of the EEG-R and ten other variables.

As in previous findings relating EEG-R results to those of other behavioral measures, none of the EEG-R correlations was found to be significantly related to such measures. However, the positive direction of the EEG-R with all measures of intellectuality was sustained, but greater variance occurred in the EEG-R relationships with personality variables.

Comparisons of mean ratings on the EEG-R for the three samples of college males are shown in Table 40.

TABLE 40
Means, SD's , and Qualitive Ratings for the Leaders, Failures, and
Beginners Samples of College Males

| | Leaders | | Failures | | Beginners | |
	Mean	SD	Mean	SD	Mean	SD
EEG-R	1.72	.96	1.97	.87	1.79	.91
Abnormal %	17%		24%		14%	

The EEG-R values for the three samples did not produce significant differences, statistically speaking. However, the negative direction of the ratings and the percentage of classified abnormals lend some credence to the view that neurological functioning, as represented by the EEG, has some possible causal and correlative relationships with academic achievement.

Moving from two variable relationships to multiple correlations in keeping with the convictions noted in an earlier chapter, several combinations of predictor variables were set up to study the GPA outcomes. In view of the exhaustive attempts to eke out relationships between intellectual variables and academic achievement which have been reported for the past 30 years, the present multiple correlations and analysis of variance in such instances were confined to searching for so-called non-intellective correlates of academic achievement.

The first combination of variables examined follows:

Variable	Mean	SD
1. GPA	2.42	.62
2. MMPI-Ma	58.83	10.43
3. SSA-Mi	79.93	36.76
4. MMPI-Mf	59.7	9.66
5. Allport-Rel.	44.26	6.38
6. EEG-R	1.79	.91

The regression equation for the above variables is:

$$X_1 = -.013X_2 + .005X_3 + .006X_4 + .019X_5 + .191X_6 + 1.244$$

$$R_{1.23456} = .5974$$

$$\sigma est\ X_1 \cdot X_2\ X_3\ X_4\ X_5\ X_6 = .50$$

The above data produces the following picture of the total variance of GPA:

4.84 percent by correlation with MMPI-Ma
9.00 percent by correlation with SSA-Mi
1.00 percent by correlation with MMPI-Mf
4.00 percent by correlation with Allport-Rel
7.84 percent by correlation with EEG-R
9.02 percent by indirect correlation of the above variables.
64.30 percent by correlation with variables other than above.

A second combination of variables was used in which the MMPI-Pd scale was substituted for the MMPI-Ma. The multiple correlation read as follows:

$$R_1 123456 = .5891$$

$$\sigma est\ X_1 \cdot X_2\ X_3\ X_4\ X_5\ X_6 = .50$$

The variance percentages in the two instances were practically the same, and the regression equation read:

$$X_1 = -.012X_2 + .005X_3 + .007X_4 + .023X_5 + .117X_6 + .988$$

Disappointing as it may appear, the search for factors explaining in a large measure the academic grade output of students continues to elude precise statistical predictability. Again, the caution must be recorded . . . that the highly selective character of the samples (all means within the top 10% of their age groups) makes it difficult to find discriminating variables for the purpose of distinguishing those who will succeed from those who will fail.

The presentation of normative data, profile configurations, and general trends are all interesting data to the scholar and the researcher. A greater urgency is noted in the concerns of parents, students, and clinicians for information that has diagnostic significance and/or differentiating value. Using the experimental sample, which has been shown to be representative of the student body at John Carroll University, a series of comparisons were made for purposes of sharpening the focus on characteristics which distinguish the successful from the unsuccessful students.

The first distinction was made in terms of students who were dismissed for academic reasons as opposed to those who distinguished themselves in academic achievement. Table 41 summarizes the findings on the major variables in this phase of the research.

Since the total assessment was carried on before actual attendance of college classes began, it can be concluded that significant differences were present in the freshman class of 1965 with respect to those students who would be achieving outstanding records as against those who would be dismissed. In both instances, 20% of the sample was found in each category.

Because of the small absolute count for each grouping (nine were found in each designation), statistical significances were difficult to obtain. However, inspectionally it can be readily noted that the outstanding students surpassed the dismissals on every measure of intellectual functioning. The personality variables produced a mixed picture in comparing the two groups. The SSA Motivation Index was distinctly higher in the outstanding group and reached statistical significance.

The surprisingly different rating earned by the dismissals versus the high achievers in terms of the EEG was not expected following the equivocal results that were secured on the Leaders and Failures in previous chapters.

On the MMPI both samples produced profiles that are within the expected range for college males. Both validity and clinical scales clustered between the 50th and 65th T values, and this pattern has been noted in numerous investigations with college populations locally and throughout the country.

TABLE 41

Means and SD's for Dismissed Students and Those Earning
Outstanding Academic Records within the First Two Years of College

Variable	'65 Sample		Dismissed		Outstanding		Sig.
	Mean	SD	Mean	SD	Mean	SD	
GPA	2.42	.62	1.56		3.53		.01
EEG-R	1.79	.91	2.71	.45	1.43	.73	.005
WAIS-V	121.9	8.14	119.3		124.9		
WAIS-P	112.0	9.57	106.71		114.6		
WAIS-FS	119.3	7.58	114.57		121.9		
SAT-V	514.9	79.9	495.3		571.0		
SAT-M	543.0	84.0	485.6		586.7		
Coop. Reading	56.6	22.1	54.4		75.7		
SSA-Mi	79.9	36.8	59.43		107.9		
MMPI-L	46.2	6.5	53.0		44.6		
MMPI-F	51.2	7.1	51.7		49.1		
MMPI-K	54.7	7.8	61.6		57.3		
MMPI-Hs	51.9	8.3	55.4		54.0		
MMPI-D	51.8	12.4	55.3		52.1		
MMPI-Hy	55.2	9.7	59.4		59.3		
MMPI-Pd	60.1	9.7	66.3		59.7		
MMPI-Mf	59.7	9.6	57.4		62.7		
MMPI-Pa	53.4	10.4	52.0		57.1		
MMPI-Pt	58.1	12.8	57.3		61.1		
MMPI-Sc	57.9	12.2	58.6		59.3		
MMPI-Ma	58.8	10.4	55.7		51.0		
MMPI-Si	49.5	11.1	46.9		55.4		
Allport-Th	41.8	7.5	42.4		42.3		
Allport-Ec	38.0	6.9	35.1		33.9		
Allport-Ae	31.3	6.8	37.9		27.4		
Allport-Soc.	41.0	7.7	38.7		45.3		
Allport-Pol.	44.2	7.1	43.1		43.1		
Allport-Rel.	44.3	6.3	43.6		47.3		

The MMPI variables that behaved in the expected manner found the poor
achievers showing higher scores on L, K. Pd, and Ma. The configuration outlined
by this quartet of scales finds the group more inclined to posturing for social
regard, highly animated or activated, and yet resistant to adult direction.
Contemporaneity is likely to loom large in the planning and execution of
programs. On the other hand, the outstanding students scored higher on Mf, Pt,
Pa, and Si. Suggested here is a quartet of scales characterizing the group as
cautious, deliberate, prone to solitary and sedentary activities, anxious about

progress and very likely to engage in much soliloquizing and rehearsing of roles in private. The Vaughn (1965) findings on the outstanding students at the University of San Francisco bear a striking resemblance to this group (see page 106.

The Allport **Study of Values** found the dismissals scoring higher than the scholars on the Ae scale, which is a measure of one's preference for sense impressions, and strikingly lower on the Soc scale, which is indicative of one's preference to relate to and serve people.

Another search was undertaken to ascertain whether any special significance or relationship could be extracted from an oft-stated, but rarely investigated or reported, causal phenomenon. It is not unusual to hear teachers, counselors, and even psychologists retreat into suggestions of probable neurological dysfunctioning when satisfactory explanations cannot be secured from psychometric or clinical procedures. Specifically, in this inquiry the question of what impact does a rating of *abnormal* on the EEG have on academic achievement and the other measures of intellectuality and personality led to an equivocal result.

All records showing abnormality for the three student samples (Leaders, Failures, and Beginners) were divided into two groupings: Those who had graduated from college or who were continuing satisfactorily toward that goal and those who had been dismissed for academic failure. The three samples included 115 males; twenty-one (21) records were judged to be abnormal by two electroencephalographers. The figure of 18% is comparable to statistics cited by Gibbs (114) for adults in this country. Table 42 will summarize the findings on the major variables used in the assessment.

Any inclination to find a "catch-all" explanation, when others fail to suffice, in the unusual brain wave configurations gains little support from this summary. In the first place, 62% of such student records were classified as having graduated or successfully pursuing degree requirements.

In the area of intellectual abilities, all of the differences were less than of statistical significance. In the personality realm, the story is quite different.

The abnormal-failures exceeded the abnormal-successfuls on the MMPI scales of Hs, Hy, Pd, Sc, Ma, and lower on the Allport-Social. The major characterization of the failure sample in this case would be one of great preoccupation with bodily functions, physical conversion states, and agitation. Closely following in a descriptive fashion would be the absence of deep emotional responsivity to peers and authority figures. The abnormal-successfuls follow very closely the configuration that is secured on the Beginner sample that maintained satisfactory progress for two years. Figure 10 in the next chapter points out the distinction in a more dramatic fashion than does Table 45. In all of the MMPI profiles to this point, no group or sub-group had produced clinical scales which exceeded 70. In this instance, the abnormal-failure sample had two: Pd and Ma.

TABLE 42
Means and SD's for GPA, WAIS, Reading, MMPI, and Study of Values Variables for Academically Achieving and Failing Students Who Had Abnormal EEG's

Variable	Successful (N = 13) Mean	SD	Dismissed Failing (N = 8) Mean	SD	Sig.
GPA	2.30	.54	1.49	.28	
WAIS-V	121.6	8.6	117.3	8.8	
WAIS-P	111.3	9.1	108.8	6.5	
WAIS-FS	118.5	8.5	114.3	5.6	
Coop. Reading	45.6	7.3	51.2	6.3	
MMPI-L	44.6	6.7	46.5	5.1	
MMPI-F	53.4	5.2	54.8	3.5	
MMPI-K	54.7	3.7	57.2	3.4	
MMPI-Hs	47.8	5.7	52.5	1.7	.05
MMPI-D	48.3	9.2	52.3	2.9	
MMPI-Hy	53.4	2.7	59.7	3.4	.05
MMPI-Pd	52.5	6.9	71.3	5.5	.001
MMPI-Mf	64.1	11.97	56.5	5.8	
MMPI-Pa	52.2	6.6	57.0	10.7	
MMPI-Pt	55.8	9.3	61.0	5.5	
MMPI-Sc	54.8	14.2	64.5	5.2	.05
MMPI-Ma	58.1	15.9	74.0	11.4	.05
MMPI-Si	49.3	10.8	47.0	11.5	
Allport-Th	39.8	7.9	38.0	2.6	
Allport-Ec	37.2	9.3	44.0	11.1	
Allport-Ae	34.2	5.9	37.5	6.9	
Allport-Soc.	39.6	8.2	32.3	1.7	.05
Allport-Pol.	45.7	3.1	45.8	3.8	
Allport-Rel.	42.8	6.5	40.5	4.8	

When the Normal-EEG dismissed group was compared with the Abnormal EEG-dismissed group, the following differences were noted:

1. Twenty-five percent (25%) of the total student group having normal EEG's were dismissed from studies; 38% of the abnormal EEG's were dismissed for poor scholastic achievement.
2. In terms of intellectual abilities, both groups were drawn from the same population of abilities.

3. With reference to personality variables, the abnormal-EEG group was significantly higher on MMPI-Pd, Ma. The constancy with which the Pd and Ma scales distinguished the successful from the failing students suggests that the thrust or overactivity of the poor student may, in part, be related to provocations which are physical as well as psychological.

In Table 42 the subdued or depressed scores for the abnormal EEG-success group are conspicuous. In every case this sample showed greater restraint, passivity, or moderation. The abnormal EEG dismissed group and normal EEG dismissed group had more common features than did the abnormal EEG success group. Comparable profiles do not necessarily derive from common antecedents, but must be interpreted in terms of contemporaneous functioning, when etiology is vague or missing. The caution cannot be overemphasized that "organicity," which is a favorite refuge for diagnosticians, is not diagnostically specific as it relates to academic achievement, intellectual abilities, and personality traits.

CHAPTER 10

Some Portraits and Last Thoughts

No attempt will be made to summarize the findings of results reported in the previous three chapters because they are deemed to be summaries of studies conducted in many settings.

Recourse to profiling was made in order to sharpen the focus of the statistical findings that were presented in tables throughout the book.

INTELLECTUALITY

The distribution of subtest scores on the Wechsler Adult Intelligence Scale in Figure 6 supports the conclusion that a considerable degree of homogeneity was found in the three samples of males studied in these investigations. The mean scores for each surpassed the 90th percentile of their age peers, thereby representing a fairly high selective group. The downward range of scores placed the poorest performer at the 70th percentile for his age group.

Figure 7, using college students in liberal arts colleges as the norm group, again finds the three samples exceeding the typical student samples in such settings. No case can be made for any special inter-sample differences to account for the three statuses that were descriptive of the students.

Relatively little attention has been devoted to the possibility that low correlations between tests of ability on the one hand and grade point averages on the other *may be due to uncontrolled sources of variation in grades themselves.* Although the problem has been discussed, it has not been investigated systematically. (Lavin, 204)

The relationship between ability and academic performance has been well documented, and the majority of studies are no longer concerned primarily with showing this finding. Rather, they attempt to improve predictions through the use of additional factors of a non-intellectual nature. In this type of research it is important to ensure that non-intellectual variables are independent of ability. The present investigation did not find independence between such variables but did find low correlations to be the characteristic relationship.

TABLE OF SCALED SCORE EQUIVALENTS*

Scaled Score	Information	Comprehension	Arithmetic	Similarities	Digit Span	Vocabulary	Digit Symbol	Picture Completion	Block Design	Picture Arrangement	Object Assembly	Scaled Score
19	29	27-28		26	17	78-80	87-90					19
18	28	26		25		76-77	83-86	21		36		18

STUDENT LEADERS

Scaled Score	Information	Comprehension	Arithmetic	Similarities	Digit Span	Vocabulary	Digit Symbol	Picture Completion	Block Design	Picture Arrangement	Object Assembly	Scaled Score
17	27	25	18	24		74-75	79-82		48	35	43	17
16	26	24	17	23	16	71-73	76-78	20	47	34	42	16
15	25	23	16	22	15	67-70	72-75		46	33	41	15
14	23-24	22	15	21	14	63-66	69-71	19	44-45	32	40	14
13	21-22	21	14	19-20		59-62	66-68	18	42-43	30-31	38-39	13
12	19-20	20	13	17-18	13	54-58	62-65	17	39-41	28-29	36-37	12
11	17-18	19	12	15-16	12	47-53	58-61	15-16	35-38	26-27	34-35	11
10	15-16	17-18	11	13-14	11	40-46	52-57	14	31-34	23-25	31-33	10

STUDENT FAILURES

Scaled Score	Information	Comprehension	Arithmetic	Similarities	Digit Span	Vocabulary	Digit Symbol	Picture Completion	Block Design	Picture Arrangement	Object Assembly	Scaled Score
17	27	25	18	24		74-75	79-82		48	35	43	17
16	26	24	17	23	16	71-73	76-78	20	47	34	42	16
15	25	23	16	22	15	67-70	72-75		46	33	41	15
14	23-24	22	15	21	14	63-66	69-71	19	44-45	32	40	14
13	21-22	21	14	19-20		59-62	66-68	18	42-43	30-31	38-39	13
12	19-20	20	13	17-18	13	54-58	62-65	17	39-41	28-29	36-37	12
11	17-18	19	12	15-16	12	47-53	58-61	15-16	35-38	26-27	34-35	11
10	15-16	17-18	11	13-14	11	40-46	52-57	14	31-34	23-25	31-33	10

STUDENT BEGINNERS

Scaled Score	Information	Comprehension	Arithmetic	Similarities	Digit Span	Vocabulary	Digit Symbol	Picture Completion	Block Design	Picture Arrangement	Object Assembly	Scaled Score
15	25	23	16	22	15	67-70	72-75		46	33	41	15
14	23-24	22	15	21	14	63-66	69-71	19	44-45	32	40	14
13	21-22	21	14	19-20		59-62	66-68	18	42-43	30-31	38-39	13
12	19-20	20	13	17-18	13	54-58	62-65	17	39-41	28-29	36-37	12
11	17-18	19	12	15-16	12	47-53	58-61	15-16	35-38	26-27	34-35	11
10	15-16	17-18	11	13-14	11	40-46	52-57	14	31-34	23-25	31-33	10

Scaled Score	Information	Comprehension	Arithmetic	Similarities	Digit Span	Vocabulary	Digit Symbol	Picture Completion	Block Design	Picture Arrangement	Object Assembly	Scaled Score
2	2	4	2	1	6	9	13-14	2	3-5	6	5-7	2
1	1	3	1		4-5	8	12	1	2	5	3-4	1
0	0	0-2	0	0	0-3	0-7	0-11		0-1	0-4	0-2	0

Figure 6. Distribution of WAIS Subtest Scores for Student Leaders, Failures, and Beginners.

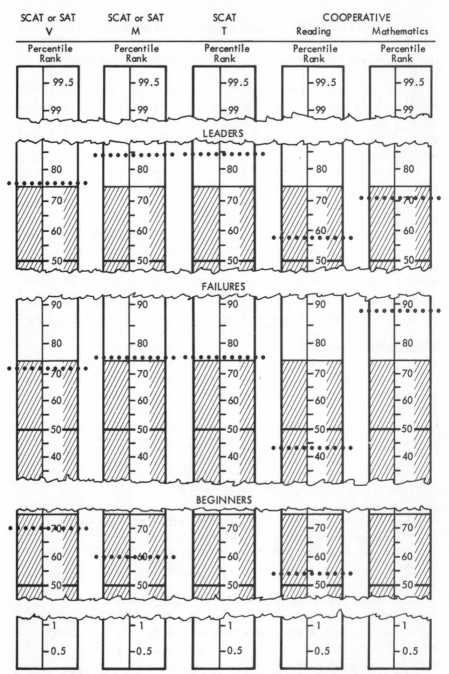

Figure 7. Distribution of Scores on Scholastic Aptitude Tests for Student Leaders, Failures, and Beginners.

Lavin's (204) extensive review of the problem of achievement and various measures of human functioning reported that three factors emerge as basic correlates of academic performance. These are ability, sex, and socioeconomic status (SES).

Brim (1965), reporting on studies at the college level, found that students with high self-estimates of intelligence had higher grade point averages than students with equal measured intelligence, but lower self-estimates of intelligence. A case for revealing to the candidate his ability scores is readily supported.

While standardized testing has come a long way both in technical proficiency and in usefulness, we have, as yet, to use the words of Robert Faris, "heard only the opening bars of the overture in the present opera on the nature and destiny of man's genius." (Faris, 1961)

The shortcomings of a standardized intelligence and other ability tests in predicting performances over long periods of time and in other than academic situations intimate that usefulness of an ability construct, at least when projected onto an increasingly fluid behavioral field, may be limited primarily to distinguishing between extremes. (Lavin, 204)

The concept of ability is still a hypothetical construct and before we go about investing any such concept with the sole responsibility for allocation of human beings to jobs and statuses with the society, we need to be sure we have described it in such a way as to maximize its usefulness.

The frequently heard maxim that is attributed to Terman for his work on gifted children, viz., that the "laws of nature are correlative, not compensatory" lulled many to sleep in working with bright young people who have been found to be casualties of various kinds, academic and societal, as well as a large number of bright people who remain undiscovered or unchallenged.

PERSONALITY

Figure 8 presents the distribution of scores for the three student samples. The major variations from a singular style were the mean scores for the Failure sample on the Economic and Religious scales. In the first case, the Failure sample was higher in valuing the economic posture more highly and devaluing the religous scale.

Despite fairly high tested abilities as found in figures 6 and 7, the absence of a "creativity" profile is striking when compared with the scores earned by three highly creative groups as reported in Table 43. The elevation of two scales, viz., theoretical and aesthetic are, in sharp distinction from those found on undergraduate males, irrespective of their academic prowess.

TABLE 43

Mean Scores on Six Values for Architects, Research
Scientists, and Women Mathematicians on the Allport-
Vernon-Lindzey Study of Values Test.

Group	Th.	EC	Ae	Soc.	Pol.	Rel.
Architects	50.8	28.4	56.2	29.8	40.0	34.8
Research Sc.	57.0	36.3	47.5	29.1	41.9	28.1
W. Math	52.9	25.7	54.7	37.3	36.3	30.7

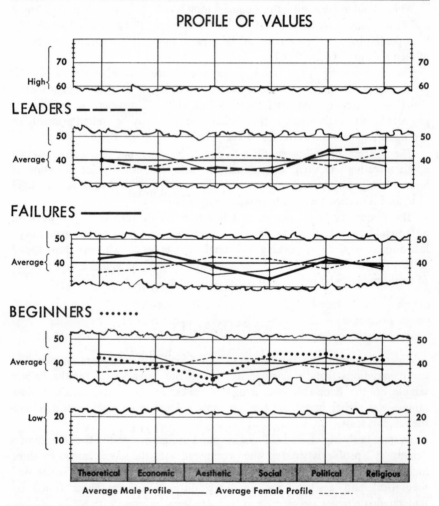

Figure 8. Distribution of Scores on Allport-Vernon-Lindzey Study of Values for Leaders,
Failures and Beginners.

The frequently repeated statement that most college men are pursuing studies primarily for vocational or economic gain rather than intellectual purposes is not supported by the evidence cited herein. On the other hand, the distinction between academic (grades) goals as distinguished from intellectual (self-development goals) cannot be judged to emerge from the data.

Figure 9 compels the conclusion that the three samples of college males used in these investigations were more alike than different insofar as personalities described. Upon closer scrutiny the distinctions between the successful students and those experiencing academic difficulties are found in scales F, D, Pd, Mf, Pt, Sc. Descriptively, the failure group tended to be more independent (obstinate) in holding to its convictions, more inclined to worry and depression, less disposed to be subject to adult authority, and more activated in conduct.

McClelland and associates (1965) reported that of 9 college studies, 4 were found to have positive correlations between achievement motivation and academic performance. All nine controlled for ability. For one sample of male students the correlation between grades and achievement motivation, as measured by the TAT, was .39. This is strikingly similar to the .37 found between the Mi index based on TAT cards and GPA for the beginning studies in the present investigation.

The findings of Travers (1965) and Bloomers (1965), which found that small positive relations have been found between the degree of introversion and academic success were not supported, in the present instance.

The literature on the MMPI is increasingly reporting that males with high points on the Mf scale have better records of achievement than would be expected from a random sample at the University of Florida and University of Wisconsin (Barger and Hall, 1964) and (Drake and Oetting, 76). High points on the Pd and Ma scales are not only predictive of poorer academic achievement and higher dropout rates than would be expected on the average, but also indicative of the fact that ability scores will be somewhat less predictive of grade point averages than are other high points. High scores on either the Pd or Ma scale, especially when both scales have high ranks in the profile, are often indicative of nonconformity, rebelliousness, and high activity level. These traits are not conducive to high achievement in most academic setting. (Dahlstrom and Welsh, 62)

ELECTROENCEPHALOGRAPHY

The consistently low positive correlations between measures of ability and EEG ratings have been reported in the previous three chapters. The inconsistency of correlations between personality variables and the EEG ratings preclude any easy generalizations especially when investigations are conducted on bright young men.

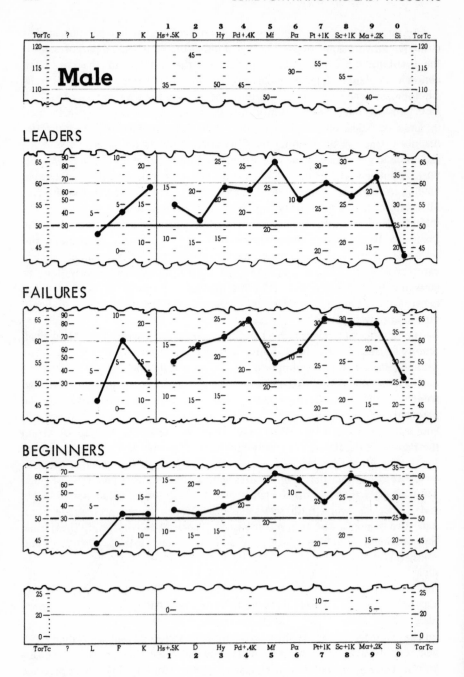

Figure 9. Distribution of Scores on the MMPI for Leaders, Failures, and Beginners.

One special combination of variables was set up to establish relationships of configurations between personality variables and EEG ratings. Figure 10 reports the distribution of MMPI values for three sub-groups of males: (1) those having abnormal EEG's who were dropped from studies, (2) those having abnormal EEG's who were continuing in studies, and (3) those males who had normal EEG's and were dropped from studies.

The abnormal EEG group which was handling academic studies in a successful manner had an MMPI profile that was indistinguishable from the normal EEG group that was in good standing. Both abnormal EEG-failing group and the normal EEG-failing group had elevations on the Pd, Pt, Sc, and Ma scales that have become widely associated with poor academic achievement, as well as lower Mf scores that are frequently associated with poor academic motivation. The interesting distinction is the exaggeration of the two scales, Pd and Ma, that are found for the abnormal EEG failing sample.

What can be concluded from widespread efforts of many investigators to explain what factors are important for academic progress? The compelling conclusion that the best combination of predictors for academic achievement (a narrow criterion of what occurs in a four-year college experience) forces the serious investigator to admit that more of the variance is unaccounted for than is known about the explanatory conditions. In other words, try as we may, repeatedly the lawful explanations of student achievement eludes the scientist. This condition may derive in part from the models that are proposed to explain man. Instead of man being viewed as erratic and sometimes inscrutable, it may well be that the theories or models are insufficient or too simplistic. Cattell (48) maintains that the theory should mirror nature, not nature mirror the theory, and Murphy (1967) cautioned against becoming enamored of numerology and quantification that result in the dehumanizing of the individual.

In a thoughtful treatment of the two major strategies in personality measurement, which are polarized by the trait-factor and clinical positions, Tomkins (364) examined the argument of whether a human being is the most real and valuable entity in nature, an end in himself—or whether that which is most real and valuable is some norm, some ideal essence quite independent of the human being.

The polarities are recognized in most fields of scholarly inquiry. In philosophy it is, on the one hand, the extreme idealistic posture which holds that the world is created by man, and, on the other hand, the extreme Platonic view that neither the world nor man is real or valuable, but that there exists an ideal set of essences, of which the world and man are imitations. In the humanistic view it is what the individual wants that defines what is good, true, and beautiful. In the normative view the individual must struggle to attain value and reality by conforming to the ideal norm. These two postures generate socializations which stress either that the child is an end in himself, that he is

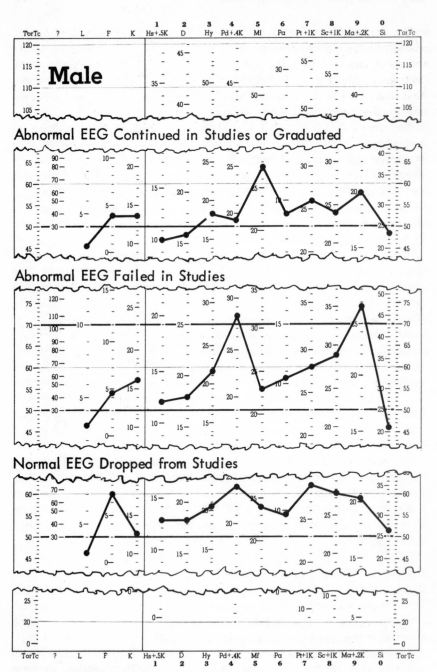

Figure 10. Distribution of MMPI Scores for Students with Abnormal EEG's versus Normal
EEG Failing Students.

loved for what he is, or which say that if he wishes to grow up to be a good human being he must conform to a norm administered by parents, whether he feels like it or not.

In theories of government there is a polarity between theories of the state as the major instrument through which men attain such limited freedom as is possible, versus theories of the state as of the people, for the people, and by the people.

In theories of education a recurrent polarity, now intensified, between education as the learning of information versus a stimulation of the potential of the individual is visible. In theories of perception in psychology we see this polarity between those who would account for perception by an analysis of the stimulus, against those who regard the percept as a personal construct. Within the Rorschach group we are confronted with the insistence on norms by Beck, and the more free-wheeling cognition of Klopfer.

Those who have insisted on the objective, whether in science or in art, have derogated man and insisted on certainty. Those who have insisted on the subjective have glorified man and stressed the value of both play and risk. It is our conviction that the humanistic ideology, in the long run, will yield both the greater and surer payoff. (Tomkins, 364).

A jest—"You don't really understand a subject until you're confused"— characterized the thinking of the investigator upon completion of the specific studies on Student Leaders, Failures, and Beginners. The more difficult task of telescoping and integrating the information into the larger fabric of college males in the United States in the middle of the Twentieth Century did not completely erase the doubts nor the confusion.

Searching for definitive clues on how to describe, interpret, and possibly counsel the college male forced the writer to collect data from diverse sources that typically are not presented to counselors for purposes of carrying out their assignments. Each excursion into the literature led the investigator to explore far beyond his initial expectations. The myth of a "college man" is quickly disposed of by any review of the current scene. Consequently, the task that confronts the educator, the professional practitioneer, and the public is more formidable than is frequently acknowledged when problems arise in that sector of the educational ladder.

REFERENCES

1. Abe, C., Holland, J.L., Lutz, S.W., & Richards, J.M. Jr., "A Description of American College Freshmen," in *ACT Research Reports, No. 1,* American College Testing Program, 62 pp., March, 1965.
2. Adelson, Joseph, "The Teacher as a Model," in Sanford, Nevitt, *The American College,* John Wiley and Sons, Inc., New York, 1962.
3. Allport, G.W., and Vernon, P.E., *A Study of Values,* Houghton, Mifflin, Boston, 1931.
4. American Council on Education, *Higher Education and National Affairs,* Washington, Vol. XVI, No. 40, December 15, 1967.
5. Anastasi, Anne, Ed., *Testing Problems in Perspective,* American Council on Education, Washington, D.C., 1966.
6. Anderson, W., "The MMPI: Low Pa Scores," in *J. Counsel. Psychol.,* No. 3, pp. 226-228, 1956.
7. Arnold, Magda B., *Story Sequence Analysis,* Columbia University Press, New York, 1962.
8. Astin, A.W., "The Functional Autonomy of Psychotherapy," in *Amer. Psychologists,* No. 16, pp. 75-79, 1961.
8a. Baldwin, A.L., *Theories of Child Development,* N.Y., John Wiley & Sons, Inc., 1967.
9. Balinsky, Benjamin, and Wescott, H. Shaw, "The Contribution of the WAIS to a Management Appraisal Program," in *Personnel Psychology,* No. 9, pp. 207-209, 1956.
10. Bandura, A., "Psychotherapy As a Learning Process," in *Psychol. Bull.,* No. 58, pp. 143-157, 1961.
11. Bass, Bernard, *Leadership, Psychology, and Organizational Behavior,* Harper and Brothers, New York, 1960.
12. Batt, H.V., "An Investigation of the Significance of the Rorschach Z Score," in Rickers-Ovsiankina, M.A., *Rorschach Psychology,* John Wiley, New York, 1960.
13. Bay, Christian, "A Social Theory of Higher Education," in Sanford, Nevitt, Ed., *The American College,* John Wiley & Sons, Inc., 1962.
14. Bayley, Nancy, in Buros, Oscar, *The Fifth Mental Measurement Yearbook,* p. 414, Gryphon Press, Highland Park, 1959.
15. Bayley, Nancy, "A New Look at the Curve of Intelligence," in Anastasi, Anne, Ed., *Testing Problems in Perspective,* pp. 384-405, American Council on Education, Washington, D.C., 1966.
16. Beck, Carlton E., Ph.D., *Philosophical Foundations of Guidance,* Prentice-Hall, Inc., Englewood Cliffs, N.J., 1965.
17. Beck, S.J., *Rorschach's Test, Volume I. Basic Processes,* Grune and Stratton, New York, 1950.
18. Beer, Michael; Buckhout, Robert; Horowitz, Milton W.; Levy, Seymour, "Some Perceived Properties of the Difference Between Leaders and Non-Leaders," in *Journal of Psychology,* No. 47, pp. 49-56, 1959.

19. Behring, Daniel W., "Predicting College Achievement with an Activities-Preference Inventory," in *Proceedings of the 73rd Annual Convention of the American Psychological Association–1965,* pp. 345-346, American Psychological Association, Inc., Washington, D.C., 1965.

20. Bier, Ernst G., "A Clinician Looks at Creativity," in *Proceedings of the 73rd Annual Convention of the American Psychological Association– 1965,* pp. 189-190, American Psychological Association, Inc., Washington, D.C., 1965.

21. Berdie, Ralph F., "Student Ambivalence and Behavior," in Dennis, Lawrence E. and Kauffman, Joseph F., *The College and the Student,* American Council on Education, Washington, D.C., 1966.

22. Berdie, Ralph, "Aptitude, Achievement, Interest, and Personality Tests: A Longitudinal Comparison," in *J. of Applied Psychol.,* vol. 39, pp. 103-114, 1955.

23. Bereiter, C., and Freedman, M.B., "Personality Differences Among College Curricular Groups," in *American Psychol.,* No. 15, p. 435, 1960.

24. Bereiter, C. and Freedmen, M.B., "Fields of Study and the People in Them," in Sanford, Nevitt, *The American College,* John Wiley and Sons, Inc., New York, 1962.

25. Bienen, S.; Bott, M.M.; Leventhal, A.M.; Magoon, T.M.; McKenzie, J.; Pavey, S.; 7 Ray, P.B., "Inter-Judge Agreement on the Use of Counseling Categories," in *The Journal of College Student Personnel,* No. 7 (July), pp. 213-217, 1966.

26. Bier, William C., "A Comparative Study of Five Catholic College Groups on the MMPI," in Welsh, G.S., and Dahlstrom, W.G., *Basic Readings on the MMPI in Psychology and Medicine,* University Minn. Press, Minneapolis, pp. 586-609, 1956.

27. Bijou, Sidney W., "Implications of Behavioral Science for Counseling and Guidance," in Krumboltz, John, Ed., *Revolution in Counseling: Implications of Behavioral Science,* 1966.

28. Black, Milton, *The Teacher and Student Action Movements,* Paper read at California Conference on Higher Education, Los Angeles, May, 1966.

29. Blaine, Graham B., Jr., "College Students and Moral Values," in Dennis, Lawrence E., and Kauffman, Joseph F., *The College and the Student,* American Council on Education, Washington, D.C., 1966.

30. Blocher, Donald H., *Developmental Counseling,* The Ronald Press Company, New York, 1966.

31. Bolton, C.D. and Kammeyer, *The University Student,* New Haven, College and University Press, 1967.

32. Brewster, Kingman, Jr., "New Responsibilities for an Old Generation," in Dennis, Lawrence E. and Kauffman, Joseph F., *The College and the Student,* American Council on Education, Washington, D.C., 1966.

33. Brink, R. Alexander, Ed.. *Heritage From Mendel,* The University of Wisconsin Press, Madison, 1967.

34. Britt, Laurence V., "Some Concepts of Student Academic Freedom," in Dennis, Lawrence E., and Kauffman, Joseph F., *The College and the Student,* American Council on Education, Washington, D.C., 1966.

35. Brower, D., "The Relation Between Intelligence and MMPI Scores," in *J. Social Psychology.,* No. 25, pp. 243-245, 1947.

36. Brown, David, "Personality, College Environments, and Academic Productivity," in Sanford, Nevitt, *The American College,* John Wiley and Sons, Inc., New York, 1962.

37. Brown, H.S., "Similarities and Differences in College Populations on the Multiphasic," in *J. Appl. Psychol.,* No. 32, pp. 541-549, 1948.

38. Bruner, Jerome S., Oliver, Rose R., and Greenfield, Patricia M., *Studies in Cognitive Growth,* John Wiley and Sons, Inc., N.Y., 1966.

39. Buber, Martin, *Between Man and Man,* Beacon Press, Boston, 1955.

40. Burgess, Elva, op. cit., Clark, Selby G., "The Rorschach and Academic Achievement," in *Personnel and Guidance Journal,* Vol. 36, pp. 339-341, 1958.

41. Burkhardt, Frederick H., "The Changing Role of the Professor," in Dennis, Lawrence E. and Kauffman, Joseph F., *The College and the Student,* American Council on Education, Washington, D.C., 1966.

42. Burks, F.W., "Some Factors Related to Social Successes in College," in *Journal of Social Psychology,* No. 9, pp. 125-140, 1938.

43. Burnham, Paul S., "Prediction and Performance," in *From High School to College: Readings for Counselors,* College Entrance Examination Board, New York, 1964.

44. Caplow, T., and McGee, R.J. *The Academic Marketplace,* Basic Books, New York, 1958.

45. Carnegie Corporation of New York, *Quarterly,* Volume IX, No. 3, July, pp. 1-8, 1961.

46. Caskey, O.L., "Freshman Drop-outs and Returnees, Part I, a Descriptive Study," in *University Counseling Services Research* Report, No. 364, 1964.

47. Cattell, J. McKeen, and Farrand, L., "Physical and Mental Measurements of the Students of Columbia University," in *Psychol. Rev.,* No. 3 (6) pp. 618-648, 1896.

48. Cattell, Raymond B., Ed., *Handbook of Multivariate Experimental Psychology,* Rand NcNally & Company, Chicago, 1966.

49. Chickering, Arthur, W., *Institutional Differences and Student Characteristics,* Paper read at American College Health Association, San Diego, May, 1966.

50. Churchill, Ruth, *Problems of Selection at a Small, Selective College,* Paper read at Association for Institutional Research, Boston, May, 1966.

51. Clark, Jerry H., "The Interpretation of the MMPI Profiles of College Students: A Comparison by College Major Subject," in *J. of Clin. Psych.,* Vol. 9, pp. 382-384, 1953.

52. Clark, K.E., "The Mountain's Mouse," in *Cont. Psychology,* pp. 72-73, March, 1960.

53. Cobb, Catherine, "Measuring Leadership in College Women by Free Association," in *Journal of Abnormal and Social Psychology,* No. 47, pp. 126-128, 1952.

54. Cogley, John, *Universe Bulletin,* Cleveland, August 18, 1967.

55. Cohen, Jacob, "The Impact of Multivariate Research in Clinical Psychology," in Cattell, Raymond B., Ed., *Handbook of Multivariate Experimental Psychology,* pp. 856-877, Rand McNally & Company, Chicago, 1966.

56. Committee on the College Student of the Group for the Advancement of Psychiatry, *Considerations on Personality Development in College Students,* Report No. 32, N.Y., May, 1955.

57. Connors, G. Keith, "Effects of Brief Psychotherapy, Drugs, and Type of Disturbance on Holtzman Inkblot Scores in Children," in *Proceedings of the 73rd Annual Convention of the American Psychological Association* −1965, pp. 201-202, American Psychological Association, Inc., Washington, D.C., 1965.

58. Coombs, R.H., & Davies, V., "Self-Conception and the Relationship Between High School and College Scholastic Achievement," in *Sociology and Social Research,* No. 50 (July) pp. 460-469, 1966.

59. Counseling and Guidance Center, *"The Relationship of Selected Factors to College Success,* Unpublished Report, John Carroll University, 1961.

60. Crawford, A.B., "Forecasting Freshman Achievement," in *Sch. & Soc.,* No. 31, pp. 125-132, 1930.

61. Crawford, A.B., and Burnham, P.S., *Forecasting College Achievement,* Yale Univ. Press, New Haven, 1946.

62. Dahlstrom, W.G., & Welsh, G.S., *An MMPI Handbook,* Univ. of Minn. Press, Minneapolis, 1960. (Appendix L: Intercorrelations among the basic scales.)

63. Dale, Edgar, "The Tangible Task," in *The News Letter,* Vol. XXXXII, No. 7, School of Education, Ohio State Univ., Columbus, April, 1967.

64. Dale, Edgar, "Why Aren't We Smarter?", *The News Letter,* Vol. XXXI, No. 6, School of Education, Ohio State University, Columbus, March, 1966.

65. Dale, Edgar, "Creating the Future," in *The News Letter,* Vol. XXXII, No. 8, School of Education, Ohio State University, Columbus, May, 1967.

66. Davis, H., and Davis, P.A., "The Human Electroencephalogram in Health and in Certain Mental Disorders," in *J. Nerv. & Ment. Dis.,* No. 85, p. 463, 1937.

67. Davis, Junius A., "Nonintellectual Factors in College Student Achievement," in *From High School to College: Readings for Counselors,* College Entrance Examination Board, Teachers College, Columbia University, New York, 1964.
68. DeMartino, H.A., "The Wechsler-Bellevue Intelligence Scale as a Predictor of Success in a College of Engineering," *Michigan Academy of Science,* No. 39, pp. 459-465, cited by Wechsler (111), 1954.
69. de Tocqueville, A., *Democracy in America,* 4 vols., Saunders and Ottey, London, 1840.
70. Dixon, James P., "The Student's Role in Educational Policy," in Dennis, Lawrence E. and Kauffman Joseph F., *The College and the Student,* American Council on Education, Washington, D.C., 1966.
71. Dizney, H.F., & Yamamoto, K., "Eight Professors—A Study on College Students' Preferences Among their Teachers," in *Journal of Educational Psychology,* No. 57 (June), pp. 146-150, 1966.
72. Dollard, J., & Miller, N.E., *Personality and Psychotherapy,* c 1950. Used by permission of McGraw-Hill Book Company.
73. Douvan, Elizabeth, "Character Processes in Adolescence," (Paper presented at American Psychological Association) August, 1957.
74. Douvan, Elizabeth, "Independence and Identity in Adolescents," in *Children,* No. 4, pp. 186-190, 1957.
75. Douvan, Elizabeth, and Kaye, Carol, "Motivational Factors in College Entrance," in Sanford, Nevitt, Ed., *The American College,* John Wiley and Sons, Inc., New York, 1962.
76. Drake, L.E., and E.R. Oetting, *An MMPI Codebook for Counselors,* Univ. of Minn. Press, Minneapolis, 1959.
77. Drake, L.E., Oetting, E.R., "An MMPI Pattern and a Suppressor Variable Predictive of Academic Achievement," in *J. Counsel. Psychol.,* No. 4, pp. 245-247, 1957.
78. Dunteman, George H.; Anderson, Harry E., Jr.; Barry, John R., *Characteristics of Students in the Health Related Professions,* University of Florida, Gainesville, Fla., No. 2, June, 1966.
79. Durflinger, G.W., "The Prediction of College Success: A Summary of Recent Findings," in *J. Amer. Assn. Col. Reg.,* No. 19, pp. 68-78, 1943.
80. Eddy, Edward D., Jr., "Some Suggestions for Student Involvement in Educational Policy," in Dennis, Lawrence E. and Kauffman, Joseph F., *The College and the Student,* American Council on Education, Washington, D.C., 1966.
81. Eddy, Edward D., Jr., *The College Influence on Student Character,* American Council on Education, Washington, D.C., 1959.
82. Ellingson, R.J., "Brain Waves and Problems in Psychology," in *Psych. Bull.,* Vol. 53, No. 1, pp. 1-34, 1956.
83. Ellingson, R.J., "Relationship between EEG and Intelligence: a Commentary," *Psychol. Bulletin,* 65: pp. 91-98, 1966.
84. Erikson, E.H., *Childhood and Society,* Norton, N.Y., 1950.
85. Eurich, A., "College Failures," in *Sch. & Soc.,* No. 37, pp. 692-696, 1933.
86. Ewing, T.N., & Gilbert, W.M., *Using Programmed Materials in a College Counseling Service,* Paper read at American Personnel and Guidance Assoc., Washington, D.C., April, 1966.
87. Eysenck, H.J., "The Effects of Psychotherapy: An Evaluation," in *J. Consult. Psychol.,* No. 16, pp. 319-324, 1952.
88. Eysenck, H.J., (Ed.) *Behaviour Therapy and The Neuroses,* Pergamon Press, New York, 1960.
89. Farnsworth, D.L., *Mental Health in College and University,* Harvard Univ. Press, Cambridge, 1957.
90. Farnsworth, D.L., "Problems of the College Student in Terms of Human Development and Motivation," in *JEA Workshop,* No. 9, Denver, July, 1965.
91. Farnsworth, D.S., "Some Non-Academic Causes of Success and Failure in College Students," in *Coll. Admissions,* No. 2, pp. 72-78, 1955.

92. Finan, John L., "Perspectives on Theory from a Refrigerator," in *GW*, The George Washington University Press, Washington, D.C., Vol. Three, Number Four, pp. 11-14, Winter, 1967.

93. Fink, Stephen, and Schontz, Franklin C., "Inference on Intellectual Efficiency from WAIS Vocabulary Subtest," in *J. Clin. Psych.*, No. 14, pp. 409-412, October, 1958.

94. Fisher, Gary M., "A Corrected Table for Determining the Significance of the Differences Between Verbal and Performance IQ's on the WAIS and the Wechsler-Bellevue," in *J. Clin, Psych.* No. 16, pp. 6-8, January, 1960.

95. Fishman, J.A., "Unsolved Criterion Problems in the Selection of College Students," in *Harvard Educ. Rev.*, No. 28, pp. 340-349, 1958.

96. Fishman, J.A., "Some Social-Psychological Theories for Selecting and Guiding College Students," in Sanford, Nevitt, *The American College*, John Wiley & Sons, Inc., N.Y., 1952.

97. Fishman, J.A., and Pasanella, A.K., "College Admission-Selections Studies," in *Rev. Educ. Research*, No. 30, pp. 298-310, 1960.

98. Fonda, C.P., "The White Space Response," in Rickers-Ovsiankina, M.A., *Rorschach Psychology*, John Wiley, pp. 80-105, New York, 1960.

99. Frank, Alan, "Patterns of Student Stress," in Dennis, Lawrence E., and Kauffman, Joseph F., *The College and the Student*, American Council on Education, Washington, D.C., 1966.

100. Frankel, Charles, "Rights and Responsibilities in the Student-College Relationship," in Dennis, Lawrence E. and Kauffman, Joseph F., *The College and the Student*, American Council on Education, Washington, D.C., 1966.

101. Frankl, Viktor, *The Doctor and the Soul: An Introduction to Logotherapy*, Alfred A. Knopf, Inc., New York, 1955.

102. Freedman, Mervin B., "Personality Growth in the College Years," in *From High School to College: Readings for Counselors*, College Entrance Examination Board, Teachers College, Columbia University, New York, 1964.

103. Freedman, M.B., *The College Experience*, Jossey-Bass, Inc., San Francisco, 1967.

104. Fricke, B.G., "Response Bias (B) Scale for the MMPI," in *J. Counsel. Psychol.*, No. 4, pp. 145-153, 1957.

105. Fricke, B.G., "Response Set as a Suppressor Variable in the OAIS and MMPI," in *J. Consult. Psychol.*, No. 20, pp. 161-169, 1956.

106. Gaito, John and Zavala, Albert, "Neurochemistry and Learning," in Helson, Harry, Ed., *Psychological Bulletin*, Vol. 61, No. 1, pp. 45-57, American Psychological Association, Washington, D.C., January, 1964.

107. Gallagher, Buell G., "The Vanguard of the Dysphoric Generation," in Dennis, Lawrence E. and Kauffman, Joseph F., *The College and the Student*, American Council on Education, Washington, D.C., 1966.

108. Gallagher, R.J., Gibbs, E.L., and Gibbs, F.A., "Relation Between Electric Activity of Cortex and Personality in Adolescent Boys," in *Psychom. Med.*, No. 4, pp. 134-139, 1942.

109. Gardiner, J., "Pursuit of Excellence," *(Special Studies Project, Report V)*, Carnegie Corporation of New York, 1958.

110. Gardner, John, "Each Man's Right to Grow," *Plain Dealer*, Cleveland, April 17, 1967.

111. Gastaut, Y., and Aird, R.B., "Occipital and Posterior Electroencephalographic Rhythms," in *EEF Clin. Neurophysiol.*, No. 11, pp. 637-656, 1959.

112. Gerth, D.R., & Jones, R.G., *Gamesmanship vs. Scholarship*, Paper read at California Conference on Higher Education, Los Angeles, May, 1966.

113. Gibbs, F.A., and Knott, John R., "Growth of the Electrical Activity of the Cortex," in *EEG Clin. Neurophysiol.*, No. 1, pp. 223-230, 1949.

114. Gibbs, F.A., and Gibbs, E.L., *Atlas of Electroencephalography*, Vol. I, 2nd. Ed., Reading, Addison-Wesley Publishing, 1951.

115. Gibson, Ben W., "Why Not Give Them Their Odds?", in *College Board Review*, No. 63, Spring, 1967.

116. Gilmer, B.H., "Industrial Psychology," in *Review of Psychology*, No. 11, pp. 323-350, 1960.
117. Glaser, Gilbert H., M.D., *EEG & Behavior*, Basic Books, Inc., New York, 1963.
118. Glaser, G.H., "The Normal Electroencephalogram and Its Reactivity," in Glaser, Gilbert H., *EEG & Behavior*, Basic Books, Inc., New York, 1963.
119. Glasser, William, *Reality Therapy*, N.Y., Harper-Row Company, 1965.
120. Goetz, Walter, and Leach, Donald, "The Disappearing Student," in *The Personnel and Guidance Journal*, Vol. 45, No. 9, pp. 883-887, American Personnel and Guidance Assoc., Washington, D.C., May, 1967.
121. Goldberger, L., "Individual Differences in the Effects of Perceptual Isolation," in Rickers-Ovsiankina, M.A., *Rorschach Psychology*, John Wiley & Sons, Inc., New York, 1960.
122. Goldman, Leo, "Construction of a Student Leadership Rating Scale," in *Personnel and Guidance Journal*, No. 36, pp. 87-94, 1957.
123. Goldsen, Rose K., "High Hopes and Campus Realities," in Dennis, Lawrence E. and Kauffman, Joseph F., *The College and the Student*, American Council on Education, Washington, D.C., 1966.
124. Goldsen, R.K., Rosenberg, M., Williams, R.M., Jr., and Suchman, E.A., *What College Students Think*, Van Nostrand, Princeton, New Jersey, 1960.
125. Goldsen, R.K., "Recent Research on the American College Student: 2," in Brown, Nicholas C., Editor, *Orientation to College Learning*, American Council on Education, Washington, D.C., 1961.
126. Golla, F.L., Hutton, E.L., and Grey, Walter, "The Objective Study of Mental Study of Mental Imagery," in *J. Ment. Science*, No. 19, pp. 216-223, 1943.
127. Goodstein, L.D., "Regional Differences in MMPI Responses among Male College Students," in Welsh, G.S., and Dahlstrom, W.G., *Basic Readings in the MMPI in Psychology and Medicine*, Univ. Minn. Press, Minneapolis, pp. 574-578, 1956.
128. Goslin, David A., *The Search for Ability* (Standardized Testing in Social Perspective) Russell Sage Foundation, N.Y., 1963.
129. Gottleber, A.B., "The Relationship Between Brain Potentials and Personality," in *J. Exp. Psych.*, No. 22, pp. 67-74, 1938.
130. Grass, *Eight Channel Electroencephalograph, Model IV*, Grass Instrument Company.
130a. Greeley, Andrew, *Cleveland Catholic Universe Bulletin*, August 18, 1967.
131. Green, N.E., "Verbal Intelligence and Effectiveness of Participation in Group Discussion," in *J. Educ. Psych.*, No. 41, pp. 440-445, 1950.
132. Greenwald, Harold, "Play Therapy for Children Over Twenty-One,' in Gendlin, Eugene T., Ed., *Psychotherapy: Theory, Research and Practice*, Vol. 4, No. 1, pp. 44-46, Psychologists Interested in the Advancement of Psychotherapy, Univ. of Chicago, Chicago, Illinois, February, 1967.
133. Grennan, Sr. Jacqueline, "The Ecumenical World of Search," in Dennis, Lawrence E. and Kauffman, Joseph F., *The College and the Student*, American Council on Education, Washington, D.C., 1966.
134. Gross, Mason W., "The Climate of Learning," in Brown, Nicholas C.., Ed., *Orientation to College Learning*, American Council on Education, Washington, D.C., 1961.
135. Grossberg, John M., "Behavior Therapy: A Review," in Helson, Harry, Ed., *Psychological Bulletin*, Vol. 62, No. 2, pp. 73-85, American Psychological Association, Washington, D.C., August, 1964.
136. Guertin, Wilson, in Buros, Oscar, *The Fifth Mental Measurements Yearbook*, Gryphon Press, Highland Park, pp. 415-416, 1959.
137. Gulvas, Joseph, *Relationship of the Wechsler Adult Intelligence Scale to Scholastic Aptitude and Academic Achievement at the College Level*, Unpublished Master's Essay, John Carroll University, 1961.
138. Gwynn, Frederick L., "And Sadly Teach," in Dennis, Lawrence E. and Kauffman, Joseph F., *The College and the Student*, American Council on Education, Washington, D.C., 1966.

139. Hackett, Herbert, "Use of the MMPI to Predict College Achievement," in *J. Coun. Psych.*, pp. 68-69, Spring, 1955.

140. Harmon, L.R., *What Escalates the Doctorates?*, Paper read at American Personnel and Guidance Association, Washington, April, 1966.

141. Harris, D., "Factors Affecting College Grades: A Review of the Literature, 1930-37," in *Psychol. Bull.*, No. 37, pp. 125-166, 1940.

142. Harris, J.G., "Validity, The Search for a Constant in a Universe of Variables," in Rickers-Ovsiankina, M.A., *Rorschach Psychology*, Wiley, pp. 380-439, 1960.

143. Hascall, O.W., *Some Practical Applications of Research Studies*, Paper read at Association for Institutional Research, Boston, May, 1966.

144. Hassenger, R., & Weiss, R., "The Catholic College Climate," in *The School Review*, No. 74 (Winter), pp. 419-445, 1966.

145. Hathaway, S.R., and McKinley, J.C., *Manual for the Minnesota Multiphasic Personality Inventory* (Rev. ed.), Psychological Corp., New York, 1951.

146. Havemann, E., and West, Patricia Salter, *They Went to College*, Harcourt Brace, New York, 1952.

147. Heist, P., "Diversity in College Student Characteristics," in *J. Educ. Soc.*, No. 33, pp. 279-291, 1960.

148. Henry, C.E., and Knott, John R., "A Note on the Relationship Between 'Personality' and the Alpha Rhythm of the Electroencephalogram," in *J. Exp. Psych.*, No. 28, pp. 362-366, 1941.

149. Henry, C.E., "Electroencephalographic Correlates with Personality," in Wilson, W.P., Ed., *Applications of Electroencephalography in Psychiatry*, Durham, Duke University Press, 1965.

150. Henry, C.E., "Electroencephalograms of Normal Children," in *Monogr. Soc. Res. Child. Developm.*, No. 49 (whole No. 39), 1944.

151. Henry, C.E., "Positive Spike Discharges in the EEG and Behavior Abnormality," in Glasser, G.H., *EEG & Behavior*, Basic Books, Inc., New York, 1963.

152. Henry, C.E., and Pribram, K.H., "Effect of Aluminum Hydroxide Cream Implantation in Cortex of Monkey on EEG and Behavior Performance," in *Electroenceph. Clin. Neurophysiol.*, No. 6, p. 693, 1954.

153. Hertz, M.R., "Organization Activity," in Rickers-Ovsiankina, M.R., *Rorschach Psychology*, Wiley, pp. 25-57, 1960.

154. Hertz, M.R., *Frequency Tables for Scoring Responses to the Rorschach Ink Blot Test*, 3rd. ed., WRU Press, Cleveland, 1951.

155. Hobbs, Nicholas, "The Art of Getting Students Into Trouble," in Dennis, Lawrence E. and Kauffman, Joseph F., *The College and the Student*, American Council on Education, Washington, D.C., 1966.

156. Hobbs, Nicholas, "Sources of Gain in Psychotherapy," in *Amer. Psychologist*, No. 17, pp. 741-747, 1962.

157. Holland, J.L., & Richards, J.M., Jr., "Academic and Non-Academic Accomplishment in a Representative Sample Taken From a Population of 612,000," in *ACT Research Reports*, No. 12, American College Testing Program, pp. 17, May, 1966.

158. Holland, J.L. and Richards, J.M., "The Prediction of College Grades from Personality and Aptitude Variables," in *Journal of Educ. Psych.*, Vol. 51, pp. 245-254, 1960.

159. Hollingsworth, Leta S., *Gifted Children*, MacMillan, New York, 1926.

160. Hood, Albert, B., "Comparison of the Academic Achievement of Certain Types of Students in Different Types of Colleges," in *Proceedings of the 74th Annual Convention of the American Psychological Association–1966*, American Psychological Assoc., Inc., Washington D.C., p. 289, 1966.

161. Hoovey, H.B., and Kooi, K.A., "Alterations in Mental Function and Paroxysmal Cerebral Activity," in *AMA Arch. Neurol. Psychiat.*, No. 78, pp. 264-271, 1957.

162. Horst, Paul, "Differential Prediction in College Admissions," in *College Board Review*, Vol. 33, pp. 19-23, 1957.

163. Horst, Paul, *Differential Prediction of Academic Success*, University of Washington, Seattle, 1959.

164. Howe, Harold, "Innovation in Higher Education Lags Behind Public Schools," in *Higher Education and National Affairs,* Vol. XVI, No. 29, American Council on Education, Washington, D.C., August 25, 1967.

165. Hughes, John, "Electroencephalographic Study of Specific Reading Disabilities," in *EEG Clin. Neurophysiol.,* No. 3, p. 176, 1951.

166. Hughes, John R., "Electroencephalography and Learning," in Myklebuste, H.R., *Progress in Learning Disabilities,* N.Y., Grune and Stratton, Inc., 1967.

167. Hunter, Edwin C., and Jordan, A.M., "An Analysis of Qualities Associated with Leadership Among College Students," in *J. Educ. Psych.,* No. 30, pp. 497-509, 1939.

168. Iffert, R.E., "What Ought Colleges and Universities Do About Student Morality?", in *Assoc. for Higher Education, Current Issues in Higher Education,* National Education Assoc., Washington, D.C., pp. 170-180, 1954.

169. Iffert, R.E., *Retention and Withdrawal of College Students,* U.S. Dept. of Health, Education and Welfare–Office of Education, Washington, D.C., 1957.

170. Industrial Relations Counselors Monograph No. 21, *Behavioral Science Research in Industrial Relations,* New York, 177 pp., 1962.

171. Jackson, C. Wesley, Jr., and Wohl, Julian, "A Survey of Rorschach Teaching in the University," in *J. of Projective Techniques & Personality Assessmennt,* The Society for Projective Techniques and Personality Assessment, Inc., Glendale, Calif., Vol. 30, No. 2, pp. 115-134, April, 1966.

172. Jackson, D.N., and Messick, S., "Acquiescence and Desirability as Response Determinants on the MMPI," in *Educ. Psychol. Measmt.,* No. 21, pp. 771-790, 1961.

173. Jacob, P., *Changing Values in College,* Harper Bros., New York, 1957.

174. Jasper, H.H., "Charting the Sea of Brain Waves," in *Science,* Vol. 108, No. 2805, pp. 343-347, October 1, 1948.

175. Jenkins, W.O., "A Review of Leadership Studies with Particular Reference to Military Problems," in *Psychol. Bull.,* No. 44, pp. 54-79, 1947.

176. Jensen, V.H., "Influence of Personality Traits on Academic Success," in *Personnel Guid. J.,* No. 36, pp. 497-500, 1958.

177. John, E.R., "High Nervous Functions: Brain Function and Learning." in *Ann. Rev. Physiol.,* No. 12, pp. 451-484, 1961.

178. Johnson, L.C., and Ulett, George, "Quantitative Study of Pattern and Stability of Resting Electroencephalographic Activity in a Young Adult Group," in *EEG. Clin. Neurophysiol.,* No. 11, pp. 233-249, 1959.

179. Kahn, H., and Singer, E., "An Investigation of the Factors Related to Success or Failure of School of Commerce Students," in *J. Educ. Psychol.,* No. 40, pp. 107-117, 1949.

180. Katz, Joseph, "Personality and Interpersonal Relations in the College Classroom," in Sanford, Nevitt, *The American College,* John Wiley and Sons, Inc., New York, 1962.

181. Katz, Joseph, "Societal Expectations and Influences," in Dennis, Lawrence E. and Kauffman, Joseph F., *The College and the Student,* American Council on Education, Washington, D.C., 1966.

182. Katz, Robert W., "The Skills of an Effective Administrator," *Harvard Bus. Review.* May, 1963.

183. Katzenback, Edward L., Jr., "Trouble is Already Here," in *College and University,* No. 41, (Summer) pp. 389-397, 1966.

184. Kauffman, Joseph F., "The Student in Higher Education" and "The Time of the Student: Shall We Overcome?", in Dennis, Lawrence E. and Kauffman, Joseph F., *The College and the Student,* American Council on Education, Washington, D.C., 1966.

185. Kawi, A.A., and Passamanik, B., "Association of Factors of Pregnancy with Reading Disorders in Childhood," *J.A.M.A.,* No. 166, pp. 1420-1423, 1958.

186. Kelly, Joseph, "A Study of Leadership in Two Contrasting Groups," *Soc. Review,* 11:3, 1963.

187. Kemp, C.G., *Intangibles in Counseling,* Houghton Mifflin Company, New York, 1967.

188. Kennard, M.A., and Schwartzman, A.E., "A Longitudinal Study of Electroencepha-lographic Frequency Patterns in Mental Hospital Patients and Normal Controls," in *EEG Clin. Neurophysiol.*, No. 9, pp. 263-274, 1957.
189. Kennard, M.A., and Schwartzman, A.E., "The Electroencephalogram and Disorders of Behavior," in *J. Nerv. Ment. Dis.*, No. 124, pp. 103-124, 1956.
190. Kennard, M.A., and Schwartzman, A.E., "A Longitudinal Study of Changes in EEG Frequency Pattern as Related to Psychological Changes," in *J. Nerv. Ment. Dis.*, No. 124, pp. 8-20, 1956.
191. Kerchin, Sheldon J., "Form Perception and Ego Functioning," in Rickers-Ovsiankina, M.A., *Rorschach Psychology*, John Wiley & Sons, Inc., New York, 1960.
192. Kilbane, Marian, *An Analysis of Personality Traits of Student Leaders*, Unpublished Master's Essay, John Carroll University, 1961.
193. Kleinmuntz, Benjamin, "Annotated Bibliography of MMPI Research Among College Populations," *J. Coun. Psych.*, Vol. 9, No. 4, N.Y., pp. 1-14, 1963.
194. Klopfer, Bruno, and Kelley, D.M., *The Rorschach Technique*, World Book Company, Yonkers-on-Hudson, 1946.
195. Knapp, R.H., and Goodrich, H.B., *Origins of American Scientists*, Univ. of Chicago Press, Chicago, 1952.
196. Knapp, R.H., and Goodrich, H.B., "Changing Functions of the College Professor," in Sanford, Nevitt, *The American College*, John Wiley & Sons, Inc., New York, 1962.
197. Knott, John R., "Comments on Some Electroencephalographic Correlates of Intelligence," in *NSSE Thirty-Ninth Yearbook, Part I: Intelligence: Its Nature and Nurture*, Public School Publishers, Bloomington, 1940.
198. Knott, J.R., Ingram, W.R., Wheatley, M.D., and Summers, T. D., "Hypothalamic Influence on Cortical Activity," in *Electroenceph. Clin. Neurophysiol.*, No. 3, pp. 102, 1951.
199. Knott, J.R., and Travis, L.E., "A Note on the Relationship Between Duration and Amplitude of Cortical Potentials," in *J. Psychol.*, No. 3, pp. 169-172, 1937.
200. Kohn, M. & Levenson, E.A., "Differences Between Accepted and Rejected Patients in a Treatment Project of College Dropouts," in *The Journal of Psychology*, No. 63 (May), pp. 143-156, 1966.
201. Kranzberg, Melvin, "The Liberal Curriculum in a Scientific and Technological Age," in Dennis, Lawrence E. and Kauffman, Joseph F., *The College and the Student*, American Council on Education, Washington, D.C., 1966.
202. Krasner, L., "Studies of the Conditioning of Verbal Behavior," in *Psychol. Bull.*, No. 55, pp. 148-170, 1958.
203. Krumboltz, John D., Ed., *Revolution in Counseling: Implications of Behavioral Science*, Houghton Miflin Company, Boston, 1966.
204. Lavin, David E., *The Prediction of Academic Performance*, Russell Sage Foundation, New York, 1965.
205. Learned, W.S., and Wood, B.D., *The Student and His Knowledge*, A report to the Carnegie Foundation on the results of the high school and college exams of 1928, 1930, and 1932, Bull. No. 29, The Carnegie Foundation for the Advancement of Teaching, New York, New York, 1938.
206. Learned, W.S., and Langmuir, C., *Misplacement in College*, Thirty- third annual report of the Carnegie Foundation for The Advancement of Teaching, Carnegie Foundation, N.Y., 1938.
207. Lennox, M.A., and Lennox, W.G., "Electrical Activity of the Brain," in *Ann. Rev. Physiol.*, No. 9, pp. 507-524, 1947.
208. Lennox, M.A., & Lennox, W.G., "Influence of Drugs on the Human Electroencepha-logram," in *EEG Clin. Neurophysiol.*, No. 1, pp. 45-51, 1949.
209. Lerner, Max, "The Revolutionary Frame of Our Time," in Dennis, Lawrence E. and Kauffman, J.F., *The College and the Student*, American Council on Education, Washington, D.C., 1966.
210. Lerner, May, "The University in an Age of Revolutions," in *Oakland Papers*, No. 52 (August) pp. 16-32, 1966.

211. Lindsley, D.B., and Cutts, K.K., "The Electroencephalograms of 'Constitutionally Inferior' and Behavior Problem Children Comparison with Normal Children and Adults," in *Arch. Neurol. Psychiat.*, No. 44, pp. 1199-1212, 1940.

212. Lindsley, D.B., "Electroencephalography," in J. McV. Hunt, Ed., *Personality and Behavior Disorders*, Vol. II, pp. 1033-1103, Ronald Press, New York, 1944.

213. Lindsley, D.B., "Emotion," in Stevens, S.S., Ed., *Handbook of Experimental Psychology*, Wiley, pp. 473-516, N.Y., 1951.

214. Loevinger, J., "Measuring Personality Patterns of Women," in *Genetic Psychology Monographs*, No. 65, pp. 35-136, 1962.

215. Loevinger, J., "A Theory of Test Response," in Anastasi, Anne, Ed., *Testing Problems in Perspective*, pp. 545-556, American Council on Education, Washington, D.C., 1966.

216. Loevinger, J., "A Theory of Test Response," *Proceedings of the Invitational Conference on Testing Problems*, Educational Testing Service, Princeton, N.J., 1959.

217. Ludeman, S.W., "Qualities of the Ideal and Effective College Student: A Study of Student Evaluation," in *J. Educ. Research*, No. 50 pp. 151-153, 1956.

218. MacArthur, Charles C., "Clinical Versus Actuarial Prediction," in Anastasi, Anne, Ed., *Testing Problems in Perspective*, pp. 617-624, American Council on Education, Washington, D.C., 1966.

219. MacKinnon, D.W., and Woodworth, D.G., *The Use of Trait Ratings in an Assessment of 100 Air Force Captains*, Washington, D.C., Office of Technical Services, U.S. Dept. of Commerce, 1958.

220. MacKinnon, Donald W., "What Do We Mean by Talent and How Do We Test for It?", in *College Admissions*, No. 7, pp. 20-29, College Entrance Examination Board, New York, 1960.

221. MacKinnon, D.W., "What Do We Mean by Talent and How Do We Test for It?", in *The Search for Talent*, College Entrance Examination Board, New York, pp. 20-29, 1960.

222. Mallery, David, "Society and the Campus," in Dennis, L.E., and Kauffman, J.F., *The College and the Student*, American Council on Education, Washington, D.C., 1955.

223. Malloy, H., "Study of Some of the Factors Underlying the Establishment of Successful Social Contacts at the College Level," in *J. Soc. Psych.*, No. 7, pp. 205-228, 1936.

224. Marsh, Lee M., "College Dropouts—A Review," in *The Personnel and Guidance J.*, Vol. XLIV, No. 5, pp. 475-481, American Personnel and Guidance Assoc., Washington, D.C., January, 1966.

225. Mann, R.D., "A Review of the Relationships Between Personality and Performance in Small Groups," in Bass, Bernard, *Leadership, Psychology, and Organizational Behavior*, Harper, N.Y., 1960.

226. Marks, E., Ashby, J.D., & Nell, G.A., "Recommended Curricular Change and Persistence in College," in *The Personnel and Guidance Journal*, No. 44 (May) pp. 974-977, 1966.

227. Martin, Warren B., "An Answer for Anomie," in *Teachers College Record*, No. 68 (October) pp. 21-32, 1966.

228. Maslow, A.H., "A Theory of Human Motivation," in *Psych. Review*, No. 50, pp. 370-396, July, 1943.

229. Mason, Evelyn P.; Adams, Henry L.; and Blood, Don F., "Personality Characteristics of Gifted College Freshmen," in *Proceedings of the 73rd Annual Convention of the American Psychological Association—1965*, pp. 301-302, American Psychological Assoc., Inc., Washington, D.C., 1965.

230. Mathewson, Robert, *Guidance Policy and Practice*, Harper and Brothers, New York, 1944.

231. May, Rollo, "The University in an Age of Anxiety," in *Oakland Papers*, No. 51 (August) pp. 33-51, 1966.

232. May, Rollo, *Existence*, Basic Books, Inc., New York, 1958.

233. May, Rollo, *Man's Search for Himself*, W.W. Norton, N.Y., 1953.

234. Mayhew, Lewis B., "Institutional Factors and the Learning Environment," in Dennis, Lawrence E. and Kauffman, Joseph F., *The College and the Student*, American Council on Education, Washington, D.C., 1966.

235. McCabe, Sheridan P., "Attitudes, Values, and Motivational Systems of the American Catholic Male College Student," in Schneiders, A.A.; Centi, P.J.; O'Halloran, W.J., S.J.; and Gorman, Mother M., *The Catholic Psychological Record*, Vol. 4, No. 1, pp. 35-41, (Spring) The Heffernan Press, Inc., Worcester, Mass., 1966.

236. McCandless, B.R., "The Rorschach as a Predictor of Academic Success," in *J. Appl. Psychol.*, No. 33, pp. 43-50, 1949.

237. McClelland, D.D., Baldwin, A.L., Bronfernbrenner, U., and Strodtbeck, F.L., *Talent and Society*, D. Van Nostrand Company, Princeton, 1958.

238. McClelland, D.D., et al., *The Achievement Motive*, Appleton-Century- Crofts, New York, 1953.

238a. McClelland, D.D., "Encouraging Excellence," *Daedalus*, 90:4, Fall, 1961.

239. McConnell, T.R., "Recent Research on Institutional Climates: 2. The Vocational College Culture," in Brown, Nicholas C., Editor, *Orientation to College Learning*, American Council on Education, Washington, D.C., 1961.

240. McConnell, T.R., and Heist, P., "Do Students Make the College?", in *Coll. Univer.*, pp. 442-452, 1959.

241. McConnell, T.R., "The Diversity of American Higher Education, a Research Program," in *Educational Record*, No. 38, pp. 300-315, 1957.

242. McConnell, T.R., and Heist, Paul, "The Diverse College Student Population," in Sanford, Nevitt, Ed., *The American College*, John Wiley and Sons, Inc., New York, 1962.

243. McCuen, T.L., "Leadership and Intelligence," in *Education*, No. 50, pp. 89-95, 1929.

244. McGrath, E.J., and Russell, Charles, *Are Liberal Arts Colleges Becoming Professional Schools?* N.Y., Teachers College Press, 1958.

245. McKeachie, Wilbert J., "Effective Teaching: The Relevance of the Curriculum," in Dennis, L.W., and Kauffman, J.F., *The College and the Student*, American Council on Educ., Washington, D.C., 1966.

246. McNeeley, J.H., "College Student Mortality Studies," in *J. American Assoc. Coll. Registrars*, No. 15, pp. 119-124, 1939.

247. Medsker, L.M., "Beyond Ability," in *The Research Reporter*, The Center for Research and Development in Higher Education, University of California, Vol. II, November 1, 1967.

248. Meehl, Paul, *Clinical Versus Statistical Prediction*, University of Minnesota Press, Minneapolis, 1954.

249. Melville, Donald S. (Ed.) *Examiner's Manual*, Cooperative School and Ability Tests, Cooperative Test Division, Educational Test Service, New Jersey, 57 pp., 1955.

250. Messick, Samuel, "Personality Measurement and College Performance," in Anastasi, Anne, Ed., *Testing Problems in Perspective*, pp. 557-572, American Council on Education, Washington, D.C., 1966.

251. Messick, Samuel, and Ross, John, Editors, *Measurement in Personality and Cognition*, John Wiley & Sons, Inc., N.Y., 1962.

252. Meyerson, Martin, "The Ethos of the American College Student: Beyond the Protests," in *Daedalus*, No. 95 (Summer) pp. 713-739, 1966.

253. Michael, J., & Meyerson, L., "A Behavioral Approach to Counseling and Guidance," in *Harv. Educ. Rev.*, No. 32, pp. 382-402, 1962.

254. Morgan, H.H., "A Psychometric Comparison of Achieving and Nonachieving College Students of High Ability," in *J. Consult. Psychol.*, No. 16, pp. 292-298, 1952.

255. Mowrer, Hobart, *Learning Theory and the Symbolic Processes*, John Wiley and Sons, Inc., New York, 1960.

256. Mundy-Castle, A.C., "The EEG and Mental Activity," in *EEG Clin. Neurophysiol.*, No. 9, pp. 643-655, 1957.

257. Mundy-Castle, A.C., "Theta and Beta Rhythms in the Electroencephalograms of Normal Adults," in *EEG Clin. Neurophysiol.*, No. 3, pp. 477-486, 1951.

258. Mundy-Castle, A.C., "Central Excitability in the Aged," in Blumenthal, H.T. (Ed.), *Medical and Clinical Aspects of Aging,* Columbia Univ. Press, New York, pp. 575-595, 1962.
259. Mundy-Castle, A.C., "Electrophysiological Correlates of Intelligence," in *J. Personality,* Vol. 26, No. 1, pp. 184-199, March, 1958.
260. Mundy-Castle, A.C., and Sugarman, L., "Factors Influencing Relations Between Tapping Speed and Alpha Rhythm," in *EEG Clin. Neurophysiol.* No. 12, pp. 895-904, 1960.
261. Mundy-Castle, A.C., & Nelson, G.K., "Intelligence, Personality and Brain Rhythms in a Socially Isolated Community," in *Nature, London,* No. 185, pp. 484-485, 1960.
262. Murray, H.A., *Thematic Apperception Test,* Harvard Univ. Press, Cambridge, Mass., 1943.
263. Murray, H.A., *Explorations in Personality,* Oxford Univ. Press, New York, 1938.
264. Nachmansohn, David, "Basic Aspects of Nerve Activity Explained by . . . Biochemical Analysis," in *J. Am. Med. Assoc.,* Vol. 179, pp. 639-643, February 24, 1962.
265. Newcomb, Theodore M., "Research on Student Characteristics: Current Approaches," in Dennis, Lawrence E. and Kauffman, Joseph F., *The College and the Student,* American Council on Education, Washington, D.C., 1966.
266. Newcomb, T.M., "Student Peer-Group Influence," in Sanford, Nevitt, *The American College,* John Wiley & Sons, Inc., New York, 1962.
267. Nicholi, A.M., "Study of Harvard Dropouts," *Education Recaps,* Princeton, ETS, Vol. 7, No. 3, p. 10, December 1967.
268. Nosal, W.S., "Five Year Comparison of Graduates in Two Professional Curricula: Eds. vs. Meds," in *J. Teach. Ed.,* No. VII, pp. 238-243, September, 1956.
269. O'Brien, Kenneth B., Jr., "The Undergraduate and American Higher Education: Notes for a Course," in *Liberal Education,* No. 52 (May) pp. 165-171, 1966.
270. Oppenheimer, R., "Analogy in Science," in *Amer. Psych.,* No. 11, pp. 127-135, 1956.
271. Ostroff, Anthony, "Economic Pressures and the Professor," in Sanford, Nevitt, *The American College,* John Wiley & Sons, Inc., New York, 1962.
272. Pace, C. Robert, "Perspectives on the Student and His College," in Dennis, Lawrence E. and Kauffman, Joseph F., *The College and the Student,* American Council on Education, Washington, D.C., 1966.
273. Pace, C.C., and Stern, G.G., "Approach to the Measurement of Psychological Characteristics of College Environment," in *J. of Educ. Psych.,* No. 49, pp. 269-277, 1958b.
274. Pace, C.C., "Five College Environments," in *Coll. Bd. Rev.,* No. 41, pp. 24-28, 1960.
275. Palmer, and Rock, "High Alpha Incidence in the EEG and Personality Patterning," in Proceedings of Central Assoc. of EEG, *EEG Clin. Neurophysiol.,* No. V, p. 374, 1951.
276. Penfield, Wilder, *The Excitable Cortex in Conscious Man,* 1958. Courtesy of Charles Thomas, Springfield, Illinois.
277. Pepinsky, Harold B., *Diagnostic Categories in Clinical Counseling,* Stanford Univ. Press for Amer. Psychological Assoc., Stanford, 1948.
278. Petraoja, Sergio D., "The Concept of Freedom in Viktor Frankl:, in Schneiders, A.A.; Centi, P.J.; O'Halloran, W.J., S.J.; and Gorman, Mother M., *The Catholic Psychological Record,* Worcester, Mass., (Fall) 1966.
279. Phay, J.E., & McDonald, D., *Four Years of Academic Achievement and Disposition of the 1961-62 Entering Freshmen at the University of Mississippi Compared with American College Test Scores,* University Miss: The University of Miss., Bureau of Institutional Research, pp. 161, 1965.
280. Piaget, J., *The Construction of Reality in the Child,* Basic Books, New York, 1954.
281. Piaget, J., *The Psychology of Intelligence,* Harcourt, Brace, New York, 1950.
282. Piaget, J., *The Origins of Intelligence in Children,* W.W. Norton and Company, Inc., New York, 1952.

283. Pinner, Frank, "The Crisis of the State Universities: Analysis and Remedies," in Sanford, Nevitt, Ed., *The American College,* John Wiley & Sons, Inc., New York, 1962.

284. Piotrowski, Zygmunt A., "The Movement Score," in Rickers-Ovisiankina, M.A., *Rorschach Psychology,* John Wiley, N.Y., 1960.

285. Plant, Walter T., and Lynd, Celia, "A Validity Study and a College Freshman Norm Group for the Wechsler Adult Intelligence Scale," in *Person. & Guid. J.,* No. 37, pp. 578-580, April, 1959.

286. Plant, W.T., and Richardson, Harold, "The IQ of the Average College Student," in *J. of Counsel. Psych.,* No. 5, pp. 229-231, 1958.

287. Pope, Ruth V., *Factors Affecting the Elimination of Women Students,* Columbia Univ. Teachers College Series, No. 485, 1931.

288. Pribram, Karl H., "The New Neurology: Memory, Novelty, Thought, and Choice," in Glaser, G.H., *EEG & Behavior,* Basic Books, Inc., New York, 1963.

289. Prouty, Helen, "Personality Factors Related to Over-and Underachievement," in *Amer. Psychologist,* No. 10, p. 304, 1955.

290. Quinn, S.B., "Relationship of Certain Personality Characteristics to College Achievement," in *Dissert. Abstr.,* No. 17, p. 809, 1957.

291. Rabinovitch, M.S., Kennard, M.A., and Fisher, W.P., "Personality Correlates of Electroencephalographic Findings," in *Can. J. Psychol.,* No. 9, pp. 29-41, 1955.

292. Rank, Otto, *Will Therapy,* Alfred A. Knopf, Inc., New York, 1936.

293. Reisman, David, and Jencke, Christopher, "The Viability of the American College," in Sanford, Nevitt, *The American College,* John Wiley & Sons, Inc., New York, 1962.

294. Renick, T.F., "Are High School Records Indicative of Success at the Doctoral Level?", *Journal* in *The of College Student Personnel,* No. 7 (July) pp. 246-247, 1966.

295. Richards, J.M., Jr., & Lutz, S.W., "The Prediction of Student Accomplishment in College," in *ACT Research Reports,* No. 13, American College Testing Program, 38 pp., June, 1966.

296. Richards, J.M., Holland, John L., Lutz, Sandra W., *The Assessment of Student Accomplishment in College,* American College Testing Program Research Reports, No. 11, Iowa City, Iowa, March, 1966.

297. Richardson, Harold, and Roebuck, Julian, "Minnesota Multiphasic Personality Inventory and California Psychological Inventory Differences between Delinquents and their Nondelinquent Siblings," in *Proceedings of the 73rd Annual Convention of the American Psychological Association— 1965,* pp. 255-256, Amer. Psych. Assoc., Inc., Washington D.C. 1965.

298. Rickers-Ovsiankina, M.A., *Rorschach Psychology,* John Wiley, New York, 1960.

299. Riesman, David; Jacob, Philip E.; and Sanford, Nevitt, *Spotlight on the College Student,* American Council on Education, Washington, D.C., 1959.

300. Roark, and Hawkes, "Electroencephalograms of Behavior Problem Children," in *EEG Clin. Neurophysiol.,* No. 3, p. 105, 1951.

301. Roe, Anne, "Analysis of Group Rorschachs of Psychologists and Anthropologists," in *Journal of Projective Techniques,* No. 16, pp. 212-224, 1952.

302. Rogers, Carl R., "Toward a Modern Approach to Values," The Valuing Process in the Mature Person," *J. of Abn. Soc. Psych.,* 68:2, February, 1964.

303. Rokeach, M., *The Open and Closed Mind,* Basic Books, New York, 1960.

304. Rorschach, Hermann, *Psychodiagnostics,* Barn, Hans Gruber, 1942.

305. Rose, H.A., & Elton, C.F., "Another Look at the College Dropout," in *Journal of Counseling Psychology,* (Summer) pp. 242-245, 1966.

306. Rosenzweig, M.R., Krech, D., and Bennett, E.L., "A Search for Relations Between Brain Chemistry and Behavior," in *Psych. Bull.,* No. 57, pp. 476-492, 1960.

307. Rosenzweig, M.R., "Environmental Complexity, Cerebral Change, and Behavior," in *Am. Psych.,* Vol. 21, No. 4, pp. 321-332, April, 1966.

308. Rossi, A.M., and Neuman, G.G., "A Comparative Study of Rorschach Norms: Medical Students:, in *Journal of Projective Techniques,* No. 25, pp. 334-338, September, 1961.

309. Roston, Ronald A., "Some Personality Characteristics of Male Compulsive Gamblers," in *Proceedings of the 73rd Annual Convention of the American Psychological Association*– 1965, pp. 263-264, American Psychological Association, Inc., Washington, D.C., 1965.

310. Rotter, Julian B., "Generalized Expectancies for Internal versus External Control of Reinforcement," in *Psych. Monographs*, No. 609, Vol. 80, No. 1, 1966.

311. Rubin, S., and Bowman, K.M., "Electroencephalographic and Personality Correlates in Peptic Ulcer," in *Psychosom. Med.*, No. 4, pp. 309-318, 1942.

312. Ruch, T.C., "Neurophysiology in Diagnosis," in *Conference on Diagnosis in Mental Retardation*, Training School, Vineland, N.J., 1958.

313. Rudolph, Frederick, "Neglect of Students as a Historical Tradition," in Dennis, Lawrence E. and Kauffman, Joseph F., *The College and the Student*, American Council on Education, Washington, D.C., 1966.

314. Sanders, M.W., "The Prediction of Academic Success Among University Freshmen in a School of Education," Unpublished Ph.D. Dissert., New York Univer., 1950. (Also abstracted in Microfilm Abstr., 11, 63-64, 1951).

315. Sanford, Nevitt, Editor, *The American College*, John Wiley & Sons, Inc., New York, 1962.

316. Sanford, Nevitt, "The Interview in Personality Appraisal," in Anastasi, Anne, Ed., *Testing Problems in Perspective*, pp. 607-616, American Council on Education, Washington, D.C., 1966.

317. Sanford, Nevitt, *Where Colleges Fail*, Jossey-Bass, Inc., San Francisco, 1967.

318. Sattin, Albert, "Article" *Plain Dealer*, Cleveland, 1967.

319. Saul, L.J., David, H., and Davis, P.A., "Psychological Correlations with the Electroencephalogram," in *Psychosom. Med.*, No. 11, pp. 361-376. 1949.

320. Saul, L.J. et al., "Psychological Correlations with the Electroencephalogram," in *EEG Clin. Neurophysiol.*, No. 1, p. 515, 1949.

321. Saunders, D.R., "Further Implications of Mundy-Castle's Correlations between EEG and Wechsler-Bellevue Variable," in *J. Nat. Inst. Personnel Res.*, No. 8, pp. 91-101, 1960.

322. Seibel, Dean W., "A Study of the Academic Ability and Performance of Junior College Students," in *Evaluation and Advisory Service Field Studies Report No. 1*, Educational Testing Service, 44 pp., October, 1965.

323. Selvin, H.C., *Effects of Leadership*, Glencoe, Ill., Free Press, 1960.

324. Shapiro, David, "A Perceptual Understanding of the Color Response," in Rickers-Ovsiankina, M.A., *Rorschach Psychology*, John Wiley, New York, 1960.

325. Shartle, Carroll L., *Executive Performance and Leadership*, Prentice- Hall, Inc., Englewood Cliffs, 1956.

326. Shaw, Dale J., *A Factor Analysis of the Collegiate WAIS*, Paper read at Midwestern Psychological Assoc., Chicago, May, 1966.

327. Sherburne, Phillip, "Before the Doctor Comes: Conditions of Stress on the Campus," in Dennis, L.E., and Kauffman, J.F., *The College and the Student*, Amer. Coun. on Educ., Washington, D.C., 1966.

328. Shoben, Edward, "Personal Worth in Education and Counseling," in Krumboltz, John, Ed., *Revolution in Counseling: Implications of Behavioral Science*, Houghton Mifflin Company, Boston, 1966.

329. Shure, G.H., & Rogers, M.S., "Note of Caution on the Factor Analysis of the MMPI," in *Psych. Bull.*, No. 63, pp. 14-18, 1965.

330. Sisson, B.D., & Ellingson, R.J., "On the Relationship Between 'Normal' EEG Patterns and Personality Variables," in *J. Nerv., Ment. Dis,.* No. 121, pp. 353-357, 1955.

331. Skager, R., Holland, J.L., & Braskamp, L.A., "Changes in Self-Ratings and Life Goals Among Students at Colleges with Different Characteristics," in *ACT Research Reports*, No. 14, American College Testing Program, 24 pp., August, 1966.

332. Slatter, K.H., "Alpha Rhythms and Mental Imagery," in *EEG Clin. Neurophvsiol.*, No. 12, pp. 851-859, 1960.

333. Smith, H.L., and Krueger, L.M., "A Brief Summary of Literature on Leadership," in *Bull. Sch. Educ.*, No. 4, Bloomington, University of Indiana, 1933.

334. Smith, Louise, "A Statistic Strikes Back," in *The Personnel and Guidance Journal*, American Personnel and Guidance Assoc., Vol. 45, No. 9, pp. 872-877, Washington, D.C., May, 1967.

335. Snitz, R.H., "Study Success, Failure, and Causes of Withdrawal of Indiana State Teachers College Students," cited in Pope, Ruth, *Factors Affecting the Elimination of Women Students*, Columbia U., Teachers College, New York, 1931.

336. Synder, Benson, R., "The Invisible Curriculum," in Dennis, Lawrence E. and Kauffman, Joseph F., *The College and the Student*, American Council on Education, Washington, D.C., 1966.

337. Spiller, G., "The Dynamics of Greatness," in *Social. Rev.*, No. 21 (3), pp. 218-232, 1929.

338. Stalnaker, Elizabeth M., "A Four Year Study of the Freshmen Class of 1935 at the West Virginia University," in *J. Educ. Res.*, No. 36, pp. 100-118, 1942.

339. Stein, Morris I., *Personality Measures in Admissions*, College Entrance Examination Board, New York, 1963.

340. Stein, Morris I., *Personality in College Admissions*, College Entrance Examination Board, New York, 1963.

341. Stennett, R.G., "The Relationship of Performance Level to Level of Arousal," in *J. Exp. Psych.*, No. 54, pp. 54-61, 1957.

342. Stern, George G., "Recent Research on Institutional Climates: 1. Continuity and Contrast in the Transition from High School to College," in Brown, Nicholas C., Ed., *Orientation to College Learning*, Amer. Council. on Educ., Washington, D.C., 1961.

343. Stern, George, "Myth and Reality in the American College," in *AAUP Bulletin*, No. 52 (Dec.), pp. 408-414, 1966.

344. Stern, George, "Of Bardot and the State of Our Colleges," in *Current Issues in Higher Education*, Assoc. for Higher Education, pp. 180-185, 1966.

345. Stern, George, "Environments for Learning," in Sanford, Nevitt, *The American College*, John Wiley & Sons, Inc., New York, 1962.

346. Stern, George, Stein, Morris I., and Bloom, Benjamin S., *Methods in Personality Assessment*, The Free Press, Glencoe, Illinois, 1956.

347. Stern, George, "Student Values and their Relationship to the College Environment," in Sprague, H.T., (Ed.), *Research on College Students*, pp. 67-104 (b), Western Interstate Commission for Higher Education, Boulder, Colorado, 1960.

348. Stewart, Campbell, "The Place of Higher Education in a Changing Society," in Sanford, Nevitt, Ed., *The American College*, John Wiley & Sons, Inc., New York, 1962.

349. Stodgill, Ralph M., "Personal Factors Associated with Leadership: A Survey of the Literature," in *Journal of Psychology*, No. XXV, pp. 35-71, 1948.

350. Strickland, Ben, "Kierkegaard and Counseling for Individuality," in *The Personnel and Guidance Journal*, Vol. XLIV, No. 5, pp. 470-474, American Personnel and Guidance Assoc., Washington, D.C., January, 1966.

351. Stuit, Dewey, Dickson, G.S., Jordan, T.F., and Schleerb, Lester, *Predicting Success in Professional Schools*, American Council on Education, Washington A.C.E. Press, Washington, D.C., 1949.

352. Sugarman, L., "Alpha Rhythm, Perception and Intelligence," in *J. Nat. Inst. Personnel Res.*, No. 8, pp. 170-179, 1961.

353. Summerskill, John, "Dropouts from College," in Sanford, Nevitt, *The American College*, John Wiley, New York, 1962.

354. Super, Donald, "Self Concepts in Vocational Development," *Career Development: Self Concept Theory*, College Examination Entrance Board, Research Monograph, No. 4, N.Y., pp. 1-14, 1963.

355. Symonds, Percival M., "The Study of Personality Measurement," in *College Admissions*, No. 4, pp. 1-9, College Entrance Examination Board, New York, 1957.

356. Taylor, Harold, "Freedom and Authority on the Campus," in Sanford, Nevitt, *The American College,* John Wiley, New York, 1962.
357. Terman, L.M., "A Preliminary Study of the Psychology and Pedagogy of Leadership," *Pedagog. Sem.,* No. 11, pp. 413-451, 1904.
358. Terman, L.M., "The Discovery and Encouragement of Exceptional Talent, ' in *Amer. Psychologist,* No. 9, pp. 221-230, 1954.
359. Terman, L.M., and Oden, Melita, H., *Genetic Studies of Genius, Vol. V., The Gifted Group at Midlife,* Stanford Univ., Stanford, 1959.
360. Thistlethwaite, D.L., "College Press and Student Achievement," in *J. Educ. Psychol.,* No. 50, pp. 183-191, 1959b.
361. Thorndike, Robert L., *The Concept of Over- and Underachievement,* Bureau of Publications, Teachers College, Columbia University, New York, 1963.
362. Thurstone, L.L., "Creative Talent," in *Proceedings, 1950 Invitational Conference on Testing Problems,* Princeton, Educ. Testing Service, pp. 55-69, 1961.
363. Thurstone, L.L., *A Factorial Study of Perception,* Univ. of Chicago Press, Chicago, 1944.
364. Tomkins, Silvan S., "Commentary: The Ideology of Research Strategies," in Messick, Samuel and Ross, John, Editors, *Measurement in Personality and Cognition,* John Wiley & Sons, Inc., N.Y., 1962.
365. Toynbee, A.J., *A Study of History,* Oxford Univ. Press, 1946, cited in Bass, Bernard, *Leadership, Psychology, and Organizational Behavior,* Harper Brothers, New York, 1960.
366. Travers, Robert M.W., "Significant Research on the Prediction of Academic Success," in Donahue, W.T., and Assoc., Editors, *The Measurement of Student Adjustment and Achievement,* Univ. of Mich. Press, Ann Arbor, Mich., 1949.
367. Trent, James W., "Encouragement of Student Development," in *NASPA,* No. 4 (July) pp. 35-45, 1966.
368. Uhr, Leonard, "Objectively Measured Behavioral Effects of Psychoactive Drugs," in Uhr, Leonard, and Miller, J.G., Eds., *Drugs and Behavior,* John Wiley, New York, 1960.
369. Ulett, G.A., Johnson, L.C., and Mills, W.B., "Pattern Stability and Relationship among Electroencephalographic 'Activation' Techniques," in *EEG Clin. Neurophysiol.,* No. 11, pp. 255-266, 1959.
370. Ulett, G.A., Johnson, L.C., Sines, J.O., and Stern, J.A., "Cortical Activity and Cognitive Functioning," in *EEG Clin. Neurophysiol.,* No. 12, pp. 861-874, 1960.
371. Varvel, W.A., "The Rorschach Test in Psychotic and Neurotic Depressions," in *Bull. Menn. Clinic,* No. 5, pp. 5-12, 1941.
372. Vaughan, Richard P., "Personality Characteristics of Exceptional College Students," in *Proceedings of the 74th Annual Convention of the American Psychological Association–1966,* Amer. Psychol. Assoc., Inc., Washington, D.C., p. 281, 1966.
373. Vogel, William, and Broverman, Donald M., "Relationship Between EEG and Test Intelligence: A Critical Review," *Psychological Bulletin,* Vol. 62, No. 2, pp. 132-144, American Psychological Association, Washington, D.C., August, 1964.
374. Vogel, W., and Broverman, D.M., A Reply to "Relationship Between EEG and Test Intelligence: a Commentary." *Psychol. Bull.,* 1966, 65: 99-109.
375. Vogel, W., Broverman, D.M., and Klaiber, E.L., "EEG and Mental Abilities," *Electroenceph. Clin. Neurophysiol.,* 24: 166-175, 1968.
376. Wald, R.M., *A Psycho-Educational Study of Top Level Business and Industrial Executives,* Doctoral Dissertation, Northwestern University, 1953.
377. Watts, William A., "The Non-Student," in *Proceedings, NASPA,* Seattle, pp. 277-292, June, 1966.
378. Webster, Harold; Freedman, Mervin B.; and Heist, Paul, "Personality Changes in College Students:, in Sanford, Nevitt, *The American College,* John Wiley & Sons, Inc., New York, 1962.
379. Wechsler, David, *The Measurement of Adult Intelligence,* Williams and Wilkins, 4th ed., Baltimore, 1958.

380. Wechsler, Davidd, *The Range of Human Capacities,* Williams and Wilkins, 2nd. ed., Baltimore, 1955.

381. Wechsler, David, "The Non-intellective Factors in General Intelligence," in *Psychol. Bull.,* No. 37, pp. 444-445, 1940.

382. Weider, Arthur, "Underachievement: The Current Crisis in Education," *Counselor Information Service,* B'Nai B'Rith Vocational Service, Washington, Vol. 22, No. 4, Supplement, December, 1967.

383. Weitz, Henry, *Behavior Change Through Guidance,* John Wiley & Sons, Inc., New York, 1964.

384. Wellington, C. Burleigh, and Wellington, Jean, *The Underachiever: Challenges and Guidelines,* Rand McNally & Co., 122 pp., 1965.

385. Wells, Charles E., "Electroencephalographic Correlates of Conditioned Responses," in Glaser, Gilbert H., *EEG & Behavior,* Basic Books, Inc., New York, 1963.

386. Wendt, G.R., and Cameron, J.S., "Chemical Studies of Behavior: V: Procedure in Drug Experimentation with College Students," in *J. Psych.,* No. 51, pp. 173-211, 1961.

387. Wescoe, W. Clarke, "Higher Education and Moral Responsibility," in Dennis, Lawrence E. and Kauffman, J.F., *The College and the Student,* American Council on Education, Washington, D.C., 1966.

388. Wexner, Louis B., "Relationship of Intelligence and the Nine Scales of the MMPI," in *J. Clin. Psychol.,* No. 17, p. 43, 1961.

389. White, R.W., "Test Responses as Measures of Personality," in Rickers- Ovsiankina, M.A., *Rorschach Psychology,* John Wiley, New York, 1960.

390. Wiggins, Jerry S., "Substantive Dimensions of Self-Report in the MMPI Item Pool," in *Psychological Monographs,* Vol. 80, No. 22, Whole No. 630, American Psychological Assoc., Washington, D.C., 1966.

391. Williams, Vernon, "The College Dropout: Qualitites of His Environment," in *The Personnel and Guidance, Journal,* Vol. 45, No. 9, pp. 878-882, American Personnel and Guidance Assoc., Washington, D.C., May, 1967.

392. Williamson, E.G., and Cowan, John L., "Academic Freedom for Students: Issues and Guidelines," in Dennis, Lawrence E. and Kauffman, Joseph F., *The College and the Student,* American Council on Education, Washington, D.C., 1966.

393. Williamson, E.G., and Hoyt, Donald, "Measured Personality Characteristics of Student Leaders," in *Educ. Psychol. Measmt.,* No. 12, pp. 65-78, 1952.

394. Wilson, Kenneth M., "Review of CRC Studies: III—Validity of a Measure of 'Academic Motivation'," in *Research Memorandum No. 66-2,* College Research Center, Vassar College, June 13, 1966, 27 p.

395. Wilson, Logan, "Is the Student Becoming the 'Forgotten Man'?" and "Freedom and Responsibility in Higher Education," in Dennis, Lawrence E. and Kauffman, Joseph F., *The College and the Student,* American Council on Education, Washington, D.C., 1966.

396. Wilson, William P., M.D., *Applications of Electroencephalography in Psychiatry,* Duke Univ. Press, Durham, N.C., 1965.

397. Wise, W. Max, "The American Student and His College," in *From High School to College: Readings for Counselors,* College Entrance Examination Board, Teachers College, Columbia University, New York, 1964.

398. Wise, W. Max, *They Come for the Best of Reasons—College Students Today,* American Council on Education, Washington, D.C., 1960.

399. Wittrig, John J.; Mehl, Mary M.; and Deter, Francis H., "Developmental Stress, Emotionality, and Survival: A New Test," in *Proceedings of the 73rd Annual Convention of the American Psychological Association—1965,* pp. 161-162, American Psychol. Assoc., Inc., Washington, D.C., 1965.

400. Wrenn, C. Gilbert, "Two Psychological Worlds: An Attempted Reapproachment," in Krumboltz, John, Ed., *Revolution in Counseling: Implications of Behavioral Science,* Houghton Mifflin Company, Boston, 1966.

401. Yeomans, W.N. & Lundin, R.W., "The Relationship Between Personality Adjustment and Scholarship Achievement in Male College Students," in *J. Genet. Psychol.*, No. 57, pp. 213-218, 1957.
402. Yoshino, I.R., "College Drop-outs at the End of Freshmen Year," in *J. Educ. Sociol.*, No. 32, pp. 42-48, 1958.
403. Zeaman, Jean B., "Some of the Personality Attributes Related to Achievement in College: A Comparison of Men and Women Students," in *Dissert. Abstr.*, No. 18, pp. 290-291, 1958.
404. Zubin, Joseph, "Clinical Versus Actuarial Prediction: A Pseudo-Problem," in Anastasi, Anne, Ed., *Testing Problems in Perspective,* pp. 625-637, American Council on Education, Washington, D.C., 1966.
405. Barger, Ben and Hall, Everett, "Personality Patterns and Achievement in College," *Educ. Psych. Meas.*, Vol. XXIV, No. 2, 1964.
406. Brozek, J., "Personality Changes with Age: an Item Analysis of the Minnesota Multiphasic Personality Inventory," *J. Geron.*, 1955, 10, 194-200.
407. Ginzberg, El., and Herma, John L., Talent and Performance, Columbia University Press, N.Y. 1964.

INDEX

INDEX

231